The Complete
Slow Cooker
Cookbook
for Beginners

800 Must-Have Affordable and Delicious
Slow Cooker Recipes for Any Taste and
Occasion

Harmelin L. Sanders

Table of Content

Chapter 4 Rice, Grains, and Beans ·············· 21

Chapter 5 Poultry················ 33

Chapter 6 Red Meat ··········· 52

Chapter 7 Fish and Seafood 75

Chapter 8 Soups, Stews, and Chilies ················ 89

Chapter 12 Stocks, Broths, and Sauces ···················· 139

Appendix 1: Measurement Conversion Chart ················ 144

Introduction

As a result of the long, low-temperature cooking, slow cookers help tenderize less-expensive cuts of meat. A slow cooker brings out the flavours in foods. A wide variety of foods can be cooked in a slow cooker, including one pot meals, soups, stews and casseroles. A slow cooker uses less electricity than an oven

Even if no one is home, your meal is almost ready thanks to your slow cooker. This small appliance, essential in many homes for over 30 years, is based on the principles of slow cooking. The concept of slow cooking is simple: put the food in a container or a closed place and let it cook slowly.

How to Choose the Right Slow Cooker for You?

1.Size:

Probably the most important consideration when buying your slow cooker is what size to buy. Since a slow cooker works best when it's at least half full, it's important to think carefully about which size is best for you before you buy.

Slow cookers come in a variety of sizes, from mini pots for dips (like these delicious 3-ingredient corn dips) / dips / dips to large pots for large families with plenty of options in between.

If you are single or a family of two, 2-Quart to 3-Quart is probably the best solution. If you have a family of three or four, the right size for you is probably 4-Quart.

Large families of four to six people will likely need 6-Quarts or larger.

I think the most versatile size is the 6-Quart Oval. It is a bit on the large side, but it is easier to use a larger slow cooker for smaller quantities than the other way around. I have found that cooking moderate amounts of food in a six-quart slow cooker works very well. Another trick when cooking a small amount of food is to simply place the food into an oven-safe dish that fits inside your slow cooker. Place the dish on the bottom of the slow cooker, cover and cook!

2.Shape:

Another slow cooker parameters to consider is the shape. Slow cookers come in two basic shapes: round and oval. Round slow cookers are great for soups, stews and chili peppers.

The ovals have a larger surface area, so there is more room for foods like pork chops and stuffed peppers. And because they have more surface area, they cook food a little faster than round slow cookers.

3.Cleaning:

Each part should be easy to clean. A stainless steel exterior may show fingerprints and requires additional cleaning.

4.Timer:

A timer is useful because it counts the time spent in your slow cooker and alerts you when cooking is done. Do not confuse this with a delayed start timer. Some members wanted a slow cooker with a delayed timer that you could turn on or off while you were away.

5.Automatic Adjustment:

This setting is useful because the process starts at a high temperature to heat up the food and then switches to low for the remaining cooking time.

Tips and Tricks for Slow Cooker Success

1.Add the Right Amount of Food: One of our most important slow cooker cooking tips: Put the appropriate amount of food in the slow cooker before turning it on, making sure the cooker is at least half full but no more than two-thirds full.

2.Layer It Right: Bottom to Top: Vegetables, meat, then liquid. Cut potatoes, carrots, parsnips and other dense vegetables into small pieces before placing them in the slow cooker. These heavier, fresh greens make a great base at the bottom of your pot. Then next the meat and finally the liquid. Tender vegetables like zucchini, broccoli, green beans or peas are best added towards the end of cooking.

3.Don't Use Frozen Uncooked Meat: Never start with frozen raw meat as bacteria grow faster in the 40 ° F to 140 ° F danger zone. Frozen meat does not reach a safe temperature quickly enough and stays in the danger zone too long to be safe to consume. Defrost meat in the refrigerator overnight or for as long as needed to avoid frozen spots.

4.Dairy and seafood go in last!

These ingredients will break down if they sit in the slow cooker for too long, so keep this in mind: seafood should be added within the last hour of cooking, and dairy within the last 15 minutes.

5.No peeking or stirring!

You might be curious about what's going on inside the crock pot, but opening that lid is a big no-no. Every time you do, you're adding up to 20 minutes additional cooking time. If you really feel the need to glance inside and check for doneness, the ideal time is 30-45 minutes before the end of the cooking time. Also: no stirring unless the recipe says otherwise!

Slow Cooker Food Safety

• Do not cook dry beans

Soak and cook the dried beans first. Dried beans contain natural toxin. These toxins are easily destroyed by boiling temperatures. Soak the beans for 12 hours, rinse, then cook on the heat for at least 10 minutes before putting the beans in a slow cooker.

• Do not cook frozen foods

Make sure frozen meat or vegetables are properly thawed before putting them in the slow cooker. Adding these ingredients to the mixture while they are still frozen can pose a serious health risk, because leaving the food in a dangerous temperature zone is a magnet for bacteria.

• Store leftovers in shallow containers and refrigerate within two hours.

Make sure you are storing them safely and eating them in a timely manner to reduce your risk of food poisoning. Store leftovers in shallow containers and refrigerate within two hours of removing from the pot

Smart Plan Ahead Makes Slow Cooking Easier

• Read the entire recipe and gather all the ingredients (and required equipment) before and start cooking. It will save you the frustration of finding out you don't have potatoes in your pantry.

• Put frozen foods in the refrigerator to defrost them the day before cooking.

• Menu-plan for the week to help you remember when to thaw frozen meat or something else.

• If you're constantly in a rush in the morning, prepare some or all parts of the recipe the night before. Store the food in an airtight container in the refrigerator, and then pop it into the slow cooker in the morning, set the timer, and off you go.

Chapter 1 Breakfasts and Brunches

Raisin Oatmeal

Prep time: 5 minutes | Cook time: 8 hours | Serves 2

¾ cup steel-cut oats
¼ cup raisins
1 teaspoon ground cinnamon
⅛ teaspoon sea salt
3 cups almond milk

1.Put the oats, raisins, cinnamon, and salt in the slow cooker and stir to combine. Pour in the almond milk and stir.
2.Cover and cook the oatmeal on low for 8 hours or overnight.
3.Serve warm.

Pear and Chai Oatmeal

Prep time: 5 minutes | Cook time: 8 hours | Serves 2

¾ cup steel-cut oats
⅛ teaspoon ground cardamom
⅛ teaspoon ground nutmeg
⅛ teaspoon ground ginger
¼ teaspoon cinnamon
⅛ teaspoon sea salt
1 ripe pear, cored, peeled, and diced
3 cups unsweetened almond milk

1.Put the oats, cardamom, nutmeg, ginger, cinnamon, and salt in the slow cooker and stir to combine. Stir in the pear and the almond milk.
2.Cover and cook the oatmeal on low for 8 hours or overnight.
3.Serve warm.

Pumpkin Oatmeal

Prep time: 5 minutes | Cook time: 8 hours | Serves 2

¾ cup steel-cut oats
1 teaspoon ground cinnamon

⅛ teaspoon ground ginger
⅛ teaspoon ground nutmeg
⅛ teaspoon ground cloves
⅛ teaspoon sea salt
1 cup pumpkin purée
2 cups unsweetened almond milk or water

1.Combine the oats, cinnamon, ginger, nutmeg, cloves, and salt in the slow cooker.
2.In a medium bowl, whisk together the pumpkin and almond milk and pour the mixture into the oat mixture. Stir gently to combine.
3.Cover and cook the oatmeal on low for 8 hours or overnight.
4.Serve warm.

Apple, Bread, and Granola Bake

Prep time: 20 minutes | Cook time: 4 to 5 hours | Serves 8

2 tablespoons vegetable oil
¼ cup coconut sugar
1 teaspoon ground cinnamon
¼ teaspoon ground cardamom
10 slices whole-wheat bread, cubed
2 Granny Smith apples, peeled and diced
8 eggs
1 cup canned coconut milk
1 cup unsweetened apple juice
2 teaspoons vanilla extract
1 cup granola

1.Grease the slow cooker with vegetable oil.
2.In a small bowl, mix the coconut sugar, cinnamon, and cardamom well.
3.In the slow cooker, layer the bread, apples, and coconut sugar mixture.
4.In a large bowl, whisk the eggs, coconut milk, apple juice, and vanilla, and mix well.
5.Pour the egg mixture slowly over the food in the slow cooker. Sprinkle the granola on top.
6.Cover and cook on low for 4 to 5 hours, or until a food thermometer inserted in the mixture registers 165ºF (74ºC).
7.Scoop the mixture from the slow cooker to serve.

Strawberry French Toast

Prep time: 10 minutes | Cook time: 2½ hours | Serves 2

1 teaspoon butter, at room temperature
2 eggs
½ cup 2% milk
1 teaspoon vanilla extract
⅛ teaspoon sea salt
4 slices whole-grain bread, crusts removed, cut into 1-inch cubes
2 cups fresh strawberries
2 ounces (57 g) low-fat cream cheese, cut into small chunks

1.Grease the slow cooker with the butter.
2.In a large bowl, whisk together the eggs, milk, vanilla, and salt. Toss the bread cubes in the mixture until they are thoroughly saturated.
3.Pour half of the bread mixture into the slow cooker. Top with the strawberries and cream cheese. Add the remaining bread mixture.
4.Cover and cook on low for 6 hours or on high for 2½ hours.
5.Serve warm.

Banana and Pecan French Toast

Prep time: 10 minutes | Cook time: 2 hours | Serves 2

1 teaspoon butter, at room temperature
2 eggs
¾ cup 2% milk
1 teaspoon vanilla extract
1 teaspoon ground cinnamon
¼ teaspoon ground nutmeg
⅛ teaspoon sea salt
2 cups sliced bananas
4 slices whole-grain bread, crusts removed, cut into 1-inch cubes
2 tablespoons finely chopped toasted pecans

1.Grease the slow cooker with the butter.
2.In a large bowl, whisk together the eggs, milk, vanilla, cinnamon, nutmeg, and salt. Gently toss the bananas and bread cubes in the mixture until the bread is thoroughly saturated.
3.Pour the bread and banana mixture into the slow cooker. Sprinkle the top with the toasted pecans.
4.Cover and cook on low for 4 hours or on high for 2 hours.
5.Serve warm.

Almond and Raisin Granola

Prep time: 10 minutes | Cook time: 4 to 5 hours | Makes 9 cups

5 cups old-fashioned rolled oats
2 cups whole almonds, chopped
½ cup vegetable oil
⅓ cup maple syrup
⅓ cup honey
⅓ cup packed light brown sugar
4 teaspoons vanilla extract
1 teaspoon ground cinnamon
½ teaspoon salt
2 cups raisins
Cooking spray

1.Spritz the slow cooker with cooking spray. Combine oats and almonds in the prepared slow cooker. Whisk oil, maple syrup, honey, sugar, vanilla, cinnamon, and salt together in a bowl.
2.Drizzle oil mixture over oat mixture and gently toss until evenly coated. Cover and cook, stirring every hour, until oat mixture is deep golden brown and fragrant, 4 to 5 hours on high.
3.Transfer oat mixture to a rimmed baking sheet and spread into even layer. Let cool to room temperature, about 30 minutes. Transfer cooled granola to large bowl, add raisins, and gently toss to combine. Serve.

Quinoa and Fruit Breakfast

Prep time: 5 minutes | Cook time: 8 hours | Serves 2

¾ cup quinoa
2 cups fresh mixed fruit
⅛ teaspoon sea salt
1 teaspoon vanilla extract
3 cups water
2 tablespoons toasted pecans, for garnish

1.Put the quinoa, mixed fruit, and salt in the slow cooker. Add the vanilla extract and water, and mix thoroughly.
2.Cover and cook on low for 8 hours or overnight.
3.Garnish with the toasted pecans before serving.

Yogurt and Blueberry Parfait

Prep time: 5 minutes | Cook time: 10 hours | Serves 4

4 cups 2% milk
¼ cup plain yogurt
2 cups blueberries
1 cup low-fat, low-sugar granola

1.Pour the milk into the slow cooker. Cover and cook on low for 2 hours.
2.Unplug the slow cooker and stir in the yogurt. Put the lid on and wrap the slow cooker in a bath towel to help insulate it. Allow the yogurt to rest for 8 hours or overnight.
3.For a thick yogurt, strain the mixture into a medium bowl through a few layers of cheesecloth for 10 to 15 minutes. Discard the whey remaining in the cheesecloth.
4.To serve, layer the strained yogurt with the berries and the granola in a serving bowl.

Potato and Tomato Strata

Prep time: 20 minutes | Cook time: 6 to 8 hours | Serves 8

8 Yukon Gold potatoes, peeled and diced
1 onion, minced
2 red bell peppers, stemmed, deseeded, and minced
3 Roma tomatoes, deseeded and chopped
3 garlic cloves, minced
1½ cups shredded Swiss cheese
8 eggs
2 egg whites
1 teaspoon dried marjoram leaves
1 cup 2% milk

1.In the slow cooker, layer the diced potatoes, onion, bell peppers, tomatoes, garlic, and cheese.
2.In a medium bowl, mix the eggs, egg whites, marjoram, and milk well with a wire whisk. Pour this mixture into the slow cooker.
3.Cover and cook on low for 6 to 8 hours, or until a food thermometer inserted in the mixture registers 165°F (74°C) and the potatoes are tender.
4.Scoop out of the slow cooker to serve.

Cheesy Bread and Ham Casserole

Prep time: 10 minutes | Cook time: 8 hours | Serves 2

1 teaspoon butter, at room temperature, or extra-virgin olive oil
2 eggs
2 egg whites
Freshly ground black pepper, to taste
2 slices whole-grain bread, crusts removed, cut into 1-inch cubes
2 ounces (57 g) aged ham, diced
2 ounces (57 g) Parmesan cheese, shredded

1.Grease the slow cooker with the butter.
2.In a small bowl, whisk together the eggs, egg whites, and black pepper.
3.Put the bread, ham, and cheese in the slow cooker. Pour the egg mixture over and stir gently to combine.
4.Cover and cook on low for 8 hours or overnight.
5.Serve warm.

Peanut Butter Oatmeal Granola

Prep time: 10 to 15 minutes | Cook time: 1½ hours | Serves 16 to 20

6 cups dry oatmeal
½ cup wheat germ
½ cup toasted coconut
½ cup sunflower seeds
½ cup raisins
1 cup butter
1 cup peanut butter
1 cup brown sugar

1.Combine oatmeal, wheat germ, coconut, sunflower seeds, and raisins in the slow cooker.
2.Melt together butter, peanut butter, and brown sugar in a small bowl. Pour them over oatmeal mixture. Mix well.
3.Cover. Cook on low for 1½ hours, stirring every 15 minutes.
4.Allow to cool in cooker, stirring every 30 minutes, or spread onto cookie sheet. When thoroughly cooled, break into chunks and store in airtight container. Serve chilled.

Broccoli and Ricotta Casseroles

Prep time: 10 minutes | Cook time: 2 to 3 hours | Serves 4

1 onion, chopped
1 tablespoon extra-virgin olive oil
3 garlic cloves, minced
1 teaspoon minced fresh thyme
8 ounces (227 g) frozen broccoli spears, thawed, patted dry, and chopped
8 ounces (227 g) whole-milk ricotta cheese
1 cup shredded Cheddar cheese
4 large eggs, lightly beaten
¼ teaspoon salt
¼ teaspoon ground black pepper
2 cups boiling water
1 tablespoon minced fresh chives

1.Grease four ramekins. Microwave onion, oil, garlic, and thyme in a large bowl, stirring occasionally, until onion is softened, about 5 minutes.
2.Stir in broccoli, ricotta, Cheddar, eggs, salt, and pepper until well combined. Divide the mixture evenly among prepared ramekins.
3.Fill the slow cooker with the water and set ramekins in the slow cooker. Cover and cook until casseroles are set, 2 to 3 hours on low.
4.Using tongs and sturdy spatula, remove ramekins from slow cooker and let cool for 15 minutes. Sprinkle with chives and serve.

Quinoa and Cherry Porridge

Prep time: 5 minutes | Cook time: 8 hours | Serves 2

¾ cup quinoa
½ cup dried cherries
⅛ teaspoon sea salt
1 teaspoon vanilla extract
3 cups almond milk

1.Put the quinoa, cherries, and salt in the slow cooker. Pour in the vanilla and almond milk, and stir them together.
2.Cover and cook on low for 8 hours or overnight.
3.Serve warm.

Simple Sausage Casserole

Prep time: 15 minutes | Cook time: 4 hours | Serves 8

1 pound (454 g) loose sausage
6 eggs
2 cups milk
8 slices bread, cubed
2 cups shredded Cheddar cheese

1.In a nonstick skillet, brown the sausage for 15 to 20 minutes. Flip the sausage halfway through. Pat the sausage dry with paper towels after cooking.
2.Mix the eggs and milk in a large bowl. Stir in the bread cubes, cheese, and cooked sausage. Refrigerate overnight.
3.Place the mixture in the greased slow cooker. Cook on low for 4 hours.
4.Serve warm.

Super Egg, Quinoa and Kale Casserole

Prep time: 20 minutes | Cook time: 6 to 8 hours | Serves 8

2 tablespoons vegetable oil
3 cups 2% milk
1½ cups vegetable broth
11 eggs
1½ cups quinoa, rinsed and drained
3 cups chopped kale
1 leek, chopped
1 red bell pepper, stemmed, deseeded, and chopped
3 garlic cloves, minced
1½ cups shredded Havarti cheese

1.Grease the slow cooker with vegetable oil and set aside.
2.In a large bowl, mix the milk, vegetable broth, and eggs, and beat well with a wire whisk.
3.Stir in the quinoa, kale, leek, bell pepper, garlic, and cheese. Pour the mixture into the prepared slow cooker.
4.Cover and cook on low for 6 to 8 hours, or until a food thermometer inserted in the mixture registers 165ºF (74ºC) and the mixture is set.
5.Serve warm.

Lush Egg and Ham Breakfast Bake

Prep time: 15 minutes | Cook time: 3 to 4 hours | Serves 10

12 eggs
1½ to 2 cups shredded Parmesan cheese
1 cup diced cooked ham
1 cup milk
1 teaspoon salt
½ teaspoon pepper

1.Beat the eggs in a bowl, then pour into the slow cooker. Mix in the remaining ingredients.
2.Cover and cook on low for 3 to 4 hours. Stir periodically.
3.Serve warm.

Apple Cobbler

Prep time: 20 minutes | Cook time: 2 to 3 hours | Serves 8 to 10

8 medium, tart apples
½ cup sugar
2 tablespoons fresh lemon juice
1 to 2 teaspoons lemon zest
Dash of ground cinnamon
1½ cups natural fat-free cereal mixed with fruit and nuts
¼ cup butter, melted
Cooking spray

1.Spritz the slow cooker lightly with cooking spray.
2.Core, peel, and slice apples into the slow cooker.
3.Add sugar, lemon juice and zest, and cinnamon.
4.Mix cereal and melted butter together, then add to the ingredients in the slow cooker. Mix thoroughly.
5.Cover. Cook on low for 6 hours, or on high for 2 to 3 hours.
6.Serve warm.

Potato, Parsnip, and Carrot Hash

Prep time: 20 minutes | Cook time: 7 to 8 hours | Serves 8

4 Yukon Gold potatoes, chopped
2 russet potatoes, chopped
3 large carrots, peeled and chopped
1 large parsnip, peeled and chopped
2 onions, chopped
¼ cup vegetable broth
2 garlic cloves, minced
1 teaspoon dried thyme leaves
½ teaspoon salt
2 tablespoons olive oil

1.In the slow cooker, mix all the ingredients. Stir to combine well. Cover and cook on low for 7 to 8 hours.
2.Stir the hash well and serve.

Eggs In Tomato Purgatory

Prep time: 15 minutes | Cook time: 7⅓ to 8⅓ hours | Serves 8

2½ pounds (1.1 kg) Roma tomatoes, chopped
2 onions, chopped
2 garlic cloves, chopped
1 teaspoon paprika
½ teaspoon ground cumin
½ teaspoon dried marjoram leaves
1 cup vegetable broth
8 large eggs
2 red chili peppers, minced
½ cup chopped flat-leaf parsley

1.In the slow cooker, mix the tomatoes, onions, garlic, paprika, cumin, marjoram, and vegetable broth, and stir to mix. Cover and cook on low for 7 to 8 hours, or until a sauce has formed.
2.One at a time, break the eggs into the sauce, then do not stir.
3.Cover and cook on high until the egg whites are completely set and the yolk is thickened, about 20 minutes. Sprinkle the eggs with the minced red chili peppers.
4.Sprinkle with the parsley and serve.

Chapter 2 Appetizers

Sumptuous Party Mix

Prep time: 10 minutes | Cook time: 3 to 4 hours | Serves 10 to 12

9 cups corn, rice, and/or wheat chex cereal
1 cup pita chips, broken into 1-inch pieces
1 cup mini pretzels
1 cup roasted peanuts
8 tablespoons unsalted butter, melted
¼ cup Worcestershire sauce
1½ teaspoons garlic powder
¼ teaspoon cayenne pepper

1.Combine cereal, pita chips, mini pretzels, and peanuts in the slow cooker.
2.Whisk melted butter, Worcestershire, garlic powder, and cayenne together in a bowl.
3.Drizzle butter mixture over cereal mixture and gently toss until evenly coated. Cover and cook, stirring every hour, until cereal mixture is toasted and fragrant, 3 to 4 hours on high.
4.Transfer cereal mixture to rimmed baking sheet and spread into even layer. Let cool to room temperature, about 20 minutes. Serve.

Herbed Mushrooms

Prep time: 10 minutes | Cook time: 1 to 2 hours | Serves 8 to 10

2 pounds (907 g) small cremini or white mushrooms, trimmed
½ cup extra-virgin olive oil. divided
4 garlic cloves, minced
3 sprigs fresh thyme
Salt and ground black pepper, to taste
2 tablespoons minced fresh tarragon
1 tablespoon Dijon mustard
1 tablespoon sherry vinegar

1.Toss mushrooms with 2 tablespoons oil in a bowl and microwave, stirring occasionally, until mushrooms release their liquid and shrink in size, about 10 minutes, then drain thoroughly.
2.Combine mushrooms, garlic, thyme sprigs, ¾ teaspoon salt, ¼ teaspoon pepper, and remaining 6 tablespoons oil in the slow cooker. Cover and cook until mushrooms are tender and flavors meld, 1 to 2 hours on low.
3.Discard thyme sprigs. Stir in tarragon, mustard, and vinegar and season with salt and pepper to taste. Serve warm or at room temperature.

Creamy Artichoke and Spinach Dip

Prep time: 15 minutes | Cook time: 1 to 2 hours | Serves 6 to 8

6 ounces (170 g) cream cheese, softened
½ cup mayonnaise
2 tablespoons water
1 tablespoon lemon juice
3 garlic cloves, minced
¼ teaspoon salt
¼ teaspoon ground black pepper
3 cups jarred whole baby artichokes packed in water, rinsed, patted dry, and chopped
10 ounces (283 g) frozen spinach, thawed and squeezed dry
2 tablespoons minced fresh chives

1.Whisk cream cheese, mayonnaise, water, lemon juice, garlic, salt, and pepper in a large bowl until well combined. Gently fold in artichokes and spinach.
2.Transfer mixture to slow cooker, cover, and cook until heated through, 1 to 2 hours on low.
3.Gently stir dip to recombine. Sprinkle with chives and serve.

Crab Dip

Prep time: 10 minutes | Cook time: 1 to 2 hours | Serves 6 to 8

1 small onion, chopped fine
2 tablespoons unsalted butter
2 teaspoons Old Bay seasoning
8 ounces (227 g) cream cheese, softened
¼ cup mayonnaise
¼ teaspoon ground black pepper
1 pound (454 g) lump crabmeat, picked over for shells and pressed dry between paper towels
2 tablespoons minced fresh chives

1.Microwave onion, butter, and Old Bay seasoning in a large bowl, stirring occasionally, until onion is softened, about 5 minutes.
2.Whisk in cream cheese, mayonnaise, and pepper until well combined. Gently fold in crabmeat.
3.Transfer mixture to slow cooker, cover, and cook until heated through, 1 to 2 hours on low.
4.Gently stir dip to recombine. Sprinkle with chives and serve.

Broccoli Dip

Prep time: 15 minutes | Cook time: 2 hours | Makes 5½ cups

1 pound (454 g) ground beef
1 pound (454 g) process cheese (Velveeta), cubed
1 (10¾-ounce / 305-g) can condensed cream of mushroom soup, undiluted
3 cups frozen chopped broccoli, thawed
2 tablespoons salsa
Tortilla chips, for serving

1.In a large skillet, cook beef over medium heat until no longer pink, then drain. Transfer to the slow cooker. Add cheese, soup, broccoli and salsa, then mix well.
2.Cover and cook on low for 2 to 3 hours or until heated through, stirring after 1 hour. Serve with chips.

Chili Dip

Prep time: 5 minutes | Cook time: 1 to 2 hours | Makes 2 cups

1 (24-ounce / 680-g) jar salsa
1 (15-ounce / 425-g) can chili with beans
2 (2¼-ounce / 64-g) cans sliced ripe olives, drained
12 ounces (340 g) process cheese (Velveeta), cubed
Tortilla chips, for serving

1.In the slow cooker, combine the salsa, chili and olives. Stir in cheese.
2.Cover and cook on low for 1 to 2 hours or until cheese is melted, stirring halfway through.
3.Serve with chips.

Black Bean and Beef Taco Dip

Prep time: 15 minutes | Cook time: 1 to 2 hours | Serves 6 to 8

1 pound (454 g) 85% lean ground beef
1 (1-ounce / 28-g) packet taco seasoning
2 garlic cloves, minced
2 (15-ounce / 425-g) cans black beans, rinsed, divided
2 (10-ounce / 283-g) cans Diced Tomatoes and Green Chilies, drained with ¼ cup juice reserved
2 cups Monterey Jack cheese, shredded, divided
2 scallions, sliced thin

1.Microwave ground beef, taco seasoning, and garlic in a bowl, stirring occasionally, until beef is no longer pink, about 5 minutes. Break up any large pieces of beef with spoon, then drain off excess fat.
2.Using potato masher, mash half of beans with reserved tomato juice in a large bowl until smooth. Stir in beef mixture, tomatoes, 1½ cups Monterey Jack, and remaining beans until well combined.
3.Transfer mixture to slow cooker, cover, and cook until heated through, 1 to 2 hours on low. Gently stir dip to recombine, then sprinkle with remaining ½ cup Monterey Jack. Cover and cook on low until cheese is melted, about 5 minutes.
4.Sprinkle with scallions and serve.

Crab and Shrimp Dip

Prep time: 15 minutes | Cook time: 1½ hours | Makes 5 cups

1 (2-pound / 907-g) package process cheese (Velveeta), cubed
2 (6-ounce / 170-g) cans lump crabmeat, drained
1 (10-ounce / 283-g) can diced tomatoes and green chilies, undrained
1 cup frozen cooked salad shrimp, thawed
French bread baguettes, sliced and toasted

1. In a greased slow cooker, combine the cheese, crab, tomatoes and shrimp.
2. Cover and cook on low for 1½ to 2 hours or until cheese is melted, stirring occasionally.
3. Serve with baguettes.

Cheesy Jalapeño Poppers

Prep time: 15 minutes | Cook time: 2 hours | Makes 24 poppers

8 ounces (227 g) cream cheese, at room temperature
¼ cup sour cream
¼ cup grated Cheddar cheese
12 jalapeños, rinsed, deseeded, and halved lengthwise
24 slices bacon
⅓ cup chicken stock

1. In a medium bowl, mix the cream cheese, sour cream, and grated Cheddar cheese until well blended.
2. Divide the cheese mixture evenly among the jalapeño halves, and wrap each stuffed jalapeño half with a slice of bacon, then secure the bacon with a toothpick.
3. In the slow cooker, pour in the chicken stock and add the stuffed jalapeños.
4. Cover and cook on low for 4 hours or on high for 2 hours.
5. Using a slotted spoon, remove the stuffed jalapeños from the slow cooker and serve hot or at room temperature.

Rosemary White Bean Dip

Prep time: 10 minutes | Cook time: 1 to 2 hours | Serves 6 to 8

3 (15-ounce / 425-g) cans cannellini beans, rinsed, divided
¼ cup extra-virgin olive oil, plus extra for serving
1 garlic clove, minced
1 teaspoon minced fresh rosemary
¼ teaspoon grated lemon zest plus 1 tablespoon juice
¼ teaspoon salt

1. Process two-thirds of beans, oil, garlic, rosemary, lemon zest and juice, and salt in a food processor. Pulse until smooth, about 10 seconds, scraping down sides of bowl as needed.
2. Add remaining beans and pulse until just incorporated and chunky, about 2 pulses.
3. Transfer mixture to slow cooker, cover, and cook until heated through, 1 to 2 hours on low.
4. Gently stir dip to recombine and adjust consistency with hot water as needed. Drizzle dip with extra oil and serve.

Simple Marinated Wings

Prep time: 5 minutes | Cook time: 3 to 4 hours | Serves 20

20 whole chicken wings (about 4 pounds / 1.8 kg in total)
1 cup soy sauce
¼ cup white wine or chicken broth
2 garlic cloves, minced
1 teaspoon ground ginger
3 tablespoons sugar
¼ cup canola oil

1. Cut chicken wings into three sections, then discard wing tips. Place in a large resealable plastic bag. In a small bowl, whisk remaining ingredients until blended. Add to chicken, then seal bag and turn to coat. Refrigerate overnight.
2. Transfer chicken and marinade to the slow cooker. Cook, covered, on low for 3 to 4 hours or until chicken is tender.
3. Using tongs, remove wings to a serving plate.

Catalina Marmalade Meatballs

Prep time: 10 minutes | Cook time: 4 to 5 hours | Makes 5 dozen

1 (1-pound / 454-g) bottle Catalina salad dressing
1 cup orange marmalade
3 tablespoons Worcestershire sauce
½ teaspoon crushed red pepper flakes
1 (2-pound / 907-g) package frozen cooked meatballs, thawed

1.In the slow cooker, combine the salad dressing, marmalade, Worcestershire sauce and pepper flakes.
2.Stir in meatballs. Cover and cook on low for 4 to 5 hours or until heated through.
3.Serve warm.

Chicken Nachos

Prep time: 15 minutes | Cook time: 4 hours | Serves 8

2 pounds (907 g) boneless, skinless chicken breast
2 large tomatoes, diced
1 medium onion, chopped
3 medium jalapeños, deseeded and chopped
1 cup cooked black beans, drained and rinsed
1 tablespoon chili power
½ teaspoon garlic powder
½ teaspoon sea salt
½ teaspoon freshly ground black pepper
1 tablespoon packed brown sugar
½ cup chicken stock
8 ounces (227 g) grated pepper Jack cheese
8 ounces (227 g) grated Colby or Cheddar cheese
Tortilla chips, for serving

1.In the slow cooker, combine the chicken, tomatoes, onion, and jalapeños. Spoon the black beans over the chicken and vegetables.
2.In a medium bowl, mix the chili powder, garlic powder, salt, black pepper, brown sugar, and chicken stock. Pour the mixture over the chicken, vegetables, and beans.
3.Sprinkle the cheeses over.
4.Cover and cook on low for 8 hours or on high for 4 hours.
5.Remove the lid and shred the chicken, then mix it back in with the other ingredients. Serve hot with tortilla chips.

Posh Southwest Pork Nachos

Prep time: 40 minutes | Cook time: 7¼ hours | Serves 30

2 (3½-pounds / 1.6-kg) boneless whole pork loin roasts
1 cup unsweetened apple juice
6 garlic cloves, minced
1 teaspoon salt
1 teaspoon liquid smoke, optional
2½ cups barbecue sauce, divided
⅓ cup packed brown sugar
2 tablespoons honey
1 (10-ounce / 283-g) package tortilla chips
1½ cups frozen corn
1 (15-ounce / 425-g) can black beans, rinsed and drained
1 medium tomato, deseeded and chopped
1 medium red onion, chopped
⅓ cup minced fresh cilantro
1 jalapeño pepper, deseeded and chopped
2 teaspoons lime juice
1 (1-pound / 454-g) package process cheese (Velveeta), cubed
2 tablespoons 2% milk

1.Cut each roast in half, then place in two slow cookers. Combine apple juice, garlic, salt and liquid smoke if desired. Pour the mixture over meat. Cover and cook on low for 7 to 8 hours or until tender.
2.Preheat oven to 375ºF (190ºC). Shred pork with two forks, then place in a large bowl. Stir in 2 cups of barbecue sauce, brown sugar and honey. Divide tortilla chips between two greased baking dishes. Top with pork mixture.
3.Combine corn, beans, tomato, onion, cilantro, jalapeño and lime juice in a medium bowl. Spoon them over pork mixture. Bake, uncovered, 15 to 20 minutes or until heated through.
4.Meanwhile, in a small saucepan, melt cheese with milk.
5.Drizzle cheese sauce and remaining barbecue sauce over nachos before serving.

BBQ Glazed Chicken Wings

Prep time: 1½ hours | Cook time: 3 to 4 hours | Makes 4 dozen

5 pounds (2.3 kg) chicken wings
2½ cups hot ketchup
⅔ cup white vinegar
½ cup plus 2 tablespoons honey
½ cup molasses
1 teaspoon salt
1 teaspoon Worcestershire sauce
½ teaspoon onion powder
½ teaspoon chili powder
½ to 1 teaspoon liquid smoke, optional

1. Cut the chicken wings into three sections, then discard wing tip sections. Place wings in two greased baking pans. Bake, uncovered, at 375°F (190°C) for 30 minutes, then drain. Turn wings, then bake for 20 to 25 minutes longer or until juices run clear.
2. Meanwhile, in a large saucepan, combine the ketchup, vinegar, honey, molasses, salt, Worcestershire sauce, onion powder and chili powder. Add liquid smoke if desired. Bring to a boil. Reduce heat and simmer, uncovered, for 25 to 30 minutes.
3. Drain the wings, then place a third of wings in the slow cooker. Top with about 1 cup of sauce mixture. Repeat layers twice. Cover and cook on low for 3 to 4 hours. Stir before serving.

Tequila Sausage Queso

Prep time: 10 minutes | Cook time: 2¼ hours | Serves 4 to 6

8 ounces (227 g) chorizo sausage
1 tablespoon olive oil
½ cup diced poblano pepper, seeds removed and discarded
¼ cup diced onion
⅓ cup tequila
2 cups shredded Monterey Jack
Salsa, chopped fresh cilantro, and diced tomatoes, for serving

1. Cook the chorizo in a nonstick skillet over medium-high heat, breaking up the sausage with a spoon, for 3 to 4 minutes, or until fully cooked. Remove from the heat. Place the cooked sausage on a plate lined with paper towels to drain.
2. Drain the fat from the skillet, add the oil to it, and warm it over medium-high heat. Add the poblano pepper and onion and sauté for 2 to 3 minutes until the onion is light and translucent. Remove from the heat.
3. Return the pan to medium-high heat and carefully add the tequila. Reduce the heat to low and simmer for 2 minutes, or until the tequila evaporates. Remove from the heat.
4. Combine the chorizo and sautéed poblano pepper–onion mixture in the slow cooker. Add the cheese, cover, and cook, stirring occasionally, on low for 2 hours.
5. Reduce the setting to warm. Garnish with the salsa, cilantro, and tomatoes and serve warm.

Sweet Smoked Chicken Wings

Prep time: 20 minutes | Cook time: 3¼ to 3¾ hours | Makes 2½ dozen

3 pounds (1.4 kg) chicken wingettes (about 30)
½ teaspoon salt, divided
Ground black pepper, to taste
1½ cups ketchup
¼ cup packed brown sugar
¼ cup red wine vinegar
2 tablespoons Worcestershire sauce
1 tablespoon Dijon mustard
1 teaspoon minced garlic
1 teaspoon liquid smoke

1. Sprinkle chicken wings with a dash of salt and pepper. Broil from the heat for 5 to 10 minutes on each side or until golden brown. Transfer to a greased slow cooker.
2. Combine the ketchup, brown sugar, vinegar, Worcestershire sauce, mustard, garlic, liquid smoke, and remaining salt in a bowl. Stir to mix well. Pour the mixture over wings. Toss to coat.
3. Cover and cook on low for 3¼ to 3¾ hours or until chicken juices run clear.
4. Serve warm.

Lush BBQ Sausage Bites

Prep time: 10 minutes | Cook time: 2½ to 3 hours | Serves 12 to 14

¾ pound (340 g) smoked kielbasa or Polish sausage, cut into ½-inch slices
¾ pound (340 g) fully cooked bratwurst links, cut into ½-inch slices
1 (1-pound / 454-g) package miniature smoked sausages
1 (18-ounce / 510-g) bottle barbecue sauce
⅔ cup orange marmalade
½ teaspoon ground mustard
⅛ teaspoon ground allspice
1 (20-ounce / 567-g) can pineapple chunks, drained

1.In the slow cooker, combine the sausages. In a small bowl, whisk the barbecue sauce, marmalade, mustard and allspice. Pour over sausage mixture, then stir to coat.
2.Cover and cook on high for 2½ to 3 hours or until heated through. Stir in pineapple. Serve using toothpicks.

Crunchy Snack Mix

Prep time: 10 minutes | Cook time: 2½ hours | Makes 2½ quarts

4½ cups crispy chow mein
4 cups Rice Chex cereal
1 (9¾-ounce / 276-g) can salted cashews
1 cup flaked coconut, toasted
½ cup butter, melted
2 tablespoons soy sauce
2¼ teaspoons curry powder
¾ teaspoon ground ginger

1.In the slow cooker, combine the chow mein, cereal, cashews and coconut. In a small bowl, whisk the butter, soy sauce, curry powder and ginger, then drizzle over cereal mixture and mix well.
2.Cover and cook on low for 2½ hours, stirring every 30 minutes. Serve warm or at room temperature.

Salsa Bulgur and Black Bean Bowls

Prep time: 20 minutes | Cook time: 8½ to 9½ hours | Serves 6

Salsa:
6 ounces (170 g) cherry tomatoes, quartered
2 tablespoons minced fresh cilantro
1 tablespoon lime juice
2 tablespoons extra-virgin olive oil
Salt and ground black pepper, to taste

Beans:
1 onion, chopped fine
4 garlic cloves, minced
1 tablespoon extra-virgin olive oil
1 tablespoon ground cumin
2 teaspoons chili powder
3 cups vegetable broth
3 cups water
1 pound (454 g) dried black beans, picked over and rinsed
Salt and ground black pepper, to taste
1 cup medium-grind bulgur, rinsed
1 cup queso fresco, crumbled

For the salsa:
1.Combine all ingredients in a small bowl and season with salt and pepper to taste. Refrigerate until ready to serve.

For the beans:
2.Microwave onion, garlic, oil, cumin, and chili powder in a bowl, stirring occasionally, until onion is softened, about 5 minutes. Transfer them to the slow cooker.
3.Stir broth, water, beans, and 1 teaspoon salt into the slow cooker. Cover and cook until beans are tender, 8 to 9 hours on high.
4.Stir bulgur into beans, cover, and cook on high until bulgur is tender and most of liquid is absorbed, 20 to 30 minutes. Season with salt and pepper to taste. Top with salsa and queso fresco before serving.

Ritzy Black Bean and Quinoa Salad

Prep time: 20 minutes | Cook time: 2 to 3 hours | Serves 4 to 6

1½ cups white quinoa, rinsed
1 jalapeño chile, stemmed, deseeded, and minced
3 tablespoons extra-virgin olive oil, divided
1 garlic clove, minced
1 teaspoon ground cumin
1 teaspoon ground coriander
1¾ cups water
1 (15-ounce / 425-g) can black beans, rinsed
Salt and ground black pepper, to taste
2 red bell peppers, stemmed, deseeded, and chopped
1 mango, peeled, pitted, and cut into ¼-inch pieces
⅓ cup fresh cilantro leaves
3 scallions, sliced thin
¼ cup lime juice (2 limes)
Cooking spray

1.Spritz the slow cooker with cooking spray. Microwave quinoa, jalapeño, 1 tablespoon oil, garlic, cumin, and coriander in a bowl, stirring occasionally, until quinoa is lightly toasted and fragrant, about 3 minutes. Transfer to the prepared slow cooker.
2.Stir in water, beans, and 1 teaspoon salt. Cover and cook until quinoa is tender and all water is absorbed, 3 to 4 hours on low or 2 to 3 hours on high.
3.Fluff quinoa with fork, transfer to a large serving bowl, and let cool slightly. Add bell peppers, mango, cilantro, scallions, lime juice, and remaining 2 tablespoons oil and gently toss to combine. Season with salt and pepper to taste. Serve.

Turkish Eggplant Bulgur Casserole

Prep time: 20 minutes | Cook time: 2 to 3 hours | Serves 4 to 6

Sauce:
1 cup plain yogurt
2 tablespoons chopped fresh mint
¼ cup chopped fresh parsley
1 garlic clove, minced
Salt and ground black pepper, to taste

Bulgur:
2 teaspoons paprika
1½ teaspoons ground cumin
Salt, to taste
⅛ teaspoon cayenne pepper
⅛ teaspoon ground cinnamon
1½ pounds (680 g) eggplant, sliced into ½-inch-thick rounds
¼ cup extra-virgin olive oil, divided
1 onion, chopped fine
4 garlic cloves, minced
1 tablespoon tomato paste
1 cup medium-grind bulgur, rinsed
1 cup vegetable broth
4 tomatoes, cored and sliced ½ inch thick
Cooking spray

For the sauce:
1.Combine all ingredients in a small bowl and season with salt and pepper to taste. Refrigerate until ready to serve.

For the bulgur:
2.Adjust oven rack 6 inches from broiler element and heat broiler. Combine paprika, cumin, ¾ teaspoon salt, cayenne, and cinnamon in a bowl. Arrange eggplant in single layer on aluminum foil–lined rimmed baking sheet, brush both sides with 3 tablespoons oil, and sprinkle with spice mixture.
3.Broil eggplant until softened and beginning to brown, 10 to 12 minutes, flipping eggplant halfway through broiling.
4.Spritz slow cooker with cooking spray. Microwave onion, garlic, tomato paste, ¾ teaspoon salt, and remaining 1 tablespoon oil in a separate bowl, stirring occasionally, until onion is softened, about 5 minutes. Transfer to the prepared slow cooker. Stir in bulgur and broth.

Shingle alternating slices of eggplant and tomato into 3 tightly fitting rows on top of bulgur mixture.
5.Cover and cook until eggplant and bulgur are tender and all broth is absorbed, 3 to 4 hours on low or 2 to 3 hours on high. Serve, passing sauce separately.

Quinoa and Cucumber Lettuce Wraps

Prep time: 20 minutes | Cook time: 2 to 3 hours | Serves 4

2 tablespoons extra-virgin olive oil, divided
1 tablespoon minced fresh oregano or 1 teaspoon dried
2 garlic cloves, minced
1½ cups vegetable broth
1 cup white quinoa, rinsed
⅔ cup plain yogurt
½ cup feta cheese, crumbled
¼ cup minced fresh mint, divided
2 tablespoons red wine vinegar
Salt and ground black pepper, to taste
2 tomatoes, cored, deseeded, and chopped
1 cucumber, peeled, halved lengthwise, deseeded, and cut into ¼-inch pieces
1 small shallot, halved and sliced thin
2 (8-ounce / 227-g) heads Bibb lettuce, leaves separated
Cooking spray

1.Spritz the slow cooker with cooking spray. Microwave 1 tablespoon oil, oregano, and garlic in a bowl until fragrant, about 1 minute. Transfer to the prepared slow cooker.
2.Stir in broth and quinoa, cover, and cook until quinoa is tender and all broth is absorbed, 3 to 4 hours on low or 2 to 3 hours on high.
3.Fluff quinoa with fork, transfer to a large serving bowl, and let cool slightly.
4.Combine yogurt, feta, 2 tablespoons mint, vinegar, ½ teaspoon salt, ¼ teaspoon pepper, and remaining 1 tablespoon oil in a separate bowl as dressing.
5.Add half of dressing, tomatoes, cucumber, shallot, and remaining 2 tablespoons mint to quinoa and gently toss to combine. Season with salt and pepper to taste.
6.Serve the quinoa salad over the lettuce leaves, dress with remaining dressing separately.

Braised Eggplant and Lentils

Prep time: 20 minutes | Cook time: 2 to 3 hours | Serves 4 to 6

2 pounds (907 g) eggplant, cut into 1-inch pieces
1 onion, chopped fine
3 tablespoons extra-virgin olive oil, divided
1 tablespoon tomato paste
2 garlic cloves, minced
2 teaspoons minced fresh thyme or ½ teaspoon dried
Salt and ground black pepper, to taste
2 cups vegetable broth
1 cup French green lentils, picked over and rinsed
2 tablespoons red wine vinegar, divided
10 ounces (283 g) cherry tomatoes, halved
½ cup feta cheese, crumbled
¼ cup minced fresh parsley

1.Adjust oven rack 6 inches from broiler element and heat broiler. Line rimmed baking sheet with aluminum foil.
2.Toss eggplant and onion with 1 tablespoon oil, tomato paste, garlic, thyme, and ½ teaspoon salt in a bowl.
3.Spread eggplant mixture evenly over the prepared baking sheet. Broil until eggplant is softened and beginning to brown, 10 to 12 minutes, rotating sheet halfway through broiling.
4.Combine broth, lentils, and 1 tablespoon vinegar in the slow cooker. Spread eggplant mixture and tomatoes evenly on top of lentils.
5.Cover and cook until lentils are tender, 3 to 4 hours on low or 2 to 3 hours on high. Stir in remaining 2 tablespoons oil and remaining 1 tablespoon vinegar. Season with salt and pepper to taste. Sprinkle with feta and parsley and serve.

Enchilada Casserole

Prep time: 10 minutes | Cook time: 3½ hours | Serves 6

2 zucchini, diced
1 medium onion, chopped
1½ medium jalapeños, deseeded and chopped, or more as desired
2 cups fresh or frozen corn
2 pounds (907 g) tempeh, chopped
½ cup chopped fresh cilantro

1 teaspoon ground cumin
1 teaspoon ancho chili powder
½ teaspoon garlic powder
½ cup sliced black olives
8 Roma tomatoes, chopped, or 1 (28-ounce / 794-g) can diced fire-roasted tomatoes
6 blue corn or other corn tortillas
Cooking spray

1.Spritz the slow cooker with cooking spray.
2.In a large bowl, combine all the ingredients except the tortillas. Spoon a thin layer of the vegetable mixture on the bottom of the slow cooker. Cover the mixture with a layer of tortillas.
3.Spoon a thicker layer of the vegetable mixture on the tortillas. Cover with another layer of tortillas and repeat until the ingredients are used up, ending with a layer of tortillas.
4.Cover and cook on low for 6 hours or on high for 3½ hours.
5.Cut the casserole into slices and serve hot.

Caponata

Prep time: 15 minutes | Cook time: 5½ hours | Serves 6

1 pound (454 g) plum tomatoes, chopped
1 eggplant, not peeled, cut into ½-inch pieces
2 medium zucchini, cut into ½-inch pieces
1 large yellow onion, finely chopped
3 stalks celery, sliced
½ cup chopped fresh parsley
2 tablespoons red wine vinegar
1 tablespoon brown sugar
¼ cup raisins
¼ cup tomato paste
1 teaspoon sea salt
¼ teaspoon black pepper
¼ cup pine nuts
2 tablespoons capers, drained

1.Combine the tomatoes, eggplant, zucchini, onion, celery, and parsley in the slow cooker. Add the vinegar, brown sugar, raisins, and tomato paste. Sprinkle with the salt and pepper.
2.Cover and cook on low for 5½ hours, or until thoroughly cooked.
3.Stir in the pine nuts and capers. Serve hot.

North African Pumpkin and Cauliflower Stew

Prep time: 15 minutes | Cook time: 7 to 8 hours | Serves 6

1 tablespoon extra-virgin olive oil
2 cups diced pumpkin
2 cups chopped cauliflower
1 red bell pepper, diced
½ sweet onion, diced
2 teaspoons minced garlic
2 cups coconut milk
2 tablespoons natural peanut butter
1 tablespoon ground cumin
1 teaspoon ground coriander
¼ cup chopped cilantro, for garnish

1.Lightly grease the slow cooker with the olive oil.
2.Add the pumpkin, cauliflower, bell pepper, onion, and garlic to the slow cooker.
3.In a small bowl, whisk together the coconut milk, peanut butter, cumin, and coriander until smooth.
4.Pour the coconut milk mixture over the vegetables in the slow cooker.
5.Cover and cook on low for 7 to 8 hours.
6.Serve topped with the cilantro.

Hearty Tempeh Carnitas

Prep time: 15 minutes | Cook time: 3 hours | Serves 6

1½ pounds (680 g) tempeh, cut into bite-size cubes
5 garlic cloves
1 teaspoon ground cumin
1 teaspoon dried oregano
½ teaspoon smoked paprika
1 teaspoon chipotle powder
½ teaspoon sea salt
¾ cup fresh orange juice
2 tablespoons fresh lime juice
3 tablespoons chopped chipotles in adobo
12 flour tortillas
6 lime wedges
Cooking spray
Toppings:

1 medium onion, chopped
1 cup chopped fresh cilantro
3 jalapeños, deseeded and chopped
2 medium avocados, chopped

1.Spray the slow cooker with cooking spray. Add the tempeh, garlic, cumin, oregano, smoked paprika, chipotle powder, and salt.
2.In a medium bowl, mix the orange juice, lime juice, and chipotles, mashing the chipotles into the liquids. Pour this mixture over the ingredients in the slow cooker.
3.Cover and cook on low for 6 hours or on high for 3 hours.
4.Warm the tortillas in a dry skillet over medium heat or in the microwave. Fill the warm tortillas with the filling and top with your favorite ingredients.
5.Serve with lime wedges to squeeze over the carnitas.

Creamed Cauliflower, Beans, and Asparagus

Prep time: 15 minutes | Cook time: 6 hours | Serves 6

1 tablespoon extra-virgin olive oil
½ head cauliflower, cut into small florets
2 cups green beans, cut into 2-inch pieces
1 cup asparagus spears, cut into 2-inch pieces
½ cup sour cream
½ cup shredded Cheddar cheese
½ cup shredded Swiss cheese
3 tablespoons butter
¼ cup water
1 teaspoon ground nutmeg
Pinch freshly ground black pepper, to taste

1.Lightly grease the slow cooker with the olive oil.
2.Add the cauliflower, green beans, asparagus, sour cream, Cheddar cheese, Swiss cheese, butter, water, nutmeg, and pepper into the slow cooker.
3.Cover and cook on low for 6 hours.
4.Serve warm.

Broccoli Casserole

Prep time: 15 minutes | Cook time: 6 hours | Serves 6

1 tablespoon extra-virgin olive oil
1 pound (454 g) broccoli, cut into florets
1 pound (454 g) cauliflower, cut into florets
¼ cup almond flour
2 cups coconut milk
½ teaspoon ground nutmeg
Pinch freshly ground black pepper
1½ cups shredded Gouda cheese, divided

1. Lightly grease the slow cooker with the olive oil.
2. Place the broccoli and cauliflower in the slow cooker.
3. In a small bowl, stir together the almond flour, coconut milk, nutmeg, pepper, and 1 cup of the cheese.
4. Pour the flour mixture over the vegetables and top the casserole with the remaining ½ cup of the cheese.
5. Cover and cook on low for 6 hours.
6. Serve warm.

Zucchini and Tomato Casserole

Prep time: 10 minutes | Cook time: 4½ hours | Serves 4

1 medium red onion, sliced
1 green bell pepper, cut into thin strips
4 medium zucchini, sliced
1 (15-ounce / 425-g) can diced tomatoes, with the juice
1 teaspoon sea salt
½ teaspoon black pepper
½ teaspoon basil
1 tablespoon extra-virgin olive oil
¼ cup grated Parmesan cheese

1. Combine the onion slices, bell pepper strips, zucchini slices, and tomatoes in the slow cooker. Sprinkle with the salt, pepper, and basil.
2. Cover and cook on low for 3 hours.
3. Drizzle the olive oil over the casserole and sprinkle with the Parmesan.
4. Cover and cook on low for 1½ hours more. Serve hot.

Barley-Stuffed Cabbage Rolls

Prep time: 15 minutes | Cook time: 3½ hours | Serves 4

1 large head green cabbage, cored
1 tablespoon olive oil
1 large yellow onion, chopped
3 cups cooked pearl barley
3 ounces (85 g) feta cheese, crumbled
½ cup dried currants
2 tablespoons pine nuts, toasted
2 tablespoons chopped fresh flat-leaf parsley
½ teaspoon sea salt, divided
½ teaspoon black pepper, divided
½ cup apple juice
1 tablespoon apple cider vinegar
1 (15-ounce / 425-g) can crushed tomatoes, with the juice

1. Steam the cabbage head in a large pot over boiling water for 8 minutes. Remove to a cutting board and let cool slightly.
2. Remove 16 leaves from the cabbage head (reserve the rest of the cabbage for another use). Cut off the raised portion of the center vein of each cabbage leaf (do not cut out the vein).
3. Heat the oil in a large nonstick lidded skillet over medium heat. Add the onion, cover, and cook 6 minutes, or until tender. Remove to a large bowl.
4. Stir the barley, feta cheese, currants, pine nuts, and parsley into the onion mixture. Season with ¼ teaspoon of the salt and ¼ teaspoon of the pepper.
5. Place cabbage leaves on a work surface. On 1 cabbage leaf, spoon about ⅓ cup of the barley mixture into the center. Fold in the edges of the leaf over the barley mixture and roll the cabbage leaf up as if you were making a burrito. Repeat for the remaining 15 cabbage leaves and filling.
6. Arrange the cabbage rolls in the slow cooker.
7. Combine the remaining ¼ teaspoon salt, ¼ teaspoon pepper, the apple juice, apple cider vinegar, and tomatoes. Pour the apple juice mixture evenly over the cabbage rolls.
8. Cover and cook on high for 2 hours or on low for 6 to 8 hours. Serve hot.

Summer Super Veg Mélange

Prep time: 15 minutes | Cook time: 6 hours | Serves 6

½ cup extra-virgin olive oil
¼ cup balsamic vinegar
1 tablespoon dried basil
1 teaspoon dried thyme
¼ teaspoon salt
2 cups cauliflower florets
2 zucchini, diced into 1-inch pieces
1 yellow bell pepper, cut into strips
1 cup halved button mushrooms

1. In a large bowl, whisk together the oil, vinegar, basil, thyme, and salt, until blended.
2. Add the cauliflower, zucchini, bell pepper, and mushrooms, and toss to coat.
3. Transfer the vegetables to the slow cooker.
4. Cover and cook on low for 6 hours.
5. Serve warm.

Cauliflower and Zucchini Vindaloo

Prep time: 15 minutes | Cook time: 6 hours | Serves 6

1 tablespoon extra-virgin olive oil
4 cups cauliflower florets
1 carrot, diced
1 zucchini, diced
1 red bell pepper, diced
2 cups coconut milk
½ sweet onion, chopped
1 dried chipotle pepper, chopped
1 tablespoon grated fresh ginger
2 teaspoons minced garlic
2 teaspoons ground cumin
1 teaspoon ground coriander
½ teaspoon turmeric
¼ teaspoon cayenne pepper
¼ teaspoon cardamom
1 cup Greek yogurt, for garnish
2 tablespoons chopped cilantro, for garnish

1. Lightly grease the slow cooker with the olive oil.
2. Place the cauliflower, carrot, zucchini, and bell pepper in the slow cooker.
3. In a small bowl, whisk together the coconut milk, onion, chipotle pepper, ginger, garlic, cumin, coriander, turmeric, cayenne pepper, and cardamom until well blended.
4. Pour the coconut milk mixture into the slow cooker and stir to combine.
5. Cover and cook on low for 6 hours.
6. Serve each portion topped with the yogurt and cilantro.

Beans and Couscous Stuffed Peppers

Prep time: 15 minutes | Cook time: 4 hours | Serves 4

4 large bell peppers, any color
1 (15-ounce / 425-g) can cannellini beans, rinsed and drained
1 cup crumbled feta cheese
½ cup uncooked couscous
4 green onions, white and green parts separated, thinly sliced
1 garlic clove, minced
1 teaspoon oregano
Coarse sea salt and freshly ground black pepper, to taste
1 lemon cut into 4 wedges, for serving

1. Slice a very thin layer from the base of each bell pepper so they sit upright. Slice off the tops just below stem and discard the stem only. Chop the remaining top portions and place in a medium bowl. With a spoon, scoop out the ribs and seeds from the peppers.
2. Add the beans, feta, couscous, white parts of the green onions, garlic, and oregano to a medium bowl. Season with salt and pepper and toss to combine.
3. Stuff the peppers with bean mixture, and place them upright in the slow cooker. Cover and cook on high for 4 hours, or until the peppers are tender and the couscous is cooked.
4. To serve, sprinkle the peppers with the green parts of the green onions and plate with 1 lemon wedge alongside each pepper.

Sumptuous Chinese Vegetable Mix

Prep time: 10 minutes | Cook time: 3 to 6 hours | Serves 6

1 (12-ounce /340-g) package chop-suey vegetables
1 (1-pound / 454-g) can bean sprouts, drained
2 (4-ounce / 113-g) cans sliced mushrooms, drained
1 (8-ounce / 227-g) can water chestnuts, drained
1 bunch celery, sliced on the diagonal
1 large onion, sliced
3 tablespoons soy sauce
1 tablespoon sugar
¼ teaspoon black pepper, or to taste
¾ cup water
Cooking spray

1.Spritz the slow cooker with cooking spray.
2.Combine all ingredients in the slow cooker.
3.Cover. Cook on low for 3 to 6 hours, depending upon how soft or crunchy you like the vegetables.
4.Serve warm.

Tofu with Greens

Prep time: 20 minutes | Cook time: 6 hours | Serves 6

1 pound (454 g) firm tofu, drained and crumbled
½ cup onion, chopped
½ cup celery, chopped
2 cups bok choy, chopped
2 cups napa cabbage, chopped
½ cup pea pods, cut in half

1.Combine all the ingredients in the slow cooker. Gently stir to mix well.
2.Cook on low for 6 hours.
3.Serve warm.

Chapter 4 Rice, Grains, and Beans

Cheesy Basil Brown Rice

Prep time: 10 minutes | Cook time: 2 to 3 hours | Serves 6

3 cups boiling water
2 cups long-grain brown rice, rinsed
1 tablespoon unsalted butter
Salt and ground black pepper, to taste
1 cup Parmesan cheese, grated
½ cup chopped fresh basil
2 teaspoons lemon juice
Cooking spray

1.Spritz the slow cooker with cooking spray. Combine boiling water, rice, butter, ½ teaspoon salt, and ½ teaspoon pepper in prepared slow cooker. Gently press a sheet of parchment paper onto surface of water, folding down edges as needed. Cover and cook until rice is tender and all water is absorbed, 2 to 3 hours on high.
2.Discard parchment. Fluff rice with a fork, then gently fold in Parmesan, basil, and lemon juice. Season with salt and pepper to taste. Serve.

Mexican Jalapeño Rice Bowl

Prep time: 15 minutes | Cook time: 2 to 3 hours | Serves 6

1 onion, chopped fine
2 jalapeño chiles, stemmed, deseeded, and minced
3 tablespoons tomato paste
2 tablespoons extra-virgin olive oil
4 garlic cloves, minced
½ teaspoon ground cumin
Salt and ground black pepper, to taste
3 cups vegetable or chicken broth
2 cups long-grain white rice, rinsed
¼ cup chopped fresh cilantro
2 scallions, sliced thin
1 tablespoon lime juice
Cooking spray

1.Spritz the slow cooker with cooking spray.

Microwave onion, jalapeños, tomato paste, oil, garlic, cumin, and ½ teaspoon salt in a bowl, stirring occasionally, until vegetables are softened, about 5 minutes. Transfer to the prepared slow cooker.
2.Microwave broth in a separate bowl until steaming, about 5 minutes. Stir broth and rice into the slow cooker. Gently press a sheet of parchment paper onto surface of broth, folding down edges as needed. Cover and cook until rice is tender and all broth is absorbed, 2 to 3 hours on high.
3.Discard parchment. Fluff rice with fork, then gently fold in cilantro, scallions, and lime juice. Season with salt and pepper to taste. Serve.

Basmati Rice Pilaf

Prep time: 10 minutes | Cook time: 2 to 3 hours | Serves 6

1 tablespoon extra-virgin olive oil
2 garlic cloves, minced
½ teaspoon ground turmeric
¼ teaspoon ground cinnamon
3 cups boiling water
2 cups basmati rice, rinsed
⅓ cup dried currants
Salt and ground black pepper, to taste
¼ cup sliced almonds, toasted
Cooking spray

1.Spritz the slow cooker with cooking spray. Microwave oil, garlic, turmeric, and cinnamon in a bowl until fragrant, about 1 minute, stirring halfway through microwaving. Transfer to the prepared slow cooker.
2.Stir boiling water, rice, currants, and ½ teaspoon salt into the slow cooker. Gently press a sheet of parchment paper onto surface of water, folding down edges as needed. Cover and cook until rice is tender and all water is absorbed, 2 to 3 hours on high.
3.Fluff rice with fork, then gently fold in almonds. Season with salt and pepper to taste. Serve warm.

Simple Cheesy Polenta

Prep time: 10 minutes | Cook time: 2 to 3 hours | Serves 6

3 cups water, plus extra as needed
1 cup whole milk
1 cup ground cornmeal
2 garlic cloves, minced
Salt and ground black pepper, to taste
1 cup Parmesan cheese, grated
2 tablespoons unsalted butter
Cooking spray

1.Spritz the slow cooker with cooking spray. Whisk water, milk, cornmeal, garlic, and 1 teaspoon salt together in the prepared slow cooker. Cover and cook until polenta is tender, 3 to 4 hours on low or 2 to 3 hours on high.
2.Whisk Parmesan and butter into polenta until combined. Season with salt and pepper to taste. Serve.

Easy Parmesan Arborio Risotto

Prep time: 15 minutes | Cook time: 2 to 3 hours | Serves 6

1 onion, chopped fine
4 tablespoons unsalted butter
3 garlic cloves, minced
1 teaspoon minced fresh thyme or ¼ teaspoon dried
Salt and ground black pepper, to taste
5 cups vegetable or chicken broth, plus extra as needed
½ cup dry white wine
2 cups Arborio rice
1 cup Parmesan cheese, grated
2 tablespoons minced fresh chives
1 teaspoon lemon juice
Cooking spray

1.Spritz the slow cooker with cooking spray. Microwave onion, 2 tablespoons butter, garlic, thyme, and ½ teaspoon salt in a bowl, stirring occasionally, until onion is softened, about 5 minutes. Transfer to the prepared slow cooker.
2.Microwave 2 cups broth and wine in 4-cup liquid measuring cup until steaming, about 5 minutes. Stir broth mixture and rice into the slow cooker. Gently press a sheet of parchment paper onto surface of broth mixture, folding down edges as needed. Cover and cook until rice is almost fully tender and all liquid is absorbed, 2 to 3 hours on high.
3.Microwave remaining 3 cups broth in the now-empty measuring cup until steaming, about 5 minutes. Discard parchment. Slowly stream broth into rice, stirring gently, until liquid is absorbed and risotto is creamy, about 1 minute. Gently stir in remaining 2 tablespoons butter, Parmesan, chives, and lemon juice until combined. Adjust consistency with extra hot broth as needed. Season with salt and pepper to taste. Serve warm.

Butternut Squash Risotto with White Wine

Prep time: 10 minutes | Cook time: 2½ hours | Serves 4 to 6

½ cup (1 stick) unsalted butter, divided
2 tablespoons olive oil
½ cup finely chopped shallots (about 4 medium)
2 cups diced, peeled, and deseeded butternut squash
1½ cups Arborio or Carnaroli rice
¼ cup dry white wine or vermouth
4¼ cups chicken broth
½ cup freshly grated Parmesan cheese, divided
Cooking spray

1.Spritz the slow cooker with nonstick cooking spray.
2.Heat ¼ cup of the butter with the oil in a large saucepan over medium-high heat. Add the shallots and squash and sauté until the shallots are softened, about 3 minutes.
3.Add the rice and cook, tossing to coat with the butter, until the rice is opaque. Add the wine and cook until the wine evaporates.
4.Transfer the mixture to the slow cooker and stir in the broth. Cover and cook on high for 2½ hours. Check the risotto at 2 hours to make sure the broth hasn't evaporated. Stir in the remaining ¼ cup butter and ¼ cup of the cheese.
5.Serve the risotto immediately with the remaining cheese on the side.

Pine Nut Pilaf

Prep time: 10 minutes | Cook time: 2½ hours | Serves 8 to 10

2 tablespoons unsalted butter
1 cup pine nuts
3 cups converted white rice
4½ cups chicken or vegetable broth
1 teaspoon freshly ground black pepper
½ cup finely chopped fresh basil, plus additional whole leaves for garnishing
Nonstick cooking spray

1. Spritz the slow cooker with nonstick cooking spray.
2. Melt the butter in a small sauté pan over medium-high heat. Add the pine nuts and sauté until they begin to color, about 4 minutes. Set aside.
3. Combine the rice, 4½ cups broth, and the pepper in the slow cooker. Cover and cook on high for 1 hour.
4. Stir in the pine nuts and chopped basil. Cover and cook for 1½ hours, until the rice is tender and liquid is absorbed.
5. Serve warm, garnished with the whole basil leaves.

Wild Rice and Fruit Pilaf

Prep time: 15 minutes | Cook time: 2¾ to 3¾ hours | Serves 8 to 10

2 cups wild rice, rinsed with cold water and drained twice
½ cup (1 stick) unsalted butter
1 medium onion, finely chopped
3 stalks celery, finely chopped
1 teaspoon dried marjoram
4 to 5 cups chicken broth
½ cup finely chopped dried apricots
½ cup dried cranberries
½ teaspoon freshly ground black pepper
½ cup sliced almonds, toasted
Cooking spray

1. Spritz the slow cooker with nonstick cooking spray.
2. Pour the rice into the slow cooker. Melt the butter in a large skillet over medium-high heat. Add the onion, celery, and marjoram and sauté until the vegetables are softened, about 4 minutes.
3. Transfer the vegetables to the slow cooker. Stir in the broth, apricots, cranberries, and pepper. Cover and cook on high for 2½ to 3 hours or on low for 7 hours, until the rice is tender. Check at intervals to make sure there is still liquid in the slow cooker and add more broth if needed. Uncover the slow cooker and cook for another 30 to 45 minutes on low. Stir in the almonds.
4. Serve warm.

Orzo with Peas

Prep time: 15 minutes | Cook time: 1 to 2 hours | Serves 4 to 6

1 cup orzo
1 onion, chopped fine
6 garlic cloves, minced
3 tablespoons unsalted butter, divided
Salt and ground black pepper, to taste
2½ cups vegetable or chicken broth, divided, plus extra as needed
¼ cup dry white wine
1 cup frozen peas, thawed
1 cup Parmesan cheese, grated
1½ teaspoons grated lemon zest

1. Microwave orzo, onion, garlic, 1 tablespoon butter, and ½ teaspoon salt in a bowl, stirring occasionally, until orzo is lightly toasted and onion is softened, 5 to 7 minutes. Transfer to the slow cooker.
2. Microwave 2 cups broth and wine in a separate bowl until steaming, about 5 minutes. Stir broth mixture into slow cooker, cover, and cook until orzo is al dente, 1 to 2 hours on high.
3. Sprinkle peas over orzo, cover, and let sit until heated through, about 5 minutes. Microwave remaining ½ cup broth in a third bowl until steaming, about 2 minutes. Stir broth, Parmesan, lemon zest, and remaining 2 tablespoons butter into orzo until mixture is creamy. Adjust consistency with extra hot broth as needed. Season with salt and pepper to taste. Serve.

Barley Pilaf with Dates

Prep time: 15 minutes | Cook time: 2 to 3 hours | Serves 6

1 onion, chopped fine
1½ cups pearl barley, rinsed
2 tablespoons extra-virgin olive oil, divided
2 teaspoons grated fresh ginger
Salt and ground black pepper, to taste
⅛ teaspoon ground cinnamon
⅛ teaspoon ground cardamom
3½ cups vegetable or chicken broth
½ cup pitted dates, chopped
⅓ cup chopped fresh parsley
2 teaspoons lemon juice
Cooking spray

1.Spritz the slow cooker with cooking spray. Microwave onion, barley, 1 tablespoon oil, ginger, ½ teaspoon salt, cinnamon, and cardamom in a bowl, stirring occasionally, until onion is softened and barley is lightly toasted, about 5 minutes. Transfer to the prepared slow cooker.
2.Stir in broth, cover, and cook until barley is tender and all broth is absorbed, 3 to 4 hours on low or 2 to 3 hours on high.
3.Fluff barley with fork, then gently fold in dates, parsley, lemon juice, and remaining 1 tablespoon oil. Season with salt and pepper to taste. Serve.

Wild Rice, Bacon, and Cherries

Prep time: 10 minutes | Cook time: 6 hours | Serves 2

1 teaspoon extra-virgin olive oil
¾ cup wild rice
½ cup minced onion
1 piece applewood-smoked bacon, cooked and crumbled
1 teaspoon minced fresh rosemary
¼ cup dried cherries
2 cups chicken broth
⅛ teaspoon sea salt

1.Grease the slow cooker with the olive oil.
2.Put all the ingredients into the slow cooker and stir them to mix thoroughly.
3.Cover and cook on low for 6 hours until the rice has absorbed all the water and is tender.
4.Serve warm.

Pearl Barley Pilaf

Prep time: 10 minutes | Cook time: 2 to 3 hours | Serves 6

1 onion, chopped fine
1½ cups pearl barley, rinsed
2 tablespoons extra-virgin olive oil, divided
2 garlic cloves, minced
1 teaspoon minced fresh thyme or ¼ teaspoon dried
Salt and ground black pepper, to taste
3½ cups vegetable or chicken broth
¼ cup chopped fresh basil, dill, or parsley
Cooking spray

1.Spritz the slow cooker with cooking spray. Microwave onion, barley, 1 tablespoon oil, garlic, thyme, and ½ teaspoon salt in a bowl, stirring occasionally, until onion is softened and barley is lightly toasted, about 5 minutes. Transfer to the prepared slow cooker. Stir in broth, cover, and cook until barley is tender, and all broth is absorbed, 3 to 4 hours on low or 2 to 3 hours on high.
2.Fluff barley with fork, then gently folds in basil and remaining 1 tablespoon oil. Season with salt and pepper to taste. Serve warm.

Barley and Mushroom Risotto

Prep time: 15 minutes | Cook time: 7 to 8 hours | Serves 8

2¼ cups hulled barley, rinsed
1 onion, finely chopped
4 garlic cloves, minced
1 (8-ounce / 227-g) package button mushrooms, chopped
6 cups vegetable broth
½ teaspoon dried marjoram leaves
⅛ teaspoon freshly ground black pepper
⅔ cup grated Parmesan cheese

1.In the slow cooker, mix the barley, onion, garlic, mushrooms, broth, marjoram, and pepper.
2.Cover and cook on low for 7 to 8 hours, or until the barley has absorbed most of the liquid and is tender, and the vegetables are tender.
3.Stir in the Parmesan cheese and serve.

Herbed Parmesan Polenta

Prep time: 5 minutes | Cook time: 7 hours | Makes 7 cups

5 cups vegetable broth
2 onions, chopped
4 garlic cloves, minced
1½ teaspoons salt
¼ cup butter
1½ cups cornmeal
¼ cup chopped fresh flat-leaf parsley
3 tablespoons minced fresh basil
2 tablespoons minced fresh thyme
1 cup grated Parmesan cheese

1.In a large saucepan over high heat, bring the broth, onions, garlic, salt, and butter to a boil. Turn down the heat and simmer for 5 minutes, or until the onions are crisp-tender.
2.Carefully pour the hot broth mixture into the slow cooker. Add the cornmeal, stirring constantly with a wire whisk until well combined.
3.Cover and cook on low for 7 hours.
4.Stir in the parsley, basil, thyme, and cheese, and serve immediately.

Farro with Mushrooms

Prep time: 15 minutes | Cook time: 2 to 3 hours | Serves 4 to 6

2 shallots, minced
½ ounce (14 g) dried porcini mushrooms, rinsed and minced
2 tablespoons extra-virgin olive oil, divided
3 garlic cloves, minced
2 teaspoons minced fresh thyme or ½ teaspoon dried
Salt and ground black pepper, to taste
2½ cups vegetable or chicken broth, divided, plus extra as needed
¼ cup dry sherry
8 ounces (227 g) cremini mushrooms, trimmed and sliced thin
1 cup whole farro
½ cup Parmesan cheese, grated
2 tablespoons chopped fresh parsley
Cooking spray

1.Spritz the slow cooker with cooking spray. Microwave shallots, porcini mushrooms, 1 tablespoon oil, garlic, thyme, ½ teaspoon salt, and ½ teaspoon pepper in a bowl, stirring occasionally, until shallots are softened, about 5 minutes. Transfer to the prepared slow cooker.
2.Microwave 2 cups broth and sherry in a separate bowl until steaming, about 5 minutes. Stir broth mixture, cremini mushrooms, and farro into the slow cooker. Cover and cook until farro is tender, 3 to 4 hours on low or 2 to 3 hours on high.
3.Microwave remaining ½ cup broth in a third bowl until steaming, about 2 minutes. Stir broth and Parmesan into farro until mixture is creamy. Adjust consistency with extra hot broth as needed. Stir in parsley and remaining 1 tablespoon oil. Season with salt and pepper to taste. Serve.

Quinoa with Corn

Prep time: 15 minutes | Cook time: 2 to 3 hours | Serves 6

1½ cups white quinoa, rinsed
1 onion, chopped fine
2 jalapeño chiles, stemmed, deseeded, and minced
2 tablespoons extra-virgin olive oil
Salt and ground black pepper, to taste
1¾ cups water
1 cup frozen corn, thawed
⅓ cup minced fresh cilantro
2 tablespoons lime juice
Cooking spray

1.Spritz the slow cooker with cooking spray. Microwave quinoa, onion, jalapeños, 1 tablespoon oil, and 1 teaspoon salt in a bowl, stirring occasionally, until quinoa is lightly toasted and vegetables are softened, about 5 minutes. Transfer to the prepared slow cooker. Stir in water, cover, and cook until quinoa is tender, and all water is absorbed, 3 to 4 hours on low or 2 to 3 hours on high.
2.Sprinkle corn over quinoa, cover, and let sit until heated through, about 5 minutes. Fluff quinoa with fork, then gently folds in cilantro, lime juice, and remaining 1 tablespoon oil. Season with salt and pepper to taste. Serve.

Citrus Wheat Berries

Prep time: 15 minutes | Cook time: 3 to 4 hours | Serves 6 to 8

5 cups water
1½ cups wheat berries
1 bay leaf
Salt and ground pepper, to taste
⅛ teaspoon grated orange zest, plus 1 peeled and pitted orange
1 shallot, minced
3 tablespoons red wine vinegar
2 tablespoons extra-virgin olive oil
1½ tablespoons Dijon mustard
1½ teaspoons honey
1 garlic clove, minced
3 carrots, peeled and shredded
1 tablespoon chopped fresh tarragon

1.Combine the water, wheat berries, bay leaf, and ½ teaspoon salt in the slow cooker. Cover and cook until the wheat berries are tender, 4 to 5 hours on low or 3 to 4 hours on high.
2.Drain the wheat berries, transfer to a large serving bowl, and let cool slightly. Quarter the orange, then slice crosswise into ¼-inch-thick pieces.
3.Whisk the shallot, vinegar, oil, mustard, honey, garlic, ½ teaspoon salt, and orange zest together in separate bowl. Add the orange and any accumulated juices, vinaigrette, carrots, and tarragon to wheat berries, and toss to combine. Season with salt and pepper to taste. Serve.

Bulgur with Tomato

Prep time: 15 minutes | Cook time: 5 to 6 hours | Serves 8

2 cups medium bulgur
2 tablespoons extra-virgin olive oil
1 medium onion, finely chopped
3 cloves garlic, minced
Pinch of red pepper flakes
1 (14- to 15-ounce / 397- to 425-g) can chopped tomatoes, drained but juice reserved
3½ cups chicken or vegetable broth
1 teaspoon salt
¼ cup finely chopped fresh basil
¼ cup finely chopped fresh mint
Nonstick cooking spray

1.Spritz the slow cooker with nonstick cooking spray and add the bulgur. Heat the oil in a large skillet over medium-high heat. Add the onion, garlic, and red pepper flakes and sauté until the onion is softened, about 3 minutes. Add the drained tomatoes and cook until there is no liquid left in the pan.
2.Pour the broth in the skillet and scrape up any browned bits on the bottom of the pan. Transfer them to the slow cooker and stir in the reserved tomato juice and the salt. Cover and cook on low for 5 to 6 hours, until the bulgur is tender and the liquid is absorbed.
3.Stir in the basil and mint and serve from the cooker set on warm.

Lush Bulgur and Mushroom Pilaf

Prep time: 10 minutes | Cook time: 5 to 6 hours | Serves 8

2 cups medium bulgur
2 tablespoons extra-virgin olive oil
1 medium onion, finely chopped
2 cloves garlic, minced
8 ounces (227 g) fresh shiitake mushrooms, stems removed, caps sliced
¼ cup soy sauce
4 cups beef broth (substitute vegetable or chicken broth if desired)
4 ounces (113 g) dried shiitake mushrooms, crumbled
Nonstick cooking spray

1.Spritz the slow cooker with nonstick cooking spray and add the bulgur. Heat the oil in a large skillet over medium-high heat.
2.Add the onion, garlic, and fresh mushrooms and sauté until the onion is softened and translucent and the liquid in the pan has evaporated.
3.Remove from the heat, pour in the soy sauce, and scrape up any remaining bits from the bottom of the pan.
4.Transfer the contents of the skillet to the slow cooker and stir in the broth and dried mushrooms. Cover and cook on low for 5 to 6 hours, until the bulgur is tender and the broth is absorbed.
5.Serve warm.

Quinoa with Mushrooms and Carrots

Prep time: 10 minutes | Cook time: 5 to 6 hours | Serves 8

2 cups quinoa, rinsed and drained
2 onions, chopped
2 carrots, peeled and sliced
1 cup sliced cremini mushrooms
3 garlic cloves, minced
4 cups vegetable broth
½ teaspoon salt
1 teaspoon dried marjoram leaves
⅛ teaspoon freshly ground black pepper

1. In the slow cooker, mix all the ingredients. Cover and cook on low for 5 to 6 hours, or until the quinoa and vegetables are tender.
2. Stir the mixture and serve.

Rice, Farro, and Barley Medley

Prep time: 15 minutes | Cook time: 7 hours | Serves 2

1 tablespoon extra-virgin olive oil
1 onion, chopped
2 garlic cloves, minced
1 carrot, sliced
⅓ cup wild rice, rinsed and drained well
⅓ cup farro, rinsed and drained well
⅓ cup pearl barley, rinsed and drained well
3 cups vegetable broth
1 bay leaf
½ teaspoon dried basil leaves
½ teaspoon salt
⅛ teaspoon freshly ground black pepper
⅓ cup grated Parmesan cheese

1. In a small saucepan over medium heat, heat the olive oil. Add the onion, garlic, and carrot, and sauté until crisp-tender, about 5 to 6 minutes.
2. In the slow cooker, combine the onion mixture, rice, farro, and barley.
3. Stir in the broth, bay leaf, basil, salt, and pepper.
4. Cover and cook on low for 7 hours, or until the grains are tender. Remove and discard the bay leaf, stir in the cheese, and serve.

Brown Rice Risotto with Starch Vegetables

Prep time: 20 minutes | Cook time: 4 to 5 hours | Serves 8

1 large sweet potato, peeled and chopped
1 onion, chopped
5 garlic cloves, minced
2 cups short-grain brown rice
1 teaspoon dried thyme leaves
7 cups vegetable broth
2 cups green beans, cut in half crosswise
2 cups frozen baby peas
3 tablespoons unsalted butter
½ cup grated Parmesan cheese

1. In the slow cooker, mix the sweet potato, onion, garlic, rice, thyme, and broth. Cover and cook on low for 3 to 4 hours, or until the rice is tender.
2. Stir in the green beans and frozen peas. Cover and cook on low for 30 to 40 minutes or until the vegetables are tender.
3. Stir in the butter and cheese. Cover and cook on low for 20 minutes, then stir and serve.

Buckwheat with Lush Mushrooms

Prep time: 20 minutes | Cook time: 5 to 6 hours | Serves 2

1 cup buckwheat groats
1 egg, beaten
1 onion, chopped
½ cup sliced button mushrooms
½ cup sliced shiitake mushrooms
½ cup sliced cremini mushrooms
2½ cups vegetable broth or chicken stock
1 bay leaf
½ teaspoon dried basil leaves
½ teaspoon salt
⅛ teaspoon freshly ground black pepper

1. In a medium bowl, mix the buckwheat groats with the egg, combining well.
2. In a medium saucepan over low heat, sauté the buckwheat mixture until the groats smell toasted, about 5 minutes.
3. In the slow cooker, combine all the ingredients.
4. Cover and cook on low for 5 to 6 hours, or until the buckwheat is tender.
5. Remove and discard the bay leaf and serve.

Grits Casserole

Prep time: 10 minutes | Cook time: 8 hours | Serves 8

1 cup stone-ground grits
4½ cups chicken broth
4 tablespoons (½ stick) unsalted butter, melted and slightly cooled
2 large eggs, beaten
½ cup heavy cream
2 cups finely shredded mild Cheddar cheese
Nonstick cooking spray

1. Spritz the slow cooker with nonstick cooking spray.
2. Stir the grits, broth, and butter together in the slow cooker. Cover and cook on low for 4 hours.
3. Stir in the eggs, cream, and cheese. Cover and cook for an additional 4 hours, until the grits are creamy and the cheese has melted.
4. Serve warm.

Super Baked Beans

Prep time: 20 minutes | Cook time: 8¾ hours | Serves 2

4 slices bacon
1 onion, chopped
1 cup whole small cremini mushrooms
2 garlic cloves, minced
⅓ cup dried lima beans, sorted and rinsed
⅓ cup dried pinto beans, sorted and rinsed
⅓ cup dried cannellini beans, sorted and rinsed
⅓ cup dried great northern beans, sorted and rinsed
3 cups vegetable broth
2 tablespoons honey
1 bay leaf
½ teaspoon salt
¼ teaspoon freshly ground black pepper
½ cup tomato sauce
¼ cup whole black olives, pitted
¼ cup chopped fresh flat-leaf parsley

1. In a small skillet over medium-high heat, cook the bacon until crisp, about 10 minutes. Drain the bacon on paper towels, break it into pieces, and refrigerate.
2. In the same skillet, sauté the onion in the bacon drippings until crisp-tender, about 5 minutes.
3. In the slow cooker, combine the onion, mushrooms, garlic, all the beans, broth, honey, bay leaf, salt, and pepper.
4. Cover and cook on low for 8 hours.
5. Stir in the tomato sauce and olives. Cover and cook on high for 30 minutes.
6. Remove and discard the bay leaf, garnish with the parsley and bacon, and serve.

Chickpeas with Swiss Chard

Prep time: 15 minutes | Cook time: 4½ to 5 hours | Serves 2 to 3

½ cup dried chickpeas
1 (1½-pound / 680-g) bunch Swiss chard, rinsed, stems discarded, leaves coarsely chopped
2 cups water
¼ cup olive oil
2 small white onions, finely chopped
2 tablespoons tomato paste
½ teaspoon fine sea salt, to taste
Pinch of cayenne pepper
Ground black pepper, to taste

1. Place the chickpeas in a colander and rinse under cold running water, then pick over for damaged beans and small stones. Transfer to the slow cooker. Cover with 3 inches of cold water and soak for 6 to 12 hours.
2. Blanch the chopped Swiss chard leaves in boiling water for 3 minutes.
3. Drain the chickpeas, add the 2 cups of water, cover, and cook on high until just tender, 3 to 3½ hours. The chickpeas need to be covered with liquid at all times to cook properly.
4. In a small skillet over medium-high heat, heat the olive oil, then cook the onions, stirring, until almost golden and browned around the edges, about 8 minutes.
5. When the chickpeas are tender, add the onions and oil, the wilted chard, tomato paste, salt, cayenne, and black pepper. Cover and continue to cook on high for another 1½ hours. Serve hot.

Simple Grits

Prep time: 5 minutes | Cook time: 8 hours | Serves 8

1¼ cups stone-ground grits
5½ cups water
1 teaspoon salt
2 tablespoons unsalted butter, melted, plus more for serving
Nonstick cooking spray

1. Spritz the slow cooker with nonstick cooking spray.
2. Stir all the ingredients together in the slow cooker. Cover and cook on low for 8 hours, until the grits are creamy.
3. Serve warm with additional butter on the side.

Tuscan Chickpeas with Kale and Chard

Prep time: 15 minutes | Cook time: 8½ hours | Serves 2

1 tablespoon extra-virgin olive oil
1 onion, chopped
4 garlic cloves, minced
1½ cups dried chickpeas, sorted and rinsed
3½ cups vegetable broth
1 sprig fresh rosemary
1 teaspoon dried oregano leaves
1 teaspoon lemon zest
1 teaspoon salt
⅛ teaspoon freshly ground black pepper
2 cups chopped kale
1 cup chopped Swiss chard
1 large tomato, deseeded and chopped
½ cup grated Parmesan cheese

1. In a small saucepan over medium heat, heat the olive oil. Add the onion and garlic and sauté, stirring, until tender, about 6 minutes.
2. In the slow cooker, combine the onion and garlic mixture, chickpeas, broth, rosemary, oregano, lemon zest, salt, and pepper.
3. Cover and cook on low for 8 hours, or until the chickpeas are tender.
4. Stir in the kale, Swiss chard, and tomato. Cover and cook on low for 30 minutes more, or until the greens are tender. Stir in the cheese and serve.

Pinto Beans with Jalapeño and Chipotle

Prep time: 15 minutes | Cook time: 7 to 8 hours | Makes 7 cups

1½ cups dried pinto beans, sorted and rinsed
1 onion, chopped
2 garlic cloves, minced
1 jalapeño pepper, minced
1 chipotle pepper in adobo sauce, minced
3½ cups vegetable broth
1 bay leaf
½ teaspoon salt
⅛ teaspoon freshly ground black pepper
⅛ teaspoon ground cayenne pepper
Nonstick cooking spray

1. Spray the slow cooker with the nonstick cooking spray.
2. In the slow cooker, combine all the ingredients.
3. Cover and cook on low for 7 to 8 hours, or until the beans are very tender.
4. Remove and discard the bay leaf and serve.

Lemony Herbed Chickpeas

Prep time: 15 minutes | Cook time: 9 hours | Serves 2

1 onion, chopped
2 garlic cloves, minced
1½ cups dried chickpeas, sorted and rinsed
4 cups chicken stock or vegetable broth
1 sprig fresh rosemary
½ teaspoon dried oregano leaves
½ teaspoon salt
⅛ teaspoon freshly ground black pepper
½ cup crumbled feta cheese
2 tablespoons freshly squeezed lemon juice
½ teaspoon lemon zest
Nonstick cooking spray

1. Spray the slow cooker with the nonstick cooking spray.
2. In the slow cooker, combine the onion, garlic, chickpeas, stock, rosemary, oregano, salt, and pepper.
3. Cover and cook on low for 8 to 9 hours, or until the chickpeas are tender. Drain.
4. Add the feta, lemon juice, and lemon zest, and serve.

Refried Pinto Beans

Prep time: 10 minutes | Cook time: 2 to 4 hours | Serves 4 to 6

1 (1-pound / 454-g) can refried pinto beans
1¼ cups rinsed and drained whole pinto beans
2 to 3 tablespoons unsalted butter

1.Put the refried beans, whole beans, and butter in the slow cooker, then stir with a wooden spoon to combine a bit.
2.Cover and cook on low or until hot, 2 to 4 hours. Stir and serve immediately.

Navy Bean Bake

Prep time: 15 minutes | Cook time: 11½ to 13½ hours | Serves 6 to 8

1 pound (454 g) dried white navy beans
¼ cup ketchup
¼ cup pure maple syrup
¼ cup molasses
1¼ teaspoons dried summer or winter savory
1 teaspoon baking soda
1 teaspoon salt
¼ teaspoon freshly ground black pepper
1 medium-size white onion, peeled, left whole, scored with an X at the root end, and studded with 4 cloves
Boiling water to cover
½ cup (1 stick) butter, cut into pieces

1.Rinse the beans in a colander under cold running water, then pick over for damaged beans and small stones. Transfer to the slow cooker. Cover with cold water by 2 inches, soak overnight, and drain.
2.Cover the beans with fresh water by 3 inches. Cover and cook on high for 1½ hours, until still undercooked. Drain.
3.Return the beans to the cooker and add the ketchup, maple syrup, molasses, savory, baking soda, salt, and pepper, then stir to mix well. Press the whole onion down into the center of the beans. Add boiling water to cover by ½ inch, then stir gently.
4.Cover and cook on high to bring to a boil, then reduce the heat to low and cook until the beans are soft, thick, and bubbling, 10 to 12 hours.
5.Remove the onion and stir in the butter until melted. Serve hot.

Orange Black Beans

Prep time: 15 minutes | Cook time: 1½ hours | Serves 2 to 4

2 (15-ounce / 425-g) cans black beans, rinsed and drained
2 tablespoons firmly packed light or dark brown sugar
1 medium-size shallot, minced
1 rib celery, minced
½ cup orange juice
½ cup chicken broth
½ teaspoon ground cumin
Pinch of ground cinnamon or cardamom
Salt and freshly ground black pepper, to taste
For Serving:
Hot cooked white rice
¼ cup chopped fresh cilantro leaves
½ cup chopped fresh tomatoes

1.Combine the beans, brown sugar, shallot, celery, orange juice, broth, cumin, and cinnamon in the slow cooker. Cover and cook on high for about 1½ hours.
2.Season with salt and pepper and serve hot, ladled over rice and garnished with the cilantro and tomatoes to serve.

Herbed Black Beans with Onions

Prep time: 10 minutes | Cook time: 7 to 9 hours | Serves 8

3 cups dried black beans, rinsed and drained
2 onions, chopped
8 garlic cloves, minced
6 cups vegetable broth
1 teaspoon dried basil leaves
½ teaspoon dried thyme leaves
½ teaspoon dried oregano leaves
½ teaspoon salt

1.In the slow cooker, mix all the ingredients. Cover and cook on low for 7 to 9 hours, or until the beans have absorbed the liquid and are tender.
2.Remove and discard the bay leaf before serving.

Bean and Pea Medley

Prep time: 15 minutes | Cook time: 6 to 8 hours | Serves 8

1¼ cups dried black beans, rinsed and drained
1¼ cups dried kidney beans, rinsed and drained
1¼ cups dried black-eyed peas, rinsed and drained
1 leek, chopped
2 carrots, peeled and chopped
1 onion, chopped
2 garlic cloves, minced
6 cups vegetable broth
½ teaspoon dried thyme leaves
1½ cups water

1.In the slow cooker, mix all the ingredients. Cover and cook on low for 6 to 8 hours, or until the beans are tender and the liquid is absorbed.
2.Serve warm.

Black-Eyed Peas and Greens and Sausage

Prep time: 15 minutes | Cook time: 9 to 11 hours | Serves 4

1 pound (454 g) dried black-eyed peas
1 large white onion, finely chopped
3 ribs celery, finely chopped
½ red bell pepper, finely chopped
½ green bell pepper, finely chopped
1 pound (454 g) smoked chicken-apple sausage, sliced ½-inch thick
1 (14½-ounce / 411-g) can diced tomatoes, with their juice
1 (4-ounce / 113-g) can diced roasted green chiles, drained
4 cups chicken broth
1 bunch collard greens
1 teaspoon fine sea salt
Ground black pepper, to taste

1.Put the black-eyed peas in a colander and rinse under cold running water, then pick over for damaged beans and small stones. Transfer to the slow cooker and cover with 3 inches of cold water. Soak for 6 to 12 hours.
2.Drain the beans and return them to the slow cooker. Add the onion, celery, bell peppers, sausage, tomatoes with their juice, green chiles, and broth.
3.Separate the collard green leaves and rinse well under running water. Remove the thick stems and inner ribs. Stack the leaves and roll them up, then slice into 2-inch-thick strips.
4.Add the collard greens to the slow cooker. Cover and cook on low for 9 to 11 hours, until just tender. Add the salt and pepper and serve.

Southwestern Bean and Ham Pot

Prep time: 10 minutes | Cook time: 5 to 6 hours | Serves 8

1 pound (454 g) dried Christmas lima, cranberry, pinto, or anasazi beans
7 cups water
1 large yellow onion, chopped
1 (12-ounce / 340-g) ham hock or leftover meaty ham bone
1 (8-ounce / 227-g) can or jar green chile salsa, tomato sauce, or stewed tomatoes
1 teaspoon salt, or to taste

1.Put the beans in a colander and rinse under cold running water, then pick over for damaged beans and small stones. Transfer to the slow cooker. Cover with 3 inches of cold water, then soak for 6 to 12 hours, and drain.
2.Add the 7 cups of water, onion, and ham hock. Cover and cook on high for 3½ hours, then stir in the salsa.
3.Cover and continue to cook on high for another 1½ to 2½ hours. The beans should be covered with liquid at all times to cook properly, but the mixture should be thick. When done, the beans will tender and hold their shape, rather than fall apart.
4.Remove the ham hock or bone and pick off the meat. Return the meat to the slow cooker and stir to combine. Season with the salt and serve.

Puy Lentils with Leek

Prep time: 10 minutes | Cook time: 4 to 5 hours | Serves 8

3 cups puy lentils, rinsed and drained
1 onion, chopped
1 leek, chopped
8 garlic cloves, minced
6 cups vegetable broth
1 bay leaf
½ teaspoon dried oregano leaves

1. In the slow cooker, mix all the ingredients. Cover and cook on low for 4 to 5 hours, or until the lentils are tender.
2. Remove and discard the bay leaf before serving.

Garlicky Northern Beans

Prep time: 15 minutes | Cook time: 6 to 8 hours | Serves 16

1 pound (454 g) great northern beans, rinsed and drained
1 onion, finely chopped
3 cloves garlic, minced
1 large sprig fresh rosemary
½ teaspoon salt
⅛ teaspoon white pepper
4 cups water
2 cups vegetable broth

1. Combine the beans, onion, garlic, rosemary, salt, water, and vegetable broth in the slow cooker.
2. Cover and cook on low for 6 to 8 hours or until the beans are tender.
3. Remove the rosemary stem and discard. Stir the mixture gently and serve.

French White Beans

Prep time: 10 minutes | Cook time: 6 to 7 hours | Serves 2

1½ cups dried great northern beans, sorted and rinsed
2 carrots, sliced
1 onion, chopped
3 garlic cloves, minced
3 cups chicken stock or vegetable broth
½ teaspoon dried thyme leaves
1 teaspoon salt
⅛ teaspoon freshly ground black pepper
2 tablespoons extra-virgin olive oil
1 tablespoon minced fresh thyme leaves
⅓ cup grated Parmesan cheese

1. In the slow cooker, combine all the ingredients except the fresh thyme and cheese, and stir.
2. Cover and cook on low for 6 to 7 hours, or until the beans are tender.
3. Stir in the fresh thyme and cheese, and serve.

Peppery Chicken Thighs with Bacon

Prep time: 20 minutes | Cook time: 6 to 8 hours | Serves 6 to 8

6 strips thick-cut bacon, cut into 1-inch pieces
10 chicken thighs, skin removed
1½ teaspoons salt
½ teaspoon freshly ground black pepper
2 tablespoons olive oil
2 medium onions, cut into half rounds
2 medium red bell peppers, deseeded and cut into ½-inch-thick slices
1 medium yellow bell pepper, deseeded and cut into ½-inch-thick slices
1 medium orange bell pepper, deseeded and cut into ½-inch-thick slices
2 cloves garlic, minced
1½ teaspoons smoked paprika
1 (14- to 15-ounce / 397- to 425-g) can double-strength chicken broth (not diluted)
1 (14- to 15-ounce / 397- to 425-g) can chopped tomatoes, drained
½ cup finely chopped fresh Italian parsley

1.Cook the bacon in a large skillet over medium heat for 4 minutes, or until crisp and remove it to paper towels to drain, leaving the drippings in the pan.
2.Sprinkle the chicken evenly with the salt and pepper and add to the bacon drippings. Brown the chicken on all sides, for about 7 to 10 minutes.
3.Transfer the browned chicken pieces to a slow cooker. Heat the oil in the same skillet over medium-high heat. Add the onions, bell peppers, and garlic and sauté until the vegetables begin to soften, for 4 to 6 minutes. Add the paprika and sauté for 2 minutes. Add the broth and scrape up any browned bits from the bottom of the skillet.
4.Transfer the contents of the skillet to the slow cooker. Add the tomatoes and stir to combine. Cover and cook on low for 6 to 8 hours, until the chicken is cooked through and tender. Skim off any fat from the top of the sauce.
5.Stir in the reserved bacon and the parsley and serve warm.

Asian Napa Cabbage Wraps

Prep time: 15 minutes | Cook time: 1½ to 2 hours | Serves 8

1 head Napa cabbage
2 cups chicken broth
½ cup soy sauce
4 slices fresh ginger
2 tablespoons vegetable oil
2 cloves garlic, minced
1 teaspoon freshly grated ginger
6 canned water chestnuts, finely chopped
2 chicken breast halves, skin and bones removed, finely chopped
4 green onions, finely chopped, using the white and tender green parts
2 tablespoons hoisin sauce
1 tablespoon cornstarch mixed with 2 tablespoons water

1.Core the cabbage and separate the leaves, being careful not to tear them. Put the broth, soy sauce, and ginger in a large stockpot and bring to a boil.
2.Blanch the cabbage leaves, one at a time, for 30 seconds until limp. Drain the leaves and set aside. Add the broth mixture to a slow cooker. Cover and set on warm while preparing the filling.
3.Heat the oil in a sauté pan over high heat. Add the garlic, ginger, and water chestnuts and sauté for 30 seconds. Add the chicken and cook until the chicken turns white, for 3 to 5 minutes.
4.Transfer the contents of the pan to a bowl and stir in the green onions and hoisin sauce. Place 2 to 3 tablespoons of filling at the stem end of a cabbage leaf and roll up, tucking in the sides of the leaf as you go. Place the cabbage wraps on a rack in the slow cooker.
5.Cover and cook on high for 1½ to 2 hours, until the chicken is cooked through. Remove the wraps and set aside. Strain the broth through a fine-mesh sieve into a saucepan and bring to a boil. Add the cornstarch mixture and bring back to a boil.
6.Serve the wraps with the sauce on the side.

Merlot Chicken with Mushrooms

Prep time: 10 minutes | Cook time: 5 to 6 hours | Serves 5

¾ pound (340 g) fresh mushrooms, sliced
1 large onion, chopped
2 garlic cloves, minced
3 pounds (1.4 kg) boneless, skinless chicken thighs
1 (6-ounce / 170-g) can tomato paste
¾ cup chicken broth
¼ cup Merlot wine
2 tablespoons quick-cooking tapioca
2 teaspoons sugar
1½ teaspoons dried basil
½ teaspoon salt
¼ teaspoon pepper
2 tablespoons grated Parmesan cheese
Hot cooked pasta, for serving

1. Place the mushrooms, onion and garlic in a slow cooker. Top with chicken.
2. In a small bowl, combine the tomato paste, broth, wine, tapioca, sugar, basil, salt and pepper. Pour over chicken. Cover and cook on low for 5 to 6 hours or until chicken is tender.
3. Sprinkle with cheese. Serve with pasta.

Chicken Taco with Black Beans

Prep time: 20 minutes | Cook time: 4¼ to 5⅓ hours | Serves 6

1 (8-ounce / 227-g) can crushed pineapple
½ cup salsa
2 green onions, sliced
1 teaspoon grated lime peel
¼ cup lime juice
½ teaspoon chili powder
¼ teaspoon garlic powder
¼ teaspoon ground cumin
⅛ teaspoon salt
⅛ teaspoon cayenne pepper
⅛ teaspoon pepper
1 pound (454 g) boneless, skinless chicken thighs
1 (15-ounce / 425-g) can black beans, rinsed and drained
12 flour tortillas (6 inches), warmed

Toppings:
Shredded Mexican cheese blend
Shredded lettuce
Chopped avocado

1. In a small bowl, combine the first five ingredients; stir in seasonings. Place chicken in a slow cooker; add pineapple mixture. Cook, covered, on low for 4 to 5 hours or until chicken is tender.
2. Remove chicken; cool slightly. Shred meat with two forks; return to slow cooker. Stir in beans. Cook, covered, on low for 15 to 20 minutes longer or until heated through. Using a slotted spoon, serve chicken mixture in tortillas with toppings.

Spiced Chicken with Potatoes

Prep time: 15 minutes | Cook time: 5 to 6 hours | Serves 4

1 pound (454 g) red potatoes (about 6 medium), cut into wedges
1 large onion, chopped
2 teaspoons salt
1 teaspoon paprika
½ teaspoon onion powder
½ teaspoon garlic powder
½ teaspoon dried thyme
½ teaspoon white pepper
½ teaspoon cayenne pepper
¼ teaspoon pepper
1 broiler/fryer chicken (3½ to 4 pounds / 1.5 to 1.8 kg)

1. Place potatoes and onion in a slow cooker. In a small bowl, mix seasonings. Tuck wings under chicken; tie drumsticks together. Rub seasoning mixture over outside and inside of chicken. Place chicken over vegetables.
2. Cook, covered, on low for 5 to 6 hours or until a thermometer inserted in thickest part of thigh reads 170ºF (77ºC) to 175ºF (79ºC). Remove chicken from slow cooker; tent with foil. Let stand for 15 minutes before carving.
3. Transfer vegetables to a platter; keep warm. If desired, skim fat and thicken cooking juices for gravy. Serve with chicken.

Balsamic Chicken with Figs

Prep time: 10 minutes | Cook time: 2¼ hours | Serves 6 to 8

2 tablespoons vegetable oil
8 chicken breast halves, skin and bones removed
1½ teaspoons salt
½ teaspoon freshly ground black pepper
½ cup balsamic vinegar
½ cup Ruby Port
½ cup chicken broth
1 teaspoon dried thyme
16 dried figs, cut in half

1. Heat the oil in a large skillet over medium-high heat. Sprinkle the chicken evenly with the salt and pepper.
2. Add the chicken to the skillet and brown on all sides, for 12 to 15 minutes.
3. Transfer the chicken to a slow cooker. Deglaze the skillet with the vinegar and port, scraping up any browned bits from the bottom of the skillet. Add the broth and transfer the contents of the skillet to the slow cooker.
4. Add the thyme and figs and stir to combine. Cover and cook on high for 2 hours, until the chicken is cooked through and the sauce is syrupy.
5. Serve warm.

Orange-Flavored Chicken

Prep time: 25 minutes | Cook time: 4½ to 4⅔ hours | Serves 8

1 cup chicken stock
1 cup orange juice
1 cup orange marmalade
½ cup ketchup
¼ cup Dijon mustard
2 tablespoons brown sugar
2 tablespoons rice vinegar
2 tablespoons reduced-sodium soy sauce
1 tablespoon minced fresh ginger
1 teaspoon garlic powder
¾ teaspoon crushed red pepper flakes
2 tablespoons molasses (optional)
2 pounds (907 g) boneless, skinless chicken breasts, cut into ¾-inch pieces
½ cup cornstarch
¾ teaspoon salt
½ teaspoon pepper

1 large sweet red pepper, cut into 1-inch pieces
2 cups fresh broccoli florets
Hot cooked rice, for serving

Optional Toppings:
Chopped green onions
Peanuts   Fresh cilantro

1. In a small bowl, combine the first 11 ingredients; stir in molasses, if desired. In a slow cooker, combine chicken, cornstarch, salt and pepper; toss to coat. Top with red pepper. Pour stock mixture over top. Cover and cook on low for 4 hours or until the chicken is tender.
2. Stir in the broccoli. Cover and cook on high 30 to 40 minutes longer or until broccoli is crisp-tender. Serve with rice. Sprinkle with toppings of your choice.

Lush Casablanca Chutney Chicken

Prep time: 25 minutes | Cook time: 7 to 8 hours | Serves 4

1 pound (454 g) boneless, skinless chicken thighs, cut into ¾-inch pieces
1 (14½-ounce / 411-g) can chicken broth
⅓ cup finely chopped onion
⅓ cup chopped sweet red pepper
⅓ cup chopped carrot
⅓ cup chopped dried apricots
⅓ cup chopped dried figs
⅓ cup golden raisins
2 tablespoons orange marmalade
1 tablespoon mustard seed
2 garlic cloves, minced
½ teaspoon curry powder
¼ teaspoon crushed red pepper flakes
¼ teaspoon ground cumin
¼ teaspoon ground cinnamon
¼ teaspoon ground cloves
2 tablespoons minced fresh parsley
2 tablespoons minced fresh mint
1 tablespoon lemon juice
4 tablespoons chopped pistachios

1. In a slow cooker, combine the first 16 ingredients. Cover and cook on low for 7 to 8 hours or until the chicken is tender.
2. Stir in the parsley, mint and lemon juice; heat through. Sprinkle each serving with pistachios.

Balsamic Chicken with Potatoes

Prep time: 10 minutes | Cook time: 3⅓ hours | Serves 6 to 8

6 medium Yukon gold potatoes, quartered
8 strips bacon, cut into ½-inch pieces
8 chicken thighs, skin removed
Salt and freshly ground black pepper, to taste
2 tablespoons finely chopped fresh rosemary
8 cloves garlic, quartered
1 cup balsamic vinegar
½ cup chicken broth

1. Put the potatoes in a slow cooker. Cook the bacon in a large skillet over medium heat for 4 minutes, or until crisp and remove it to paper towels to drain, leaving the drippings in the pan.
2. Sprinkle the chicken evenly with 1½ teaspoons salt and ½ teaspoon pepper and add to the bacon drippings.
3. Brown the chicken on all sides, for 12 to 15 minutes. Add the rosemary and garlic and sauté for 1 to 2 minutes. Deglaze the skillet with the vinegar, scraping any browned bits from the bottom, and transfer the contents of the skillet to the slow cooker.
4. Add the broth. Cover and cook on high for 3 hours or on low for 5 to 6 hours, until the chicken and potatoes are tender. Season with salt and pepper.
5. Sprinkle the reserved bacon over the top of the chicken and potatoes before serving.

Wine-Glazed Chicken Thighs

Prep time: 10 minutes | Cook time: 6⅓ to 8⅓ hours | Serves 6 to 8

10 chicken thighs, skin removed
1½ teaspoons salt
½ teaspoon freshly ground black pepper
2 tablespoons extra-virgin olive oil
2 tablespoons unsalted butter
2 medium onions, coarsely chopped
3 cloves garlic, minced
2 teaspoons dried thyme
1 cup red wine
1 (14- to 15-ounce / 397- to 425-g) can crushed tomatoes, with their juice
½ cup finely chopped fresh Italian parsley

1. Sprinkle the chicken evenly with the salt and pepper. Heat the oil in a large skillet over medium heat. Add the chicken and brown on all sides, for 12 to 15 minutes.
2. Transfer the browned meat to a slow cooker. Melt the butter in the same skillet. Add the onions, garlic, and thyme and sauté for about 5 minutes, until the onion is softened.
3. Add the wine and tomatoes and scrape up any browned bits from the bottom of the skillet. Transfer the contents of the pan to the slow cooker. Cover and cook on low for 6 to 8 hours, until the chicken is cooked through and tender, falling off the bone. Skim off any fat from the top of the sauce.
4. Stir in the parsley and serve warm.

Slow Cooked Chicken with Olives

Prep time: 10 minutes | Cook time: 4 to 5 hours | Serves 6

½ cup all-purpose flour
Salt and freshly ground black pepper, to taste
8 chicken thighs, skin and bones removed
¼ cup extra-virgin olive oil
4 garlic cloves, sliced
¾ cup dry white wine or vermouth
1½ cups chicken broth
1 cup pitted Niçoise olives
1 lemon, cut into ½-inch-thick slices
1 bay leaf

1. Combine the flour, ½ teaspoon salt, and ½ teaspoon pepper in a large plastic bag. Add the chicken to the bag and shake to coat. Heat the oil in a large skillet over high heat.
2. Add the chicken and brown on all sides, for 7 to 10 minutes.
3. Transfer the browned chicken to a slow cooker. Add the garlic to the same skillet and cook until it is fragrant, for about 30 seconds.
4. Add the wine and deglaze the skillet, scraping up any browned bits from the bottom. Transfer the contents of the skillet to the slow cooker. Add the remaining ingredients and stir to combine. Cover the slow cooker and cook on low for 4 to 5 hours, until the chicken is tender.
5. Season with salt and pepper before serving.

Chicken and Ham Stew

Prep time: 20 minutes | Cook time: 7⅓ hours | Serves 6 to 8

½ cup all-purpose flour
Salt, to taste
¼ teaspoon sweet paprika
Pinch of cayenne pepper
8 chicken thighs, skin removed
3 tablespoons olive oil
1 ham steak, cut into 1-inch pieces (1 pound / 454 g)
1 medium onion, coarsely chopped
1 medium red bell pepper, deseeded and coarsely chopped
1 teaspoon dried thyme
1 (15-ounce / 425-g) can chopped tomatoes
1 tablespoon Worcestershire sauce
1 cup chicken broth
6 medium red potatoes, quartered
1 (10-ounce / 284-g) package frozen lima beans, thawed
1 (16-ounce / 454-g) package frozen corn, thawed
2 cups fresh okra, cut into ½-inch slices
6 drops hot sauce
Freshly ground black pepper, to taste

1. Put the flour, 1½ teaspoons salt, the paprika, and cayenne in a large plastic bag. Add the chicken to the bag and toss to coat. Remove the chicken from the bag and shake off any excess flour.
2. Heat the oil in a large skillet over high heat. Add the chicken a few pieces at a time and brown on all sides, for 12 to 15 minutes. Transfer the browned pieces to a slow cooker.
3. Add the ham to the same skillet and sauté for 3 minutes, until it begins to color. Transfer to the slow cooker. Add the onion, bell pepper, and thyme to the skillet and sauté until the vegetables begin to soften, for about 3 minutes. Add the tomatoes and Worcestershire, stirring up any browned bits from the bottom of the pan.
4. Transfer the mixture to the slow cooker. Add the broth, potatoes, lima beans, and corn to the cooker and stir to combine. Cover and cook the stew on low for 6 hours.
5. Remove the cover and add the okra and hot sauce. Cover and cook for an additional 1 hour, until the potatoes and chicken are tender.
6. Season with salt and pepper before serving.

Teriyaki Chicken with Water Chestnuts

Prep time: 10 minutes | Cook time: 4 to 5 hours | Serves 6

1 pound (454 g) boneless, skinless chicken thighs, cut into chunks
1 pound (454 g) boneless, skinless chicken breasts, cut into large chunks
1 (10-ounce / 284-g) bottle teriyaki sauce
½ pound (227 g) snow peas (optional)
1 (8-ounce / 227-g) can water chestnuts, drained (optional)

1. Place the chicken in a slow cooker. Cover with the teriyaki sauce. Stir until the sauce is well distributed.
2. Cover and cook on low for 4 to 5 hours, or until chicken is tender. Add the snow peas and water chestnuts, if desired.
3. Cover and cook for another hour on low.
4. Serve warm.

Spiced Italian Chicken Breast

Prep time: 10 minutes | Cook time: 4 to 5 hours | Serves 6

1 medium onion, chopped
½ cup fat-free Italian dressing
½ cup water
¼ teaspoon salt
½ teaspoon garlic powder
1 teaspoon chili powder
½ teaspoon paprika
¼ teaspoon black pepper
6 boneless, skinless chicken breast halves
2 tablespoons cornstarch
2 tablespoons cold water
Cooking spray

1. Spritz the inside of the slow cooker with cooking spray. Combine all the ingredients, except for the chicken, cornstarch, and water in a slow cooker.
2. Add the chicken. Turn to coat.
3. Cover. Cook on low for 4 to 5 hours.
4. Remove the chicken and keep warm.
5. In a saucepan, combine the cornstarch and cold water.
6. Add cooking juices to the pan gradually. Stir and bring to a boil until thickened.
7. Pour the sauce over chicken and serve warm.

Apple-Cranberry Chicken

Prep time: 10 minutes | Cook time: 6 to 8 hours | Serves 6

6 boneless, skinless chicken breast halves
1 cup fresh cranberries
1 green apple, peeled, cored, and sliced
1 tablespoon brown sugar
1 cup unsweetened apple juice or cider

1. Place the chicken in a slow cooker.
2. Sprinkle with cranberries and apples.
3. Mix the brown sugar and apple juice in a bowl. Pour over the chicken and fruit.
4. Cover. Cook on low for 6 to 8 hours.
5. Serve warm

Slow Cooked Chicken in Stout

Prep time: 20 minutes | Cook time: 6¾ to 7 hours | Serves 6 to 8

1 whole chicken (about 4 pounds / 1.8 kg), cut into 8 pieces, or 8 pieces of your favorite chicken parts, skin removed
1 teaspoon salt
½ teaspoon freshly ground black pepper
3 tablespoons vegetable oil
2 medium onions, coarsely chopped
2 teaspoons freshly grated ginger
2 cloves garlic, minced
¼ cup soy sauce
2 cups baby carrots
1 (12-ounce / 340-g) can Guinness stout
1 cup chicken broth
½ pound (227 g) shiitake mushrooms, stems removed and caps sliced in half
2 tablespoons cornstarch mixed with ¼ cup water
Chopped green onions, for garnish

1. Sprinkle the chicken evenly with the salt and pepper. Heat the oil in a large skillet over high heat. Add the chicken and brown on all sides, for 12 to 15 minutes.
2. Transfer the browned chicken to a slow cooker. Add the onions, ginger, and garlic to the skillet and sauté until the onions are softened, for 3 to 4 minutes. Add the soy sauce and scrape up any browned bits from the bottom of the skillet.
3. Transfer the contents of the skillet to the slow cooker. Add the carrots, Guinness, broth, and mushrooms to the cooker. Cover and cook on low for 6 hours.
4. Remove the cover and stir in the cornstarch mixture. Cover and cook for an additional 30 to 45 minutes, until the stew is thickened, and the chicken is tender.
5. Serve the stew garnished with the green onions.

Chicken Tagine with Dried Fruit

Prep time: 20 minutes | Cook time: 5¼ to 6½ hours | Serves 6

8 chicken thighs, skin and bones removed
1½ teaspoons salt
⅛ teaspoon cayenne
¼ cup olive oil
1 medium onion, coarsely chopped
1 teaspoon ground turmeric
2 cloves garlic, minced
½ teaspoon ground cumin
½ teaspoon ground ginger
1 tablespoon brown sugar
½ cup dried apricots, cut into quarters
½ cup dried plums
½ cup orange juice
Grated zest of 1 orange
1½ cups chicken broth
¼ cup water mixed with 2 tablespoons cornstarch
3 cups cooked couscous

1. Sprinkle the chicken with the salt and cayenne. Heat the oil in a large skillet over high heat. Add the chicken a few pieces at a time and brown on all sides, for 12 to 15 minutes.
2. Transfer the browned chicken to a slow cooker. Add the onion, turmeric, garlic, cumin, ginger, and brown sugar to the skillet and sauté until the onion begins to soften, for about 4 minutes.
3. Transfer the contents of the skillet to the slow cooker. Add the apricots, plums, orange juice, orange zest, and broth to the cooker. Cover and cook on high for 4½ to 5½ hours, until the chicken is tender and the fruit is plump.
4. Stir in the cornstarch mixture and cook for an additional 30 to 45 minutes, until the sauce is thickened.
5. Serve the chicken, fruit, and sauce over a bed of the couscous.

Simple Poached Chicken Breasts

Prep time: 10 minutes | Cook time: 4 to 5 hours | Serves 8

2 cups chicken broth
3 whole black peppercorns
½ teaspoon dried thyme
12 chicken breast halves, skin and bones removed

1.Mix together the broth, peppercorns, and thyme in a slow cooker. Place the chicken breasts in the slow cooker, stacking them in an even layer.
2.Cover and cook on low for 4 to 5 hours, until the chicken is cooked through and tender. Let the chicken cool and remove it from the slow cooker. Refrigerate for 2 days or freeze for up to 10 weeks.

Traditional Chicken Pot Pie

Prep time: 15 minutes | Cook time: 3¾ to 5 hours | Serves 6 to 8

3 cups chicken broth
1 teaspoon dried thyme
4 medium Yukon gold potatoes, cut into ½-inch cubes
2 cups baby carrots
4 cups cooked chicken, cut into bite-size pieces or shredded
1½ cups frozen petite peas, thawed
1 cup frozen white corn, thawed
2 tablespoons unsalted butter, at room temperature
2 tablespoons all-purpose flour

1.Pour the broth in a slow cooker. Add the thyme, potatoes, and carrots, and stir to combine. Cover and cook on high for 3 to 4 hours, until the potatoes are tender.
2.Add the chicken, peas and corn and stir to combine. In a small bowl, stir the butter and flour and make a paste. Add the paste to the slow cooker and stir to combine. Cover and cook for an additional 45 minutes to 1 hour, until the sauce is thickened.
3.Serve warm.

Chicken with Broccoli and Miso

Prep time: 10 minutes | Cook time: 1½ to 2 hours | Serves 6

2 cups chicken broth
¼ cup white miso paste
1 clove garlic, sliced
2 thin slices fresh ginger
6 chicken breast halves, skin and bones removed
1 pound (454 g) broccoli, stalks trimmed and peeled and cut into florets

1.Pour the broth into a slow cooker. Add the miso, garlic, and ginger and stir to combine.
2.Place the chicken in the broth and place the broccoli on top of the chicken. Cover and cook on high for 1½ to 2 hours, until the chicken is cooked through and the broccoli is tender.
3.Remove the chicken from the broth and arrange it on a serving platter, surrounded by the broccoli. Strain the broth through a fine-mesh sieve and serve in bowls. The chicken can also be served in bowls.

Chicken Cacciatore

Prep time: 10 minutes | Cook time: 6 to 6½ hours | Serves 4 to 5

2 onions, sliced
2½ to 3 pounds (1.1 to 1.4 kg) chicken legs
2 garlic cloves, minced
1 (16-ounce / 454-g) can stewed tomatoes
1 (8-ounce / 227-g) can tomato sauce
1 teaspoon salt
¼ teaspoon pepper
1 to 2 teaspoons dried oregano
½ teaspoon dried basil
1 bay leaf
¼ cup white wine
Hot buttered spaghetti, linguini, or fettucini, for serving

1.Place the onions in a slow cooker.
2.Lay the chicken legs over the onions.
3.Combine the remaining ingredients in a bowl. Pour over the chicken.
4.Cover. Cook on low for 6 to 6½ hours.
5.Remove the bay leaf. Serve over hot buttered spaghetti, linguini, or fettucini.

Cheesy Italian Chicken

Prep time: 5 minutes | Cook time: 4 hours | Serves 4 to 6

2 to 3 pounds (0.9 to 1.4 kg) boneless, skinless chicken breasts, cut into chunks
1 (16-ounce / 454-g) bottle Italian dressing
¼ cup Parmesan cheese
Cooked rice, for serving

1. Place the chicken in a slow cooker and pour the dressing over the chicken. Stir together gently.
2. Sprinkle the cheese on top.
3. Cover and cook on high for 4 hours, or on low for 8 hours, or until chicken is tender but not dry.
4. Serve over cooked rice, along with extra sauce from the chicken.

Tarragon Chicken with Mushrooms

Prep time: 15 minutes | Cook time: 3 hours | Serves 6

2 tablespoons extra-virgin olive oil
8 chicken breast halves, skin and bones removed
Salt and freshly ground black pepper, to taste
1 clove garlic, minced
1 medium onion, finely chopped
1 pound (454 g) white button mushrooms, halved or quartered if large
1 teaspoon dried tarragon
¼ cup dry white wine or vermouth
1½ cups chicken broth
¼ cup Dijon mustard
½ cup heavy cream
2 teaspoons cornstarch
2 tablespoons finely chopped fresh tarragon, plus more for garnish

1. Heat the oil in a large skillet over high heat. Sprinkle the chicken evenly with 1 teaspoon salt and ½ teaspoon pepper. Add the chicken to the skillet and brown on all sides, for 12 to 15 minutes. Transfer the chicken to a slow cooker.
2. Add the garlic, onion, mushrooms, and dried tarragon to the skillet and sauté until the onion is softened and the mushroom liquid has evaporated, for 7 to 10 minutes. Deglaze the skillet with the wine, scraping up any browned bits from the bottom.
3. Transfer the contents of the skillet to the slow cooker. Add the broth and mustard to the cooker and stir to combine. Cover the slow cooker and cook on high for 2½ hours or on low for 4 to 5 hours.
4. Add cream, cornstarch, and two tablespoons fresh tarragon to the slow cooker and stir to combine. Cover and cook for an additional 15 minutes on high or 30 minutes on low, until the sauce is thickened. Season with salt and pepper.
5. Serve the chicken garnished with the additional fresh tarragon.

Classic Chicken Casablanca

Prep time: 20 minutes | Cook time: 4½ to 6½ hours | Serves 6 to 8

2 tablespoons oil
2 large onions, sliced
1 teaspoon ground ginger
3 garlic cloves, minced
3 large carrots, diced
2 large potatoes, diced
3 pounds (1.4 kg) skinless chicken pieces
½ teaspoon ground cumin
½ teaspoon salt
½ teaspoon pepper
¼ teaspoon cinnamon
2 tablespoons raisins
1 (14½-ounce / 411-g) can chopped tomatoes
3 small zucchini, sliced
1 (15-ounce / 425-g) can garbanzo beans, drained
2 tablespoons chopped parsley
Cooked rice or couscous, for serving

1. Sauté the onions, ginger, and garlic in the oil in a skillet, for 3 minutes. Reserve the oil. Transfer to a slow cooker. Add the carrots and potatoes.
2. Brown the chicken over medium heat in the reserved oil, for 12 to 15 minutes. Transfer to the slow cooker. Mix gently with the vegetables.
3. Combine the seasonings in a separate bowl. Sprinkle over the chicken and vegetables. Add the raisins and tomatoes.
4. Cover. Cook on high for 4 to 6 hours.
5. Add the sliced zucchini, beans, and parsley at the last 30 minutes.
6. Serve over cooked rice or couscous.

Asian Chicken with Cashew

Prep time: 10 minutes | Cook time: 4 to 9 hours | Serves 6

1 (14-ounce / 397-g) can bean sprouts, drained
3 tablespoons butter, melted
4 green onions, chopped
1 (4-ounce / 113-g) can mushroom pieces
1 (10¾-ounce / 305-g) can cream of mushroom soup
1 cup sliced celery
1 (12½-ounce / 354-g) can chunk chicken breast, or 1 cup cooked chicken, cubed
1 tablespoon soy sauce
1 cup cashew nuts

1.Combine all the ingredients, except for the cashew nuts, in a slow cooker.
2.Cover. Cook on low for 4 to 9 hours, or on high for 2 to 3 hours.
3.Stir in the cashew nuts before serving.

Cider Braised Chicken with Apples

Prep time: 20 minutes | Cook time: 3⅓ to 4½ hours | Serves 8

4 tablespoons unsalted butter
5 large cooking apples, peeled and cored, cut into 8 wedges each
2 medium onions, cut into half rounds
2 teaspoons dried thyme
2 tablespoons Dijon mustard
¼ cup firmly packed light brown sugar
1½ cups apple cider
2 chicken bouillon cubes
8 strips thick-cut Applewood smoked bacon, cut into 1-inch pieces
8 chicken breast halves, skin and bones removed
½ teaspoon freshly ground black pepper
½ cup heavy cream
½ cup finely chopped fresh Italian parsley

1.Melt the butter in a large skillet over medium-high heat. Add the apples, onions, and thyme and sauté until the onions begin to soften, for 5 to 7 minutes.
2.Add the mustard, sugar, and cider and stir to combine, melting the sugar. Transfer to a slow cooker. Add the bouillon cubes to the cooker, crushing them to dissolve. Set the cooker on warm while you sauté the chicken.
3.Wipe out the skillet, cook the bacon for 4 minutes, or until crisp, and remove it to paper towels to drain. Sprinkle the chicken with the pepper. Add the chicken to the bacon drippings in the skillet and brown on all sides, for 12 to 15 minutes.
4.Transfer the chicken to the slow cooker. Cover and cook on low for 3 to 4 hours, until the chicken is cooked though and the apples are tender. Add the cream and parsley and stir to combine.
5.Serve warm.

Chicken Divan with Curry

Prep time: 10 minutes | Cook time: 4 hours | Serves 6

4 tablespoons unsalted butter
1½ teaspoons curry powder
¼ cup all-purpose flour
2 cups chicken broth
1 cup evaporated milk
8 chicken breast halves, skin and bones removed
1½ cups finely shredded sharp Cheddar cheese

1.Melt the butter in a saucepan over medium-high heat. Add the curry powder and sauté for 30 seconds.
2.Add the flour and cook for 3 minutes, whisking constantly. Add the broth and bring to the mixture to a boil. Add the milk and remove the sauce from the heat and allow to cool.
3.Place the chicken in a slow cooker, stacking evenly. Pour the cooled sauce over the chicken. Cover and cook on high for 3 hours.
4.Sprinkle the cheese over the chicken, cover, and cook for an additional 1 hour, until the chicken is cooked through.
5.Serve warm.

Chicken Wings in Lemon-Rosemary Sauce

Prep time: 10 minutes | Cook time: 3 hours | Serves 8

3 pounds (1.4 kg) chicken wing drumettes
¼ cup olive oil
1½ teaspoons salt
1 teaspoon sweet paprika
Freshly ground black pepper, to taste
Cooking spray
Sauce:
½ cup lemon juice
Grated zest of 3 lemons
2 teaspoons salt
Pinch of red pepper flakes
½ cup extra-virgin olive oil
2 tablespoons red wine vinegar
6 cloves garlic, minced
1 tablespoon finely minced fresh rosemary
½ cup chicken broth

1.Spritz the insert of a slow cooker with cooking spray. Preheat the broiler to 400ºF (205ºC) for 10 minutes.
2.Combine the wings, olive oil, salt, paprika, and a generous grinding of pepper in a large mixing bowl and toss until the wings are evenly coated. Arrange the wings on a wire rack in a baking sheet and broil until the wings are crispy on one side, for about 5 minutes.
3.Turn the wings and broil until crispy and browned, for an additional 5 minutes.
4.Remove the wings from the oven. If you would like to do this step ahead of time, cool the wings and refrigerate for up to 2 days. Otherwise, put the wings in the prepared cooker insert.
5.Combine all the sauce ingredients in a mixing bowl and stir. Pour the sauce over the wings and turn to coat.
6.Cover and cook on high for 3 hours, turning the wings several times to coat with the sauce.
7.Serve warm.

Italian-Style Braised Chicken and Veggies

Prep time: 10 minutes | Cook time: 4 hours | Serves 8

8 boneless, skinless chicken breast halves
Black pepper, to taste
1 teaspoon garlic powder
1 (16-ounce / 454-g) bottle fat-free Italian salad dressing, divided
2 (15-ounce / 425-g) cans whole potatoes, drained
1 pound (454 g) frozen Italian veggies or green beans, thawed
1 (8-ounce / 227-g) can water chestnuts (optional)

1.Sprinkle the chicken with pepper and garlic powder.
2.Put the chicken in a slow cooker. Pour half of the salad dressing over meat, making sure that all pieces are glazed.
3.Add the potatoes, vegetables, and water chestnuts (if desired). Pour the remaining salad dressing over, again making sure that the vegetables are all lightly coated.
4.Cover. Cook on high for 4 hours, or on low for 7 to 8 hours.
5.Serve warm.

Slow Cooker Chicken Chili

Prep time: 5 minutes | Cook time: 6 to 8 hours | Serves 4

4 boneless, skinless chicken breast halves
1 (16-ounce / 454-g) jar salsa
2 (16-ounce / 454-g) cans Great Northern beans, drained
8 ounces (227 g) shredded cheese, Colby Jack or Pepper Jack
Cooked rice or noodles, for serving

1.Place the chicken in a slow cooker.
2.Cover with the salsa.
3.Cover and cook on low for 5½ to 7½ hours, or until the chicken is tender but not dry.
4.Shred or cube the chicken in the sauce.
5.Stir in the beans and cheese.
6.Cover and cook for another 30 minutes on low.
7.Serve over cooked rice or noodles.

Authentic Con Pollo

Prep time: 5 minutes | Cook time: 8 to 10 hours | Serves 4 to 6

3 to 4 pounds (1.4 to 1.8 kg) whole chicken
Salt, to taste
Pepper, to taste
Paprika, as needed
Garlic salt, to taste
1 (6-ounce / 170-g) can tomato paste
½ cup beer
1 (3-ounce / 85-g) jar stuffed olives, with liquid
Cooked rice or noodles, for serving

1. Wash the chicken. Sprinkle all over with salt, pepper, paprika, and garlic salt. Place in a slow cooker.
2. Combine the tomato paste and beer. Pour over the chicken. Add the olives.
3. Cover. Cook on low for 8 to 10 hours, or on high for 3 to 4 hours.
4. Serve over cooked rice or noodles.

Easy Chicken Tetrazzini

Prep time: 10 minutes | Cook time: 6 to 8 hours | Serves 4

2 to 3 cups diced cooked chicken
2 cups chicken broth
1 small onion, chopped
¼ cup sauterne, white wine, or milk
½ cup slivered almonds
2 (4-ounce / 113-g) cans sliced mushrooms, drained
1 (10¾-ounce / 305-g) can cream of mushroom soup
1 pound (454 g) spaghetti, cooked
Grated Parmesan cheese, for topping

1. Combine all the ingredients, except for the spaghetti and cheese, in a slow cooker.
2. Cover. Cook on low for 6 to 8 hours.
3. Serve over the spaghetti. Sprinkle with the Parmesan cheese.

Chicken and Turkey Sausage Jambalaya

Prep time: 20 minutes | Cook time: 6 hours | Serves 6

1 pound (454 g) uncooked boneless, skinless chicken breast, cubed
3 cups fat-free chicken broth
¾ cup water
1½ cups uncooked brown rice
4 ounces (113 g) reduced-fat, smoked turkey sausage, diced
½ cup thinly sliced celery with leaves
½ cup chopped onion
½ cup chopped green bell pepper
2 teaspoons Cajun seasoning
2 garlic cloves, minced
⅛ teaspoon hot pepper sauce (optional)
1 bay leaf
1 (14½-ounce / 411-g) can no-salt diced tomatoes, undrained

1. In a large nonstick skillet, sauté the chicken for 2 to 3 minutes.
2. Stir together the remaining ingredients in a slow cooker.
3. Add the sautéed chicken to the slow cooker.
4. Cover. Cook on high for 6 hours.
5. Serve warm.

Lemony Dill Chicken

Prep time: 5 minutes | Cook time: 3 to 4 hours | Serves 4

1 cup fat-free sour cream
1 tablespoon fresh dill, minced
1 teaspoon lemon pepper seasoning
1 teaspoon lemon zest
4 boneless, skinless chicken breast halves

1. Combine the sour cream, dill, lemon pepper, and lemon zest in a small bowl. Spoon one-fourth of the sour cream mixture into a slow cooker.
2. Arrange the chicken breasts on top in a single layer.
3. Pour the remaining sauce over the chicken. Spread evenly.
4. Cover. Cook on low for 3 to 4 hours, or until juices run clear.
5. Serve warm.

Cheesy Chicken Parmigiana

Prep time: 5 minutes | Cook time: 6⅓ to 8⅓ hours | Serves 6

1 egg, beaten
1 teaspoon salt
¼ teaspoon pepper
1 cup Italian bread crumbs
6 boneless, skinless chicken breast halves
2 to 4 tablespoons butter
1 (14-ounce / 397-g) jar pizza sauce
6 slices Mozzarella cheese
Grated Parmesan cheese, for topping

1.Combine the egg, salt, and pepper together in a bowl. Place the bread crumbs in a separate bowl.
2.Dip the chicken into the egg and coat with the bread crumbs. Sauté the chicken in the butter in a skillet for 5 minutes. Arrange the chicken in a slow cooker.
3.Pour the pizza sauce over the chicken.
4.Cover. Cook on low for 6 to 8 hours.
5.Layer the Mozzarella cheese over top and sprinkle with the Parmesan cheese. Cook for an additional 15 minutes.
6.Serve warm.

Chicken Olé Casserole

Prep time: 10 minutes | Cook time: 4½ to 5½ hours | Serves 8

1 (10¾-ounce / 305-g) can cream of mushroom soup
1 (10¾-ounce / 305-g) can cream of chicken soup
1 cup sour cream
2 tablespoons grated onion
2cups shredded Cheddar cheese, divided
12 flour tortillas, each torn into 6 to 8 pieces
3 to 4 cups cubed, cooked chicken
1 (7-ounce / 198-g) jar salsa

1.In a bowl, combine the soups, sour cream, onion, and 1½ cups of the cheese.
2.Place one-third of each of the following ingredients in layers in a slow cooker: torn tortillas, soup mixture, chicken, and salsa. Repeat layers 2 more times.
3.Cover. Cook on low for 4 to 5 hours.
4.Gently stir. Sprinkle with remaining ½ cup of the cheese. Cover. Cook on low for another 15 to 30 minutes.
5.Serve warm.

Red Pepper Chicken with Black Beans

Prep time: 10 minutes | Cook time: 4 to 6 hours | Serves 4

4 boneless, skinless chicken breast halves
1 (15-ounce / 425-g) can black beans, drained
1 (12-ounce / 340-g) jar roasted red peppers, undrained
1 (14½-ounce / 411-g) can Mexican stewed tomatoes, undrained
1 large onion, chopped
½ teaspoon salt
Pepper, to taste

1.Place the chicken in a slow cooker.
2.Combine the beans, red peppers, stewed tomatoes, onion, salt, and pepper in a bowl. Pour over the chicken.
3.Cover. Cook on low for 4 to 6 hours, or until chicken is cooked through.
4.Serve warm.

Greek Chicken with Potatoes

Prep time: 10 minutes | Cook time: 5 to 6 hours | Serves 8

6 medium potatoes, quartered
3 pounds (1.4 kg) chicken pieces, skin removed
2 large onions, quartered
1 whole bulb garlic, minced
½ cup water
3 teaspoons dried oregano
1 teaspoon salt
½ teaspoon black pepper
1 tablespoon olive oil

1.Place the potatoes in a slow cooker. Add the chicken, onions, and garlic.
2.In a small bowl, mix the water with oregano, salt, and pepper.
3.Pour over the chicken and potatoes. Drizzle with the oil.
4.Cover. Cook on high for 5 to 6 hours, or on low for 9 to 10 hours.
5.Serve warm.

Chicken Tamales

Prep time: 20 minutes | Cook time: 3 to 4 hours | Serves 6

1 medium onion, chopped
1 (4-ounce / 113-g) can chopped green chilies
2 tablespoons oil
1 (10¾-ounce / 305-g) can cream of chicken soup
2 cups sour cream
1 cup sliced ripe olives
1 cup chopped stewed tomatoes
8 chicken breast halves, cooked and chopped
1 (16-ounce / 454-g) can beef tamales, chopped
1 teaspoon chili powder
1 teaspoon garlic powder
1 teaspoon pepper
2½ cups shredded Cheddar cheese, divided

Toppings:

Fresh tomatoes   Shredded lettuce
Sour cream   Salsa
Guacamole

1.Sauté the onion and chilies in the oil in a skillet for 5 minutes.
2.Stir in all the remaining ingredients, except for ½ cup of the shredded cheese. Pour into a slow cooker.
3.Top with the remaining ½ cup of the cheese.
4.Cover. Cook on high for 3 to 4 hours.
5.Serve with your choice of toppings.

Garlicky Chicken

Prep time: 10 minutes | Cook time: 5 to 6 hours | Serves 6

¼ cup dry white wine
2 tablespoons chopped dried parsley
2 teaspoons dried basil leaves
1 teaspoon dried oregano
Pinch of crushed red pepper flakes
20 cloves of garlic (about 1 head)
4 celery ribs, chopped
6 boneless, skinless chicken breast halves
1 lemon, juiced and zested
Fresh herbs, for garnish (optional)

1.Combine the wine, parsley, basil, oregano, and red peppers in a large bowl.
2.Add the garlic cloves and celery to the bowl.

Coat well.
3.Transfer the garlic and celery to a slow cooker with a slotted spoon.
4.Add the chicken to the spice mixture. Coat well. Place the chicken on top of the vegetables in the slow cooker.
5.Drizzle with the lemon juice and sprinkle with the lemon zest in the slow cooker. Add any remaining spice mixture.
6.Cover. Cook on low for 5 to 6 hours, or until chicken is no longer pink in center.
7.Garnish with fresh herbs, if desired. Serve warm.

BBQ Chicken Legs

Prep time: 10 minutes | Cook time: 8 hours | Serves 8

10 chicken legs, skin removed
1 teaspoon salt
½ teaspoon freshly ground black pepper
2 tablespoons unsalted butter
1 medium onion, finely chopped
1 clove garlic, minced
1 tablespoon Dijon mustard
1 tablespoon Worcestershire sauce
1½ cups ketchup
½ cup chicken broth
½ cup firmly packed light brown sugar
¼ cup molasses
½ teaspoon hot sauce
Cooking spray

1.Spray the insert of a slow cooker with cooking spray.
2.Sprinkle the chicken legs evenly with the salt and pepper and transfer to the slow cooker insert.
3.Melt the butter in a large saucepan over medium-high heat. Add the onion and garlic and sauté until the onion is softened, for about 3 minutes.
4.Add the remaining ingredients and stir to combine. Pour the sauce over the chicken. Cook on low for 8 hours, until the chicken is tender and cooked through. Remove the cover from the slow cooker and skim off any fat.
5.Serve warm.

Tender Chicken with BBQ-Soda Sauce

Prep time: 5 minutes | Cook time: 8 to 10 hours | Serves 4 to 6

3 to 4 pounds (1.4 to 1.8 kg) broiler chicken
1 medium onion, thinly sliced
1 medium lemon, thinly sliced
1 (18-ounce / 510-g) bottle barbecue sauce
¾ cup cola-flavored soda

1. Place the chicken in a slow cooker.
2. Top with the onion and lemon.
3. Combine the barbecue sauce and cola in a bowl. Pour into the slow cooker.
4. Cover. Cook on low for 8 to 10 hours, or until chicken juices run clear.
5. Cut into serving-sized pieces and serve with barbecue sauce.

BBQ Chicken with Veggies

Prep time: 15 minutes | Cook time: 8 hours | Serves 6

¼ cup flour
3 whole boneless, skinless chicken breasts, cut in half
¼ cup oil
1 medium onion, sliced
1 green or yellow pepper, sliced
½ cup chopped celery
2 tablespoons Worcestershire sauce
1 cup ketchup
2 cups water
¼ teaspoon salt
¼ teaspoon paprika

1. Place the flour in a bowl. Roll the chicken breasts in the flour. Brown the chicken in the oil in a skillet, for 7 to 12 minutes. Transfer the chicken to a slow cooker.
2. Sauté the onion, pepper, and celery in the skillet, for 5 minutes, or until tender. Add the remaining ingredients and bring to a boil. Pour over the chicken.
3. Cover. Cook on low for 8 hours.
4. Serve warm.

Braised Chicken with Peas

Prep time: 5 minutes | Cook time: 3 hours | Serves 6

1½ pounds (680 g) uncooked boneless, skinless chicken breast
1 (10¾-ounce / 305-g) can fat-free, low-sodium cream of chicken soup
3 tablespoons flour
¼ teaspoon black pepper
1 (9-ounce / 255-g) package frozen peas and onions, thawed and drained
2 tablespoons chopped pimentos
½ teaspoon paprika

1. Cut the chicken into bite-sized pieces and place in a slow cooker.
2. Combine the soup, flour, and pepper in a bowl. Pour over the chicken. Do not stir.
3. Cover. Cook on high for 2½ hours, or on low for 5 to 5½ hours.
4. Stir in the peas and onions, pimentos, and paprika.
5. Cover. Cook on high for 20 to 30 minutes.
6. Serve warm.

Braised California Chicken

Prep time: 10 minutes | Cook time: 8½ to 9½ hours | Serves 4 to 6

3 pounds (1.4 kg) chicken, quartered
1 cup orange juice
⅓ cup chili sauce
2 tablespoons soy sauce
1 tablespoon molasses
1 teaspoon dry mustard
1 teaspoon garlic salt
2 tablespoons chopped green peppers
3 medium oranges, peeled and separated into slices

1. Arrange the chicken in a slow cooker.
2. In a bowl, combine the orange juice, chili sauce, soy sauce, molasses, dry mustard, and garlic salt. Pour over the chicken.
3. Cover. Cook on low for 8 to 9 hours.
4. Stir in the green peppers and oranges. Cook for 30 minutes longer.
5. Serve warm.

Southwestern Chicken with Corn

Prep time: 5 minutes | Cook time: 3 to 4 hours | Serves 6

2 (15¼-ounce / 432-g) cans corn, drained
1 (15-ounce / 425-g) can black beans, rinsed and drained
1 (16-ounce / 454-g) jar chunky salsa, divided
6 boneless, skinless chicken breast halves
1 cup low-fat shredded Cheddar cheese

1.Combine the corn, black beans, and ½ cup of the salsa in a slow cooker.
2.Top with the chicken. Pour the remaining ½ cup of the salsa over the chicken.
3.Cover. Cook on high for 3 to 4 hours, or on low for 7 to 8 hours.
4.Sprinkle with the cheese. Cover for 5 minutes until the cheese is melted.
5.Serve warm.

Slow Cooked Tex-Mex Chicken and Rice

Prep time: 15 minutes | Cook time: 4 to 4½ hours | Serves 8

1 cup uncooked converted white rice
1 (28-ounce / 794-g) can diced peeled tomatoes
1 (6-ounce / 170-g) can tomato paste
3 cups hot water
1 package dry taco seasoning mix
4 whole boneless, skinless chicken breasts, cut into ½-inch cubes
2 medium onions, chopped
1 green pepper, chopped
1 (4-ounce / 113-g) can diced green chilies
1 teaspoon garlic powder
½ teaspoon pepper

1.Combine all the ingredients, except for the chilies and seasonings, in a slow cooker.
2.Cover. Cook on low for 4 to 4½ hours, or until the rice is tender, and the chicken is cooked.
3.Stir in the green chilies and seasonings and serve.

Mediterranean Chicken with Artichokes

Prep time: 10 minutes | Cook time: 4 to 6 hours | Serves 4

1 yellow onion, thinly sliced
1 (14-ounce / 397-g) jar marinated artichoke hearts, drained
1 (14-ounce / 397-g) can low-sodium peeled tomatoes
6 tablespoons red wine vinegar
1 teaspoon minced garlic
½ teaspoon salt
½ teaspoon black pepper
4 boneless, skinless chicken breast halves

1.Combine all the ingredients, except for the chicken, in a slow cooker.
2.Place the chicken in the slow cooker, pushing down into vegetables and sauce until it's as covered as possible.
3.Cover. Cook on low for 4 to 6 hours.
4.Serve warm.

Peanut Butter Chicken Thighs

Prep time: 10 minutes | Cook time: 5 to 6 hours | Serves 4

1½ cups water
2 teaspoons chicken bouillon granules
2 ribs celery, thinly sliced
2 onions, thinly sliced
1 red bell pepper, sliced
1 green bell pepper, sliced
½ cup extra crunchy peanut butter
8 chicken thighs, skinned
Crushed chili pepper of your choice

1.Combine the water, chicken bouillon granules, celery, onions, and peppers in a slow cooker.
2.Spread the peanut butter over both sides of the chicken pieces. Sprinkle with the chili pepper. Place on top of the ingredients in the slow cooker.
3.Cover. Cook on low for 5 to 6 hours.
4.Serve warm.

Toasted Sesame Chicken Wings

Prep time: 5 minutes | Cook time: 5 hours | Serves 6 to 8

3 pounds (1.4 kg) chicken wings
Salt, to taste
Pepper, to taste
1¾ cups honey
1 cup soy sauce
½ cup ketchup
2 tablespoons canola oil
2 tablespoons sesame oil
2 garlic cloves, minced
Toasted sesame seeds, for topping

1. Rinse the wings. Cut at the joint. Sprinkle with salt and pepper. Place on a broiler pan.
2. Broil at 180ºF (82ºC) for 10 minutes on each side. Place the chicken in a slow cooker.
3. Combine the remaining ingredients, except for sesame seeds, in a bowl. Pour over the chicken.
4. Cover. Cook on low for 5 hours, or on high for 2½ hours.
5. Sprinkle the sesame seeds over top just before serving.

Chicken Wings in Plum Sauce

Prep time: 5 minutes | Cook time: 4 to 5 hours | Serves 6 to 8

3 pounds (1.4 kg) chicken wings (about 16)
1 cup bottled plum sauce
2 tablespoons butter, melted
1 teaspoon five-spice powder
Orange wedges, thinly sliced (optional)
Pineapple slices (optional)

1. In a foil-lined baking pan, arrange the wings in a single layer. Bake at 375ºF (190ºC) in the oven for 20 minutes.
2. Meanwhile, combine the plum sauce, melted butter, and five-spice powder in a slow cooker. Add the wings. Then stir to coat the wings with the sauce.
3. Cover and cook on low for 4 to 5 hours, or on high for 2 to 2½ hours.
4. Garnish with orange wedges and pineapple slices to serve, if desired.

Sweet and Sour Chicken Wings

Prep time: 10 minutes | Cook time: 5 to 6 hours | Serves 8

4 pounds (1.8 kg) chicken wings
2 large onions, chopped
2 (6-ounce / 170-g) cans tomato paste
2 large garlic cloves, minced
¼ cup Worcestershire sauce
¼ cup cider vinegar
½ cup brown sugar
½ cup sweet pickle relish
½ cup red or white wine
2 teaspoons salt
2 teaspoons dry mustard

1. Cut off the wing tips. Cut the wings at the joint. Place in a slow cooker.
2. Combine the remaining ingredients in a bowl. Add to the slow cooker and stir.
3. Cover. Cook on low for 5 to 6 hours.
4. Serve warm.

Turkey Stroganoff

Prep time: 10 minutes | Cook time: 6 to 8 hours | Serves 6

4 turkey thighs (about 4 pounds / 1.8 kg)
1 large onion, halved and thinly sliced
1 (10¾-ounce / 305-g) can condensed cream of celery soup, undiluted
⅓ cup water
3 garlic cloves, minced
2 teaspoons dried tarragon
½ teaspoon salt
½ teaspoon pepper
½ cup sour cream
Hot cooked egg noodles, for serving

1. Place the turkey and onion in a slow cooker. In a large bowl, whisk the soup, water, garlic, tarragon, salt and pepper until blended. Pour over the turkey. Cook, covered, on low for 6 to 8 hours or until the meat is tender.
2. Remove the turkey from the slow cooker. When cool enough to handle, remove the meat from bones and discard the bones. Shred the meat with two forks.
3. Whisk the sour cream into the cooking juices. Return the meat to the slow cooker. Serve with the noodles.

Turkey Breast in Onion Soup

Prep time: 5 minutes | Cook time: 8 to 10 hours | Serves 6 to 8

4 to 6 pounds (1.8 to 2.7 kg) boneless, skinless turkey breast
1 teaspoon garlic powder
1 envelope dry onion soup mix

1.Place the turkey in a slow cooker. Sprinkle with the garlic powder and pour in the onion soup mix.
2.Cover. Cook on low for 8 to 10 hours.
3.Serve warm.

Sesame-Ginger Turkey Tenderloin

Prep time: 15 minutes | Cook time: 4½ to 5½ hours | Serves 8

8 turkey breast tenderloins (4 ounces / 113 g each)
½ teaspoon ground ginger
½ teaspoon crushed red pepper flakes
1 (11-ounce / 312-g) can mandarin oranges, drained
1 cup sesame ginger marinade
½ cup chicken broth
1 (16-ounce / 454-g) package frozen stir-fry vegetable blend, thawed
1 tablespoon toasted sesame seeds
1 green onion, sliced
Hot cooked rice, for serving (optional)

1.Place the turkey in a slow cooker. Sprinkle with the ginger and pepper flakes. Top with the oranges.
2.In a small bowl, combine the marinade and broth. Pour over the turkey. Cover and cook on low for 4 to 5 hours, or until a meat thermometer reads 170ºF (77ºC).
3.Stir the vegetables into the slow cooker. Cover and cook for 30 minutes longer, or until vegetables are heated through.
4.Sprinkle with the sesame seeds and green onion. Serve with the cooked rice, if desired.

Turkey in Orange Sauce

Prep time: 5 minutes | Cook time: 7 to 8 hours | Serves 4 to 6

1 large onion, chopped
3 garlic cloves, minced
1 teaspoon dried rosemary
½ teaspoon pepper
2 to 3 pounds (0.9 to 1.4 kg) boneless, skinless turkey breast
1½ cups orange juice

1.Place the onion in a slow cooker.
2.Combine the garlic, rosemary, and pepper in a bowl.
3.Make gashes in turkey, about ¾ of the way through at 2-inch intervals. Stuff with the herb mixture. Place the turkey in the slow cooker.
4.Pour the orange juice over the turkey.
5.Cover. Cook on low for 7 to 8 hours, or until turkey is no longer pink in center.
6.Serve warm.

Sweet Potato and Turkey Casserole

Prep time: 10 minutes | Cook time: 8 to 10 hours | Serves 4

3 medium sweet potatoes, peeled and cut into 2-inch pieces
1 (10-ounce / 284-g) package frozen cut green beans, thawed
2 pounds (907 g) turkey cutlets
1 (12-ounce / 340-g) jar home-style turkey gravy
2 tablespoons flour
1 teaspoon parsley flakes
¼ to ½ teaspoon dried rosemary
⅛ teaspoon pepper

1.Layer the sweet potatoes, green beans, and turkey in a slow cooker.
2.In a bowl, whisk together the remaining ingredients until smooth. Pour over the mixture in the slow cooker.
3.Cover. Cook on low for 8 to 10 hours.
4.Remove the turkey and vegetables and keep warm. Stir the sauce. Serve with sauce over meat and vegetables, or with sauce in a gravy boat.

BBQ Turkey Cutlets

Prep time: 10 minutes | Cook time: 4 hours | Serves 6 to 8

6 to 8 turkey cutlets (1½ to 2 pounds / 680 to 907 g)
¼ cup molasses
¼ cup cider vinegar
¼ cup ketchup
3 tablespoons Worcestershire sauce
1 teaspoon garlic salt
3 tablespoons chopped onion
2 tablespoons brown sugar
¼ teaspoon pepper

1.Place the turkey cutlets in a slow cooker.
2.Combine the remaining ingredients. Pour over the turkey.
3.Cover. Cook on low for 4 hours.
4.Serve warm.

Ground Turkey with Potatoes

Prep time: 15 minutes | Cook time: 4 hours | Serves 6

1 pound (454 g) ground turkey
5 cups raw sliced potatoes
1 onion, sliced
½ teaspoon salt
Dash of black pepper
1 (14½-ounce / 411-g) can cut green beans, undrained
1 (4-ounce / 113-g) can mushroom pieces, undrained (optional)
1 (10¾-ounce / 305-g) can cream of chicken soup

1.Crumble the uncooked ground turkey in a slow cooker.
2.Add the potatoes, onions, salt, and pepper.
3.Add the beans and mushrooms. Pour the soup over top.
4.Cover. Cook on high for 4 hours, or on low for 6 to 8 hours.
5.Serve warm.

Turkey-Broccoli Supreme

Prep time: 10 minutes | Cook time: 2 to 2½ hours | Serves 8

4 cups cooked turkey breast, cubed
1 (10¾-ounce / 305-g) can condensed cream of chicken soup
1 (10-ounce / 284-g) package frozen broccoli florets, thawed and drained
1 (6.9-ounce / 196-g) package low-sodium plain rice mix
1½ cups fat-free milk
1 cup fat-free chicken broth
1 cup chopped celery
1 (8-ounce / 227-g) can sliced water chestnuts, drained
¾ cup low-fat mayonnaise
½ cup chopped onions

1.Combine all the ingredients in a slow cooker.
2.Cook, uncovered, on high for 2 to 2½ hours, or until the rice is tender.
3.Serve warm.

Spicy Turkey Sloppy Joes

Prep time: 10 minutes | Cook time: 4½ to 6 hours | Makes 6 sandwiches

1 red onion, chopped
1 sweet pepper, chopped
1½ pounds (680 g) boneless turkey, finely chopped
1 cup chili sauce or ketchup
¼ teaspoon salt
1 garlic clove, minced
1 teaspoon Dijon-style mustard
⅛ teaspoon pepper
Bread or sandwich rolls, for serving

1.Place the onion, sweet pepper, and turkey in a slow cooker.
2.Combine the chili sauce, salt, garlic, mustard, and pepper in a bowl. Pour over the turkey mixture. Mix well.
3.Cover. Cook on low for 4½ to 6 hours.
4.Serve on bread or sandwich rolls.

Super Easy Turkey Loaf

Prep time: 5 minutes | Cook time: 6 to 7 hours | Serves 10

2 pounds (907 g) fat-free ground turkey

2 tablespoons poultry seasoning

2 slices bread, cubed

1 egg

1.Combine all the ingredients in a bowl. Form the mixture into a round or oval loaf and place in a slow cooker.

2.Cook for 6 to 7 hours on low. Remove the dish from the slow cooker and allow to sit for 15 minutes before slicing and serving.

Turkey Macaroni with Corn

Prep time: 10 minutes | Cook time: 3 to 4 hours | Serves 6

1 teaspoon vegetable oil
1½ pounds (680 g) 99% fat-free ground turkey
2 (10¾-ounce / 305-g) cans condensed low-sodium tomato soup, undiluted
1 (16-ounce / 454-g) can corn, drained
½ cup onions, chopped
1 (4-ounce / 113-g) can sliced mushrooms, drained
2 tablespoons ketchup
1 tablespoon mustard
¼ teaspoon black pepper
¼ teaspoon garlic powder
2 cups dry macaroni, cooked and drained

1.Heat the oil in a medium skillet. Add the turkey and brown for 12 to 15 minutes. Drain.
2.Combine all the remaining ingredients, except for macaroni, in a slow cooker. Stir to blend.
3.Cover. Cook on high for 3 to 4 hours, or on low for 4 to 6 hours. Stir in the cooked macaroni 15 minutes before serving.
4.Serve warm.

Chapter 6 Red Meat

Mushroom Beef Roast

Prep time: 25 minutes | Cook time: 6 to 8 hours | Serves 10

1 boneless beef chuck roast (3 to 4 pounds / 1.4 to 1.8 kg)
½ teaspoon salt
¼ teaspoon pepper
1 tablespoon canola oil
1½ pounds (680 g) fresh shiitake mushrooms, sliced
2½ cups thinly sliced onions
1½ cups reduced-sodium beef broth
1½ cups dry red wine
1 (8-ounce / 227-g) can tomato sauce
¾ cup chopped peeled parsnips
¾ cup chopped celery
¾ cup chopped carrots
8 garlic cloves, minced
2 bay leaves
1½ teaspoons dried thyme
1 teaspoon chili powder
¼ cup cornstarch
¼ cup water
Mashed potatoes, for serving

1.Sprinkle the roast with salt and pepper. In a Dutch oven, brown the roast in the oil on all sides for 4 minutes. Transfer to a slow cooker. Add the mushrooms, onions, broth, wine, tomato sauce, parsnips, celery, carrots, garlic, bay leaves, thyme and chili powder. Cover and cook on low for 6 to 8 hours or until the meat is tender.
2.Transfer the meat and vegetables to a serving platter and keep warm. Discard the bay leaves. Skim fat from cooking juices and transfer to a small saucepan. Bring the liquid to a boil.
3.In a bowl, combine the cornstarch and water until smooth. Gradually stir into the pan. Bring to a boil. Cook and stir for 2 minutes or until thickened. Serve with mashed potatoes, meat and vegetables.

Feta and Spinach Stuffed Flank Steak

Prep time: 15 minutes | Cook time: 6 to 8 hours | Serves 6

1 beef flank steak (1½ pounds / 680 g)
2 cups crumbled feta cheese, divided
3 cups fresh baby spinach
½ cup oil-packed sun-dried tomatoes, drained and chopped
½ cup finely chopped onion
5 tablespoons all-purpose flour, divided
½ teaspoon salt
½ teaspoon pepper
2 tablespoons canola oil
1 cup beef broth
1 tablespoon Worcestershire sauce
2 teaspoons tomato paste
⅓ cup dry red wine
Hot cooked egg noodles, for serving (optional)

1.Starting at one long side, cut the steak horizontally in half to within ½ inch of opposite side. Open the steak flat and cover with the plastic wrap. Pound with a meat mallet to ½-inch thickness. Remove the plastic.
2.Sprinkle 1 cup of the cheese over the steak to within 1 inch of edges. Layer with the spinach, tomatoes, onion and the remaining 1 cup of the cheese. Roll up, starting with a long side and tie at 1½-inch intervals with kitchen string. Sprinkle the beef with 2 tablespoons of the flour, salt and pepper.
3.In a large skillet, heat the oil over medium heat. Brown the beef on all sides for 4 minutes and drain. Transfer to a slow cooker. In a small bowl, mix the broth, Worcestershire sauce and tomato paste. Pour over top. Cook, covered, on low for 6 to 8 hours or until meat is tender.
4.Transfer the beef to a platter and keep warm. Transfer the cooking juices to a small saucepan and skim fat. Bring the juices to a boil. Mix the remaining 3 tablespoons of the flour and the wine until smooth. Gradually stir into pan. Return to a boil. Cook and stir for 1 to 2 minutes or until thickened. Serve the beef with gravy and noodles, if desired.

Apple and Cranberry Pork Roast

Prep time: 10 minutes | Cook time: 6 to 8 hours | Serves 8

2 pounds (907 g) pork tenderloin, fat trimmed
2 tablespoons canola oil
3 cups apple juice
3 Granny Smith apples
1 cup fresh cranberries
¾ teaspoon salt
½ teaspoon black pepper

1.Brown the roast on all sides in a skillet in the canola oil, for 4 minutes. Place in a slow cooker.
2.Add the remaining ingredients.
3.Cover. Cook on low for 6 to 8 hours.
4.Serve warm.

Artichoke-Stuffed Flank Steak

Prep time: 15 minutes | Cook time: 3 hours | Serves 6 to 8

4 tablespoons unsalted butter
2 medium onions, finely chopped
3 cloves garlic, minced
1 teaspoon dried basil
½ teaspoon dried oregano
3 tablespoons all-purpose flour
2 cups full-bodied red wine
1 cup beef broth
2 (6-ounce / 170-g) jars marinated artichoke hearts, drained and coarsely chopped
6 thin slices prosciutto, cut into julienne strips
½ cup finely shredded Asiago cheese
1 cup fresh bread crumbs
1 (1½- to 2-pound / 680- to 907-g) flank steak

1.Melt the butter in a medium saucepan over medium-high heat. Add the onions, garlic, basil, and oregano and sauté until the onions are softened, for about 3 minutes. Whisk in the flour and cook for 3 minutes.
2.Add the wine and bring to a boil, whisking constantly, until the sauce is thickened. Transfer the sauce to the insert of a slow cooker and stir in the beef broth. Combine the artichoke, prosciutto, cheese, and bread crumbs together in a small bowl.

3.Place the flank steak on a cutting board and starting on one long side of the steak, cut the steak horizontally in half almost but not quite through the other side. Open the steak like a book. Spread the artichoke mixture over the flank steak. Roll the steak up from one long side and tie with kitchen string or silicone bands.
4.Arrange the steak in the slow cooker insert, cover, and cook on high for 3 hours. Remove the steak from the slow cooker, cover with aluminum foil, and allow to rest for 15 minutes. Skim off any fat from the sauce.
5.Slice the meat. Serve it with some of the sauce.

Provencal Beef Stew

Prep time: 15 minutes | Cook time: 6 to 8 hours | Serves 6

4 medium carrots, chopped
4 celery ribs, chopped
1 cup beef broth
1 (7-ounce / 198-g) jar julienned oil-packed sun-dried tomatoes, drained
1 (6-ounce / 170-g) can tomato paste
1 small onion, chopped
⅓ cup honey
¼ cup balsamic vinegar
1 garlic clove, minced
1 teaspoon dried thyme
½ teaspoon onion powder
¼ teaspoon white pepper
1 boneless beef chuck roast (2½ pounds / 1.1 kg), cut into 2-inch cubes
½ cup all-purpose flour
½ teaspoon salt
½ teaspoon pepper
2 tablespoons olive oil
Hot cooked mashed potatoes or egg noodles, for serving

1.In a slow cooker, combine the first 12 ingredients. In a large bowl, combine the beef, flour, salt and pepper. Toss to coat. In a large skillet, brown the beef in oil for 4 minutes, in batches. Transfer to the slow cooker.
2.Cover and cook on low for 6 to 8 hours or until beef is tender. Serve with mashed potatoes or egg noodles.

Onion-Celery Beef Brisket

Prep time: 10 minutes | Cook time: 6 to 7 hours | Serves 10

1 fresh beef brisket (4 pounds / 1.8 kg)
1½ teaspoons kosher salt
1½ teaspoons coarsely ground pepper
2 tablespoons olive oil
3 medium onions, halved and sliced
3 celery ribs, chopped
1 cup chili sauce
¼ cup packed brown sugar
¼ cup cider vinegar
1 envelope onion soup mix

1.Cut the brisket in half and sprinkle all sides with salt and pepper. In a large skillet, brown the brisket in oil for 4 minutes. Remove and set aside. In the same skillet, cook and stir onions over low heat for 15 to 20 minutes or until caramelized.
2.Place half of the onions in a slow cooker and top with the celery and brisket. Combine the chili sauce, brown sugar, vinegar and soup mix in a bowl. Pour over brisket and top with remaining onions.
3.Cover and cook on low for 6 to 7 hours or until meat is tender. Let stand for 5 minutes before slicing. Skim fat from cooking juices. Serve juices with meat.

Mexican Beef and Corn Stew

Prep time: 20 minutes | Cook time: 8 to 10 hours | Serves 10

1 cup all-purpose flour
¼ teaspoon salt
⅛ teaspoon pepper
1 pound (454 g) beef stew meat, cut into 1-inch cubes
2 tablespoons canola oil
1 (16-ounce / 454-g) can kidney beans, rinsed and drained
1 (15¼-ounce / 432-g) can whole kernel corn, drained
2 medium potatoes, cubed
2 small carrots, sliced
2 celery ribs, sliced
1 small onion, chopped
2 (15-ounce / 425-g) cans tomato sauce

1 cup water
1 envelope taco seasoning
½ teaspoon ground cumin
Tortilla chips and shredded Cheddar cheese, for serving

1.Combine the flour, salt and pepper in a large resealable plastic bag. Add beef, a few pieces at a time, and shake to coat.
2.Brown the meat in batches in oil in a large skillet, for 4 minutes. Drain and transfer to a slow cooker. Add the beans, corn, potatoes, carrots, celery and onion.
3.Whisk the tomato sauce, water, taco seasoning and cumin. Pour over top. Cover and cook on low for 8 to 10 hours or until meat is tender. Serve with the tortilla chips and cheese.

Italian Beef Braciole

Prep time: 10 minutes | Cook time: 6 to 8 hours | Serves 6

2 (24-ounce / 680-g) jars tomato basil pasta sauce
1 teaspoon crushed red pepper flakes
1 beef flank steak (1½ pounds / 680 g)
½ teaspoon salt
½ teaspoon pepper
2 eggs, beaten
½ cup seasoned bread crumbs
8 thin slices prosciutto or deli ham
1 cup shredded Italian cheese blend
2 tablespoons olive oil

1.In a slow cooker, combine the pasta sauce and pepper flakes. Pound the steak with a meat mallet to ½-inch Thickness. Sprinkle with salt and pepper.
2.In a small bowl, combine the eggs and bread crumbs. Spoon over the beef to within 1 inch of edges and press onto meat. Layer with prosciutto and cheese. Roll up jelly-roll style, starting with a long side. Tie at 2-inch intervals with kitchen string.
3.In a Dutch oven, brown the meat in oil on all sides, for 4 minutes. Transfer to the slow cooker and spoon sauce over meat. Cover and cook on low for 6 to 8 hours or until beef is tender.
4.Remove meat from sauce and discard the string. Cut into slices and serve with the sauce.

Savory Mexican Beef Brisket

Prep time: 15 minutes | Cook time: 10 to 12 hours | Serves 6 to 8

3 pounds (1.4 kg) beef brisket, cubed
2 tablespoons oil
½ cup slivered almonds
2 cups mild picante sauce, or hot, if you prefer
2 tablespoons vinegar
1 teaspoon garlic powder
½ teaspoon salt
¼ teaspoon cinnamon
¼ teaspoon dried thyme
¼ teaspoon dried oregano
⅛ teaspoon ground cloves
⅛ teaspoon pepper
½ to ¾ cup water, as needed

1.Brown the beef in the oil in a skillet, for 4 minutes. Place in a slow cooker.
2.Combine the remaining ingredients in a bowl. Pour over the meat.
3.Cover. Cook on low for 10 to 12 hours. Add the water as needed.
4.Serve warm.

Slow Cooked Beef in Sake

Prep time: 15 minutes | Cook time: 4 hours | Serves 8

⅔ cup soy sauce
½ cup sake
1 clove garlic, minced
½ teaspoon freshly ground black pepper
2 tablespoons sugar
2 to 3 pounds (0.9 to 1.4 kg) beef chuck, cut into 1-inch pieces
2 large onions, coarsely chopped
1 cup chicken broth
½ pound (227 g) shiitake mushrooms, stems removed and caps sliced
2 (10-ounce / 284-g) bags baby spinach
2 tablespoons cornstarch mixed with ¼ cup water or chicken broth

1.Combine the soy sauce, sake, garlic, pepper, and sugar in a large bowl and whisk.
2.Add the meat and stir to coat. Cover and refrigerate for at least 4 hours or up to 36 hours.
3.Put the beef and marinade in the insert of a slow cooker. Add the onions and chicken broth and stir to combine.
4.Cover and cook on high for 3 hours. Skim off any fat from the top of the stew. Add the mushrooms, spinach, and cornstarch mixture and stir to combine. Cover and cook on low for an additional 1 hour, until the meat is tender and the sauce is thickened.
5.Serve warm.

Beef Braised in Barolo

Prep time: 10 minutes | Cook time: 4 hours | Serves 6 to 8

4 tablespoons olive oil, divided
Salt and freshly ground black pepper, to taste
3 cloves garlic, minced
4 pounds (1.8 kg) beef chuck, cut into 1-inch pieces
2 large sweet onions, cut into half rounds
2 teaspoons sugar
1 tablespoon crushed dried rosemary
½ cup red wine, such as Chianti or Barolo
1 (32-ounce / 907-g) can crushed tomatoes, with the juice

1.Put 2 tablespoons of the oil, 1½ teaspoons salt, ½ teaspoon pepper, and the garlic in a small bowl and stir to combine. Add the meat to the bowl and toss to coat in the mixture.
2.Heat the remaining 2 tablespoons of the oil in a large skillet over high heat.
3.Add the beef and brown on all sides for 4 minutes. Transfer to a slow cooker insert. Add the onions, sugar, and rosemary to the same skillet over medium-high heat and sauté until the onions begin to soften, for 3 to 4 minutes.
4.Transfer the contents of the skillet to the slow cooker insert. Add the wine and tomatoes and stir to combine. Cover and cook on high for 4 hours, or on low for 8 hours, until the beef is tender. Remove the beef from the slow cooker with a slotted spoon and cover with aluminum foil.
5.Skim off the fat from the top of the sauce and season with salt and pepper.
6.Serve the beef with the sauce on a platter.

Slow Cooker Tri-Tip for Fajitas

Prep time: 10 minutes | Cook time: 3 hours | Serves 8

2 large onions, cut into half rounds
¼ cup firmly packed light brown sugar
2 tablespoons sweet paprika
2 teaspoons ancho chile powder
2 teaspoons garlic salt
1 teaspoon celery seeds
2 (1½- to 2-pound / 680- to 907-g) tri-tip roasts, fat trimmed, tied together with kitchen string or silicone loops
2 tablespoons olive oil
½ cup beef broth

1. Spread the onions on the bottom of the insert of a slow cooker. Combine the sugar, paprika, chile powder, garlic salt, and celery seeds in a small bowl. Rub the mixture evenly over the roasts.
2. Heat the oil in a large skillet over high heat. Add the meat and brown on all sides for 4 minutes.
3. Transfer the meat to the slow cooker insert. Deglaze the skillet with the broth and scrape up any browned bits from the bottom of the pan.
4. Pour the broth over the meat in the slow cooker insert. Cover and cook on high for 3 hours or on low for 6 to 7 hours, until the meat is tender.
5. Remove the meat from the slow cooker, cover with aluminum foil, and allow to rest. Remove the strings from the meat. Slice the meat thinly against the grain and serve.

Pork-Beef Patties with Cabbage

Prep time: 15 minutes | Cook time: 5 to 6 hours | Serves 8

1 (32-ounce / 907-g) can tomato purée
¼ cup granulated sugar
¼ cup white vinegar
½ cup golden raisins
8 ounces (227 g) lean ground pork
8 ounces (227 g) 85% lean ground beef
½ cup cooked rice
½ cup finely chopped shallot
½ cup ketchup
1 teaspoon salt
½ teaspoon freshly ground black pepper
1 large head green cabbage, cut into ½-inch-thick slices
1 large onion, sliced into half rounds
1 (15-ounce / 425-g) can sauerkraut, drained and rinsed

1. Stir the tomato purée, sugar, vinegar, and raisins together in the insert of a slow cooker. Stir the pork, beef, rice, shallot, ketchup, salt, and pepper together in a large mixing bowl. Form the mixture into 3-inch oval patties and set aside.
2. Lay half of the cabbage, onion, and sauerkraut in the bottom of the cooker with the sauce. Top with all the meat patties and spread the remaining cabbage, onion, and sauerkraut on top of the meat.
3. Cover the cooker and cook on high for 1 hour. Spoon some of the sauce over the top of the cabbage and cook on low for 4 to 5 hours, until the meat registers 165ºF (74ºC) on an instant-read thermometer.
4. Serve from the cooker set on warm.

Texas-Style Smoked Beef Brisket

Prep time: 10 minutes | Cook time: 10⅓ hours | Serves 8

4 medium onions, cut into half rounds
2 tablespoons sweet paprika
2 chipotle chiles in adobo, minced
1 teaspoon freshly ground black pepper
1 teaspoon ground cumin
¼ cup firmly packed light brown sugar
2 tablespoons Worcestershire sauce
2 tablespoons apple cider vinegar
1 (4-pound / 1.8-kg) brisket, fat trimmed
1 cup ketchup

1. Spread the onions on the bottom of the insert of a slow cooker and turn the machine on low. Stir the paprika, chiles, pepper, cumin, sugar, Worcestershire, and vinegar together in a small bowl.
2. Rub the mixture over the brisket and place the brisket on top of the onions in the slow cooker. Cover and cook for 10 hours on low, until the brisket is tender. Remove the brisket from the cooker and cover with aluminum foil.
3. Skim off any fat from the cooking liquid and strain through a fine-mesh sieve into a saucepan. Stir in the ketchup and simmer for 20 minutes, until thickened.
4. Slice the brisket across the grain to serve, accompanied by some of the sauce.

North African Beef and Bean Stew

Prep time: 15 minutes | Cook time: 8⅓ to 10½ hours | Serves 8

3 tablespoons olive oil
3 pounds (1.4 kg) beef chuck roast, cut into 1-inch pieces
1½ teaspoons salt
1 teaspoon freshly ground black pepper
1 large onion, coarsely chopped
2 cloves garlic, sliced
4 medium carrots, coarsely chopped
2 teaspoons sweet paprika
1 teaspoon ground cumin
½ teaspoon ground cinnamon
3 cups beef broth, divided
1 (15-ounce / 425-g) can garbanzo beans, drained and rinsed
1 cup dried apricots, cut into ½-inch pieces
½ cup golden raisins
2 tablespoons cornstarch mixed with ¼ cup water

1.Heat the oil in a large skillet over high heat. Sprinkle the meat evenly with the salt and pepper. Add the meat to the skillet a few pieces at a time and brown on all sides for 4 minutes. Transfer the browned meat to the insert of a slow cooker.
2.Add the onion and garlic to the same skillet and sauté until the onion begins to soften, for about 3 minutes. Add the carrots, paprika, cumin, and cinnamon and sauté until the spices are fragrant, for about 2 minutes.
3.Deglaze the skillet with 1 cup of the broth and scrape up any browned bits from the bottom of the pan. Transfer the contents of the skillet to the slow cooker insert. Add the remaining 2 cups of the broth, the beans, apricots, and raisins.
4.Cover the slow cooker and cook on low for 8 to 10 hours, until the meat is tender.
5.Skim off any fat from the top of the stew. Add the cornstarch mixture and stir to combine. Cover the slow cooker and cook for an additional 20 to 30 minutes, until the sauce is thickened.
6.Serve the stew warm from the cooker.

Braised Brisket with Dried Fruits

Prep time: 15 minutes | Cook time: 4 to 5 hours | Serves 8

Salt and freshly ground black pepper, to taste
¼ cup Dijon mustard
¼ cup firmly packed light brown sugar
1 (3- to 4-pound / 1.4- to 1.8-kg) first-cut or flat-cut brisket, fat trimmed
3 tablespoons olive oil
3 large sweet onions, thinly sliced
2 teaspoons dried thyme
½ cup red wine
½ cup beef broth
1 cup dried figs, halved
½ cup dried plums, halved
½ cup dried apricots, halved
2 tablespoons cornstarch dissolved in ¼ cup water or beef broth

1.Combine 2 teaspoons salt, 1 teaspoon pepper, the mustard, and brown sugar in a small bowl. Rub the mixture over the brisket. Heat the oil in a large skillet over medium-high heat.
2.Add the brisket and brown on all sides for 4 minutes. Remove the brisket and transfer to the insert of a slow cooker. Add the onions and thyme to the same skillet over medium-high heat and sauté until the onions are softened, for 2 to 3 minutes. Deglaze the pan with the wine and broth, scraping up any browned bits, and bring the liquid to a boil.
3.Pour the mixture into the slow cooker insert and add the dried fruits around the brisket. Cover and cook on high for 4 to 5 hours or on low for 8 to 10 hours, until the meat is fork tender. Remove the brisket and fruits from the insert and cover with aluminum foil.
4.Transfer the liquid to a saucepan or saucier. Skim off any fat from the top of the sauce.
5.Bring the sauce to a boil, add the cornstarch and stir, bringing the sauce back to a boil. Season with salt and pepper.
6.Trim any fat from the brisket and thinly slice it across the grain. Serve the brisket surrounded with the fruit and napped with some of the sauce. Serve the remaining sauce on the side.

Savory and Sweet Brisket

Prep time: 10 minutes | Cook time: 8 to 10 hours | Serves 8 to 10

3 to 3½ pounds (1.4 to 1.5 kg) fresh beef brisket, cut in half, divided
1 cup ketchup
¼ cup grape jelly
1 envelope dry onion soup mix
½ teaspoon pepper

1. Place half of the brisket in a slow cooker.
2. In a bowl, combine the ketchup, jelly, dry soup mix, and pepper.
3. Spread half the mixture over half the meat. Top with the remaining meat and then the remaining ketchup mixture.
4. Cover and cook on low for 8 to 10 hours or until meat is tender but not dry.
5. Allow meat to rest for 10 minutes. Then slice and serve with the cooking juices.

Zinfandel-Braised Beef Short Ribs

Prep time: 10 minutes | Cook time: 3½ to 4 hours | Serves 4

4½ pounds (2.0 kg) boneless short ribs, fat trimmed
2 teaspoons salt
1 teaspoon freshly ground black pepper
2 tablespoons extra-virgin olive oil
2 cups red onions, cut into half rounds
6 cloves garlic, minced
1 tablespoon dried thyme
2 cups Zinfandel wine
4 dried porcini mushrooms, crumbled

1. Sprinkle the beef ribs evenly with the salt and pepper. Heat the oil in a large skillet over medium-high heat. Add the beef a few pieces at a time and brown on all sides for 4 minutes. Transfer the meat to the insert of a slow cooker.
2. Add the onions, garlic, and thyme to the skillet and sauté until the onions are softened and fragrant, for about 3 minutes. Stir in the wine and mushrooms, stirring up any browned bits from the bottom of the skillet, and then transfer to the slow

cooker insert.
3. Cover and cook on high for 3½ to 4 hours or on low for 8 hours.
4. Remove the beef from the slow cooker and cover with aluminum foil. Let the meat rest for 10 to 15 minutes. Skim off any fat from the sauce.
5. Serve the meat with the sauce.

Traditional Beef Stew with Veggies

Prep time: 15 minutes | Cook time: 9 hours | Serves 8

6 medium Yukon gold or red potatoes, quartered
4 medium carrots, cut into 1-inch lengths
3 medium onions, quartered
Salt and freshly ground black pepper, to taste
1 cup all-purpose flour
2 to 3 pounds (0.9 to 1.4 kg) beef chuck, fat trimmed and cut into 1-inch pieces
2 tablespoons olive oil
1½ cups beef broth
2 teaspoons dried thyme leaves
2 cups frozen petite peas, thawed
2 cups frozen corn, thawed

1. Combine the potatoes, carrots, onions, 1 teaspoon salt, and ½ teaspoon pepper in the insert of a slow cooker, and toss the vegetables to distribute the seasonings.
2. Add 2 teaspoons salt, 1 teaspoon pepper, and the flour to a large plastic bag and stir to combine. Add the meat to the flour, toss to coat, and shake off any excess flour.
3. Heat the oil in a large skillet over high heat. Add the meat and brown on all sides for 4 minutes. Transfer the browned meat to the slow cooker insert.
4. Deglaze the skillet with the broth and scrape up any browned bits from the bottom of the pan. Transfer the contents of the skillet to the slow cooker insert and add the thyme. Cover and cook on low for 8 hours, until the meat is tender.
5. Add the peas and corn and cook for an additional 1 hour. Season with salt and pepper before serving.

BBQ Beef Brisket

Prep time: 10 minutes | Cook time: 6½ to 8½ hours | Serves 6 to 8

2 cups Jack Daniel's Original No. 7 Barbecue Sauce, divided
1 medium onion, cut in wedges
3 beef bouillon cubes
3 to 4 pounds (1.4 to 1.8 kg) beef roast or brisket
3 bay leaves
Sandwich buns, for serving

1. In bottom of a slow cooker, combine 1 cup of the barbecue sauce, onion, and bouillon cubes.
2. Place the roast on top of the sauce. Top with the bay leaves.
3. Cover and cook on low for 6 to 8 hours or until beef is tender enough to shred easily.
4. Remove the meat from the slow cooker. Reserve the cooking juices in the slow cooker. Shred the meat with two forks.
5. Return the meat to the slow cooker. Add the remaining 1 cup of the barbecue sauce. Mix well.
6. Cover and cook on high for 30 minutes, or until heated through.
7. Serve on sandwich buns.

Steak Fajitas

Prep time: 10 minutes | Cook time: 5 to 6 hours | Serves 8

2 tablespoons olive oil
1 teaspoon ground cumin
½ teaspoon dried oregano
1 teaspoon ancho chile powder
1 (4-pound / 1.8-kg) boneless chuck roast
2 large white onions, coarsely chopped
2 (16-ounce / 454-g) jars medium-hot salsa
½ cup lime juice
1 (12-ounce / 340-g) bottle beer

1. Add the oil, cumin, oregano, and chile powder to a small bowl and stir to combine. Rub the mixture over the meat, coating evenly. Heat a large skillet over high heat.
2. Add the meat and brown on all sides for 4 minutes. Transfer to the insert of a slow cooker. Add the onions to the skillet over medium-high heat and sauté until softened, for 3 to 5 minutes. Transfer to the slow cooker insert. Add the salsa, lime juice, and beer to the slow cooker and stir to combine.
3. Cover and cook on high for 5 to 6 hours or on low for 10 to 12 hours. Remove the meat from the slow cooker, cover with aluminum foil, and allow to rest for 20 to 30 minutes.
4. Transfer the sauce to a saucepan and bring to a boil. Boil the sauce to reduce to concentrate the flavor, for about 10 minutes. Strain the sauce through a fine-mesh sieve, if desired.
5. Shred the beef or return the sauce and beef to the slow cooker and serve from the cooker set on the warm setting.

Teriyaki Sirloin

Prep time: 10 minutes | Cook time: 4 to 5 hours | Serves 6 to 8

⅔ cup soy sauce
¼ cup vegetable oil
½ cup rice wine (mirin)
¼ cup firmly packed light brown sugar
1 teaspoon freshly grated ginger
2 cloves garlic, minced
1 (2½- to 3-pound / 1.1- to 1.4-kg) sirloin roast
2 cups beef broth
2 large sweet onions, coarsely chopped
2 teaspoons cornstarch mixed with 2 teaspoons of water
Chopped green onions, for garnish
Sesame seeds, for garnish

1. Combine the soy sauce, oil, rice wine, brown sugar, ginger, and garlic in a large zipper-top plastic bag. Add the sirloin to the bag, seal, and turn to coat the meat with the marinade. Refrigerate for at least 8 hours and up to 24 hours.
2. Pour the marinade and the meat into the insert of a slow cooker. Add the broth and onions. Cover and cook on high for 4 to 5 hours.
3. Remove the meat from the insert, cover with aluminum foil, and allow to rest for 15 minutes. Strain the sauce through a fine-mesh sieve into a saucepan and bring to a boil. Taste the sauce and dilute it with water or broth if it is too strong.
4. Add the cornstarch mixture and bring the sauce back to a boil, whisking constantly, until it is thickened. Keep the sauce warm on the stovetop, or transfer it to the slow cooker set on warm.
5. Slice the meat and serve with the sauce, and garnish with the green onions and sesame seeds.

Beef Roast Sandwiches

Prep time: 5 minutes | Cook time: 10 to 12 hours | Serves 6 to 8

3 to 4 pounds (1.4 to 1.8 kg) lean rump roast
2 teaspoons salt, divided
4 garlic cloves
2 teaspoons Romano or Parmesan cheese, divided
1 (12-ounce / 340-g) can beef broth
1 teaspoon dried oregano
Buns, for serving

1. Place the roast in a slow cooker. Cut 4 slits in top of roast. Fill each slit with ½ teaspoon salt, 1 garlic clove, and ½ teaspoon cheese.
2. Pour the broth over the meat. Sprinkle with the oregano.
3. Cover. Cook on low for 10 to 12 hours, or on high for 4 to 6 hours.
4. Remove the meat and slice or shred. Serve on buns with meat juices on the side.

Bistro Sirloin with Dijon-Wine Sauce

Prep time: 10 minutes | Cook time: 3½ hours | Serves 6

Salt and freshly ground black pepper, to taste
3 pounds (1.4 kg) beef sirloin, cut into 1-inch pieces
2 tablespoons olive oil
6 medium shallots, cut into half rounds
1 cup dry white wine or vermouth
½ cup Dijon mustard
1 teaspoon dried tarragon
1 cup beef broth
2 tablespoons finely chopped fresh tarragon
2 tablespoons unsalted butter
2 tablespoons all-purpose flour

1. Sprinkle 1½ teaspoons salt and ½ teaspoon pepper evenly over the meat. Heat the oil in a large skillet over high heat. Add the meat a few pieces at a time and brown for 4 minutes.
2. Transfer the meat to the insert of a slow cooker. Add the shallots to the same skillet over medium-high heat and sauté for 1 minute, until they begin to soften. Deglaze the pan with the wine, scraping up any browned bits from the bottom of the pan, and add the mustard and dried tarragon.
3. Transfer the mixture to the slow cooker and stir in the broth. Cover and cook on high for 3 hours, until the meat is tender. Skim off any fat from the top of the sauce and stir in the fresh tarragon.
4. Mix the butter and flour together to form a paste. Add the butter mixture in pieces to the cooker. Cover and cook for an additional 30 minutes, until the sauce is thickened.
5. Season with salt and pepper before serving.

Corned Beef Braised in Riesling

Prep time: 15 minutes | Cook time: 8 to 10 hours | Serves 6

12 small Yukon gold potatoes, scrubbed
2 cups baby carrots
3 medium sweet onions, coarsely chopped
2 cups Riesling wine
½ cup whole-grain mustard
¼ cup Dijon mustard
¼ cup firmly packed light brown sugar
4 whole black peppercorns
2 bay leaves
1 (3½- to 4-pound / 1.5- to 1.8-kg) corned beef, rinsed and fat trimmed
1 large head green cabbage, cut in half, cored and thickly sliced

1. Layer the potatoes, carrots, and onions in the insert of a slow cooker. Whisk together the Riesling, whole-grain mustard, Dijon mustard, and sugar in a large bowl. Stir in the peppercorns and bay leaves.
2. Place the brisket on top of the vegetables in the slow cooker insert. Pour the Riesling mixture over the brisket and strew the cabbage over the top of the brisket.
3. Cover the slow cooker and cook on low for 8 to 10 hours. Remove the brisket from the cooker, cover with aluminum foil, and allow to rest for about 20 minutes.
4. Using a slotted spoon, remove the vegetables and arrange them on a platter. Slice the brisket across the grain and arrange over the vegetables. Strain the liquid from the cooker through a fine-mesh sieve and ladle a bit over the meat and vegetables before serving.

Chicago-Style Flank Steaks

Prep time: 15 minutes | Cook time: 8 hours | Serves 8

3 (1½- to 2-pound / 680- to 907-g) flank steaks
4 cloves garlic
1 teaspoon dried oregano
1 teaspoon dried basil
1 bay leaf
2 shallots, coarsely chopped
½ cup soy sauce
½ cup red wine vinegar
½ teaspoon freshly ground black pepper
¼ cup extra-virgin olive oil, divided
4 large onions, cut into half rounds
2 medium green bell peppers, deseeded and thinly sliced
2 medium red bell peppers, deseeded and thinly sliced
2 (15-ounce / 425-g) cans double-strength beef broth
8 crusty rolls

1.Put the flank steaks into a 2-gallon zipper-top plastic bag. Mix the garlic, oregano, basil, bay leaf, shallots, soy sauce, vinegar, pepper, and 2 tablespoons of the oil together in a bowl. Pour the marinade into the bag and toss with the meat to coat. Seal the bag and refrigerate for at least 6 hours or overnight.
2.Remove the meat from the marinade and discard the marinade. Roll the steaks from the short side and place them in the bottom of the insert of a slow cooker.
3.Heat the remaining 2 tablespoons of the oil in a large skillet over medium-high heat. Add the onions and sauté until they are softened and begin to turn translucent, for 5 to 7 minutes. Add the bell peppers and sauté until they are softened, for about 5 minutes.
4.Transfer the onions and bell peppers to the cooker and stir in the broth. Cover and cook on low for 8 hours, until the meat is tender.
5.Remove the meat from the cooker, cover with aluminum foil, and allow to rest for at least 15 minutes. Skim off any fat from the top of the sauce. Unroll the meat on a cutting board and cut across the grain into thin slices. Return the meat to the slow cooker.
6.Serve the meat, onions, and peppers from the cooker along with the crusty rolls.

Braised Two-Meat Manicotti

Prep time: 20 minutes | Cook time: 4 to 5 hours | Serves 7

½ pound (227 g) medium fresh mushrooms, chopped
2 small green peppers, chopped
1 medium onion, chopped
1½ teaspoons canola oil
4 garlic cloves, minced
¾ pound (340 g) ground sirloin
¾ pound (340 g) bulk Italian sausage
2 (23½-ounce / 666-g) jars Italian sausage and garlic spaghetti sauce
1 (15-ounce / 425-g) carton ricotta cheese
1 cup minced fresh parsley
½ cup shredded part-skim Mozzarella cheese, divided
½ cup grated Parmesan cheese, divided
2 eggs, lightly beaten
½ teaspoon salt
¼ teaspoon pepper
⅛ teaspoon ground nutmeg
1 (8-ounce / 227-g) package manicotti shells

1.In a large skillet, sauté the mushrooms, peppers and onion in the oil for about 5 minutes, or until tender. Add the garlic and cook for 1 minute longer. Remove from the skillet.
2.In the same skillet, cook the beef and sausage over medium heat for 4 minutes, or until no longer pink. Drain. Stir in the mushroom mixture and spaghetti sauce. Set aside.
3.In a small bowl, combine the ricotta cheese, parsley, ¼ cup of the Mozzarella cheese, ¼ cup of the Parmesan cheese, eggs and seasonings. Stuff into the uncooked manicotti shells.
4.Spread 2¼ cups sauce onto the bottom of a slow cooker. Arrange five stuffed manicotti shells over sauce. Repeat two times, using four shells on the top layer. Top with the remaining sauce. Sprinkle with the remaining cheeses. Cover and cook on low for 4 to 5 hours or until pasta is tender.
5.Serve warm.

Balsamic Cherry Pork Loin

Prep time: 5 minutes | Cook time: 3 to 4 hours | Serves 8

1 boneless pork loin roast (3 to 4 pounds / 1.4 to 1.8 kg)
1 teaspoon salt
½ teaspoon pepper
1 tablespoon canola oil
¾ cup cherry preserves
½ cup dried cherries
⅓ cup balsamic vinegar
¼ cup packed brown sugar

1.Sprinkle the roast with salt and pepper. In a large skillet, heat the oil over medium-high heat. Brown the roast on all sides, for 4 minutes.
2.Transfer to a slow cooker. In a small bowl, mix the preserves, cherries, vinegar and brown sugar until blended. Pour over roast. Cook, covered, on low for 3 to 4 hours or until tender and a thermometer inserted in pork should read at least 145°F (63°C).
3.Remove the roast from the slow cooker. Tent with foil. Let stand for 15 minutes before slicing. Skim fat from the cooking juices. Serve the pork with the sauce.

Braised Beef Short Ribs

Prep time: 15 minutes | Cook time: 8 hours | Serves 4 to 6

1½ tablespoons vegetable oil
½ cup firmly packed light brown sugar, divided
4½ pounds (2.0 kg) boneless short ribs, fat trimmed
4 cups sliced sweet onions, such as Vidalia or red onions (about 4 medium to large)
6 cloves garlic, minced
1 teaspoon freshly grated ginger
2 tablespoons hoisin sauce
½ cup soy sauce
1½ cups chicken broth
½ teaspoon freshly ground black pepper
Chopped green onions, for garnish
Toasted sesame seeds, for garnish

1.Heat the oil in a large skillet over medium-high heat. Pat half of the brown sugar onto the ribs. Add the ribs a few at a time to the skillet and brown on all sides for 4 minutes, being careful not to burn the sugar.
2.Transfer the ribs to the insert of a slow cooker. Add the onions, garlic, and ginger to the skillet over medium-high heat and sauté until the onions and garlic are fragrant, for about 4 minutes.
3.Transfer the contents of the skillet to the slow cooker insert and stir in the remaining half of the sugar, the hoisin, soy sauce, and broth. Sprinkle with the pepper. Cover the slow cooker and cook on high for 8 hours or on low for 3½ to 4 hours, until the meat is tender.
4.Remove the meat from the slow cooker insert. Skim off any fat from the sauce and pour some of the sauce over the meat. Serve any remaining sauce on the side. Garnish the ribs with the green onions and sesame seeds.

BBQ Short Ribs

Prep time: 5 minutes | Cook time: 3½ to 4 hours | Serves 4 to 6

2 cups ketchup
1 tablespoon Dijon mustard
½ cup firmly packed light brown sugar
2 tablespoons Worcestershire sauce
½ teaspoon cayenne pepper
1½ tablespoons vegetable oil
4½ pounds (2.0 kg) boneless short ribs, fat trimmed
1 cup coarsely chopped red onion

1.Combine the ketchup, mustard, brown sugar, Worcestershire, and cayenne in the insert of a slow cooker. Cover and set on low while you brown the meat.
2.Heat the oil in a large skillet over high heat.
3.Add the short ribs a few at a time and brown on all sides for 4 minutes. Transfer them to the slow cooker insert. Add the onion to the same skillet and sauté until it begins to soften, for 3 to 5 minutes.
4.Transfer the onion to the insert and stir the sauce to combine. Cover, and cook on high for 3½ to 4 hours or on low for 8 hours. Remove the meat from the slow cooker insert and cover with aluminum foil. Let the meat rest for 10 to 15 minutes. Skim off any fat from the sauce.
5.Serve the beef with the sauce.

Osso Buco

Prep time: 15 minutes | Cook time: 5 hours | Serves 6

½ cup all-purpose flour

1 teaspoon salt

½ teaspoon freshly ground black pepper

6 meaty slices veal shank, cut into 1½ to 2 inches thick

2 tablespoons olive oil

2 tablespoons unsalted butter

1 medium onion, finely chopped

3 medium carrots, finely chopped

¼ cup tomato paste

⅔ cup dry white wine or vermouth

1 cup chicken broth

½ cup beef broth

2 cloves garlic, minced

Grated zest of 2 lemons

Grated zest of 1 orange

½ cup finely chopped Italian parsley

1.Mix the flour, salt, and pepper in a large zipper-top plastic bag. Coat the veal shanks in the flour mixture and shake off the excess. Heat the oil and butter in a large skillet over high heat. Add the shanks a few at a time and brown on all sides for 4 minutes.

2.Transfer the shanks to the insert of a slow cooker. Add the onion and carrots to the same skillet and sauté until the onion is softened, for about 3 minutes. Add the tomato paste and stir to combine. Add the wine and bring to a boil.

3.Transfer the contents of the skillet to the slow cooker insert Add the broths and stir. Cover and cook on low for 4 hours. Combine the garlic, citrus zests, and parsley in a small bowl. Add the garlic mixture to the stew and stir to combine. Cook the stew for another hour, until the veal is tender.

4.Taste and adjust the seasoning and serve.

Authentic German Sauerbraten

Prep time: 15 minutes | Cook time: 8 hours | Serves 6

1½ tablespoons extra-virgin olive oil

1 (4-pound / 1.8-kg) boneless beef chuck roast

2 tablespoons tomato paste

1 cup dry red wine

¾ cup cider vinegar

1½ tablespoons white sugar, plus more as needed

1 tablespoon pickling spices, wrapped in a sachet

4 carrots, chopped

1 large onion, chopped

1 cup low-sodium beef bone broth

8 gingersnap cookies, crushed

1 teaspoon kosher salt, plus more for seasoning

½ teaspoon freshly ground black pepper, plus more for seasoning

1½ tablespoons cornstarch

1½ tablespoons cold water

1.In a pan over medium-high heat, heat the oil until shimmering. Season the roast with salt and pepper, and brown for about 3 minutes per side. Transfer the meat to a plate. Add the tomato paste and cook, stirring, for 1 minute. Whisk in the wine, vinegar, and sugar. Bring to a boil and simmer for 5 minutes.

2.Add the tomato-wine mixture to a slow cooker. Add the pickling spice sachet, carrots, onion, bone broth, gingersnaps, salt, and pepper. Stir to combine. Place the meat in the slow cooker. Cover and cook on low for 8 hours.

3.About 30 minutes before serving, remove the pickling spice sachet and discard. In a small bowl, whisk together the cornstarch and water. Add to the slow cooker and gently stir. Leave the lid slightly ajar and continue cooking until the liquid is thickened and the meat is tender. Using a ladle or large spoon, skim the fat from the top of the liquid and discard the spice packet. Season with additional salt and pepper, as needed, and add more sugar if the cooking juices taste too tart. Slice the meat and serve immediately with vegetables and gravy.

Beef Roast with Stewed Tomatoes

Prep time: 5 minutes | Cook time: 8 to 10 hours | Serves 10

4 to 5 pounds (1.8 to 2.3 kg) beef roast
3 tablespoons oil
2 (14½-ounce / 411-g) cans Mexican-style stewed tomatoes
1 (16-ounce / 454-g) jar salsa
2 or 3 medium onions, cut in chunks
1 or 2 green or red bell peppers, sliced

1.Brown the roast in the oil in a skillet, for 4 minutes. Place in a slow cooker.
2.In a bowl, combine the stewed tomatoes and salsa. Spoon over the meat.
3.Cover and cook on low for 8 to 10 hours, or until the meat is tender but not dry.
4.Add the onions halfway through cooking time in order to keep fairly crisp. Push down into the sauce.
5.One hour before serving, add the pepper slices. Push down into the sauce.
6.Remove the meat from the cooker and allow to rest for 10 minutes before slicing. Place the slices on a serving platter and top with the vegetables and sauce.

Garlicky Veal Stew

Prep time: 15 minutes | Cook time: 6 to 7 hours | Serves 6

½ cup all-purpose flour
1½ teaspoons salt
½ teaspoon freshly ground black pepper
2½ pounds (1.1 kg) boneless veal shoulder or shank, cut into 1-inch pieces
3 tablespoons extra-virgin olive oil
¼ cup tomato paste
1 teaspoon dried thyme
½ cup dry white wine or vermouth
1 cup chicken broth
½ cup beef broth
1 bay leaf
40 cloves garlic, peeled

1.Mix the flour, salt, and pepper in a large zipper-top plastic bag. Add the veal, toss to coat, and shake off any excess. Heat the oil in a large skillet over high heat. Add the veal a few pieces at a time and sauté until browned on all sides for 4 minutes.
2.Transfer the browned meat to the insert of a slow cooker. When all the veal is browned, add the tomato paste, thyme, and white wine to the skillet and scrape up any browned bits from the bottom of the pan. Add both broths and stir to combine.
3.Pour the contents of the skillet over the veal in the slow cooker, add the bay leaf and garlic, and stir to distribute the ingredients. Cover and cook the veal on low for 6 to 7 hours, until it is tender. Remove the veal from the cooker with a slotted spoon.
4.Mash the garlic cloves and stir them into the sauce. Taste and adjust the seasoning. Return the veal to the cooker and serve the stew.

BBQ Beef Sandwiches

Prep time: 15 minutes | Cook time: 3 to 4 hours | Serves 8

2 tablespoons sweet paprika
1½ teaspoons salt
Pinch of cayenne pepper
2 (1½- to 2-pound / 680- to 907-g) tri tip roasts or 1 (3½- to 4-pound / 1.5- to 1.8-kg) bottom sirloin roast, rolled and tied
2 tablespoons canola or vegetable oil
1 medium onion, finely chopped
2 cloves garlic, minced
2 cups tomato sauce
1 cup ketchup
2 tablespoons Worcestershire sauce
¼ cup molasses
2 tablespoons sugar
2 tablespoons Dijon mustard
8 Kaiser rolls or soft onion rolls

1.Combine the paprika, salt, and cayenne in a small bowl, and rub the mixture evenly onto the roast. Heat the oil in a large skillet over high heat. Add the meat and brown on all sides for 4 minutes.
2.Transfer to the insert of a slow cooker. Add the onion and garlic to the same skillet over medium-high heat and sauté until the onion is softened and the garlic is fragrant, for 2 to 3 minutes. Pour in the tomato sauce and stir up any browned bits from the bottom of the pan.
3.Transfer the contents of the pan to the slow cooker and stir in the remaining ingredients, except for the rolls. Cover the slow cooker and cook on high for 3 to 4 hours or on low for 8 to 9 hours, until the meat is tender. Remove the meat from the cooker, cover with aluminum foil, and allow to rest for 10 minutes.
4.Remove the strings from the meat and slice the meat across the grain. Skim off any fat from the top of the sauce. Return the meat to the slow cooker set on warm, and serve on the rolls.

Pork Roast in Apricot Glaze

Prep time: 5 minutes | Cook time: 4 to 6 hours | Serves 10 to 12

1 (10½-ounce / 298-g) can condensed chicken broth
1 (18-ounce / 510-g) jar apricot preserves
1 large onion, chopped
2 tablespoons Dijon mustard
3½ to 4 pounds (1.5 to 1.8 kg) boneless pork loin

1.Mix the broth, preserves, onion, and mustard in a bowl.
2.Cut the roast to fit, if necessary, and place in a slow cooker. Pour the glaze over the meat.
3.Cover and cook on low for 4 to 6 hours, or on high for 3 hours, or until tender.
4.Remove the pork loin from the slow cooker to a serving platter. Discard the juices or thicken for gravy. Serve warm.

Beef Roast with Tangy Au Jus

Prep time: 10 minutes | Cook time: 6 to 8 hours | Serves 8

1½ tablespoons extra-virgin olive oil
1 (3- to 4-pound / 1.4- to 1.8-kg) boneless chuck roast
1¼ teaspoons kosher salt
1½ teaspoons freshly ground black pepper
¼ cup all-purpose flour
4 tablespoons unsalted butter
10 pepperoncini
2 tablespoons mayonnaise
1 tablespoon sour cream
2 teaspoons apple cider vinegar
1 teaspoon buttermilk
½ teaspoon dried dill
½ teaspoon dried chives

1.In a pan over medium-high heat, heat the oil until shimmering. Season the roast with and pepper, and coat with the flour. Brown the roast on both sides to create a crust, for about 4 minutes per side.
2.Place the roast in the slow cooker, along with the butter, pepperoncini, mayonnaise, sour cream, cider vinegar, buttermilk, dill, and chives. Cover and cook on low for 6 to 8 hours, until tender.

3.Transfer the meat to a cutting board. Using two forks, shred the meat and discard any fat. Return the meat to the slow cooker and mix the meat with the liquid inside, or plate the meat and drizzle the tangy au jus on top.

Pork Tenderloin with Sauerkraut

Prep time: 20 minutes | Cook time: 2 to 3 hours | Serves 4

¼ pound (113 g) center-cut bacon strips, chopped
1 cup sliced leeks (white portion only)
1 cup cubed peeled sweet potato
1 tablespoon water
1 (14-ounce / 397-g) can sauerkraut, rinsed and well drained
1 medium apple, peeled and finely chopped
½ cup frozen cranberries, thawed
½ cup sweet white wine or unsweetened apple juice
¼ cup packed brown sugar
1 teaspoon caraway seeds
¾ teaspoon salt, divided
1 pork tenderloin (1 pound / 454 g)
¼ teaspoon pepper

1.In a large skillet, cook the bacon and leeks over medium heat for 6 to 8 minutes, or until bacon is crisp, stirring occasionally. Remove with a slotted spoon and drain on paper towels.
2.Place the sweet potato and water in a large microwave-safe dish. Microwave, covered, on high for 2 to 3 minutes or until potatoes are almost tender. Drain. Stir in the bacon mixture, sauerkraut, apple, cranberries, wine, brown sugar, caraway seeds and ¼ teaspoon of the salt.
3.Transfer half of the sauerkraut mixture to a greased slow cooker. Sprinkle the pork with pepper and remaining ½ teaspoon of the salt. Place in the slow cooker. Top with the remaining sauerkraut mixture. Cook, covered, on low for 2 to 3 hours or until pork is tender and a thermometer inserted in pork should read at least 145ºF (63ºC).
4.Remove the pork from the slow cooker and tent with foil. Let stand for 10 minutes before slicing. Serve the pork with the sauerkraut.

Pork Loin Roast with Apples

Prep time: 10 minutes | Cook time: 6 to 8 hours | Serves 6

1 boneless pork loin roast (2 to 3 pounds / 0.9 to 1.4 kg)
½ teaspoon salt
¼ teaspoon pepper
1 tablespoon canola oil
3 medium apples, peeled and sliced, divided
¼ cup honey
1 small red onion, halved and sliced
1 tablespoon ground cinnamon
Minced fresh parsley (optional)

1.Sprinkle the roast with salt and pepper. In a large skillet, brown the roast in oil on all sides for 4 minutes. Cool slightly. With a paring knife, cut about sixteen 3-inch-deep slits in sides of roast. Insert one apple slice into each slit.
2.Place half of the remaining apples in a slow cooker. Place the roast over the apples. Drizzle with the honey. Top with the onion and remaining apples. Sprinkle with the cinnamon.
3.Cover and cook on low for 6 to 8 hours or until meat is tender. Remove the pork and apple mixture. Keep warm.
4.Transfer the cooking juices to a small saucepan. Bring to a boil and cook until the liquid is reduced by half. Serve with the pork and apple mixture. Sprinkle with the parsley, if desired.

BBQ Ribs in Root Beer

Prep time: 10 minutes | Cook time: 6 to 8 hours | Serves 5

1 cup root beer
1 cup ketchup
¼ cup orange juice
3 tablespoons Worcestershire sauce
2 tablespoons molasses
1 teaspoon onion powder
1 teaspoon garlic powder
½ teaspoon ground ginger
½ teaspoon paprika
¼ teaspoon crushed red pepper flakes
4½ pounds (2.0 kg) pork baby back ribs
1 teaspoon salt

½ teaspoon pepper

1.In a small saucepan, combine the first 10 ingredients. Bring to a boil over medium heat. Reduce heat and simmer, uncovered, for 10 minutes or until sauce is reduced to 2 cups. Set aside.
2.Cut the ribs into five serving-size pieces and sprinkle with salt and pepper. Place in a slow cooker. Pour the sauce over the ribs. Cover and cook on low for 6 to 8 hours or until meat is tender. Serve with the sauce.

Asian Braised Pork Chops

Prep time: 15 minutes | Cook time: 3 to 4 hours | Serves 4

4 boneless pork loin chops (5 ounces / 142 g each)
¼ teaspoon salt
⅛ teaspoon pepper
1 medium onion, chopped
1 medium green pepper, chopped
4 green onions, chopped
¼ cup packed brown sugar
¼ cup white wine or chicken broth
¼ cup soy sauce
1 tablespoon finely chopped crystallized ginger
1½ teaspoons sesame oil
1 garlic clove, minced
2 tablespoons cornstarch
2 tablespoons cold water
Hot cooked rice, for serving (optional)

1.Sprinkle the pork chops with salt and pepper. Place in a slow cooker. Add the onion, green pepper and green onions. In a small bowl, combine the brown sugar, wine, soy sauce, ginger, sesame oil and garlic. Pour over the chops. Cover and cook on low for 3 to 4 hours or until meat is tender.
2.Remove the meat to a serving platter and keep warm. Skim fat from cooking juices and transfer to a small saucepan. Bring the liquid to a boil. Combine the cornstarch and water until smooth. Gradually stir into the pan. Bring to a boil. Cook and stir for 2 minutes or until thickened. Serve with the pork and rice, if desired.

Asian-Flavored Pork Ribs

Prep time: 15 minutes | Cook time: 6 to 7 hours | Serves 6

6 pounds (2.7 kg) pork baby back ribs, cut into serving-size pieces
1⅓ cups packed brown sugar
1 cup reduced-sodium soy sauce
¼ cup rice vinegar
¼ cup sesame oil
¼ cup minced fresh ginger
6 garlic cloves, minced
1 teaspoon crushed red pepper flakes
¼ cup cornstarch
¼ cup cold water
Thinly sliced green onions and sesame seeds, for garnish (optional)

1.Place the ribs in a slow cooker. In a small bowl, combine the brown sugar, soy sauce, vinegar, oil, ginger, garlic and pepper flakes. Pour over the ribs. Cover and cook on low for 6 to 7 hours or until the meat is tender.
2.Remove the meat to a serving platter and keep warm. Skim fat from cooking juices and transfer to a small saucepan. Bring to a boil.
3.Combine the cornstarch and water until smooth. Gradually stir into the pan. Bring to a boil. Cook and stir for 2 minutes or until thickened. Serve with the ribs. Garnish with the onions and sesame seeds, if desired.

Pork Chops with Potatoes and Onions

Prep time: 10 minutes | Cook time: 8 to 10 hours | Serves 6

4 medium potatoes, peeled and thinly sliced
6 bone-in pork loin chops (7 ounces / 198 g each)
1 tablespoon canola oil
2 large onions, sliced and separated into rings
2 teaspoons butter
3 tablespoons all-purpose flour
¼ teaspoon salt
¼ teaspoon pepper
1 (14½-ounce / 411-g) can reduced-sodium chicken broth
1 cup fat-free milk
Cooking spray

1.Place the potatoes in a slow cooker coated with cooking spray. In a large nonstick skillet, brown the pork chops in oil for 4 minutes, in batches.
2.Place the chops over the potatoes. Sauté the onions in drippings for 3 minutes, or until tender. Place over the chops. Melt the butter in the skillet. Combine the flour, salt, pepper and broth until smooth. Stir into the pan. Add the milk. Bring to a boil. Cook and stir for 2 minutes or until thickened.
3.Pour the sauce over the onions. Cover and cook on low for 8 to 10 hours or until pork is tender. Skim fat and thicken cooking juices if desired.
4.Serve warm.

Traditional German Pork Roast

Prep time: 15 minutes | Cook time: 8 to 10 hours | Serves 8

16 small red potatoes
1 (14-ounce / 397-g) can sauerkraut, rinsed and well drained
2 large tart apples, peeled and cut into wedges
1 pound (454 g) smoked kielbasa or Polish sausage, cut into 16 slices
2 tablespoons brown sugar
1 teaspoon caraway seeds
1 teaspoon salt, divided
1 teaspoon pepper, divided
1 boneless pork loin roast (3 pounds / 1.4 kg)
3 tablespoons canola oil

1.Place the potatoes in a greased slow cooker. Top with the sauerkraut, apples and kielbasa. Sprinkle with the brown sugar, caraway seeds, ½ teaspoon salt and ½ teaspoon pepper.
2.Cut the roast in half and sprinkle with remaining salt and pepper. In a large skillet, brown the meat in oil on all sides for 4 minutes. Transfer to the slow cooker.
3.Cover and cook on low for 8 to 10 hours or until the meat and vegetables are tender. Skim fat and thicken cooking liquid if desired.
4.Serve warm.

Sumptuous Pork with Veggies

Prep time: 10 minutes | Cook time: 6 to 8 hours | Serves 6

1 pound (454 g) pork roast, cut into strips ½-inch thick
1 large onion, chopped
1 small green bell pepper, sliced
8 ounces (227 g) fresh mushrooms, sliced
1 (8-ounce / 227-g) can low-sodium tomato sauce
4 carrots, sliced
1½ tablespoons vinegar
1 teaspoon salt
2 teaspoons Worcestershire sauce
Hot rice, for serving

1.Brown the pork in a skillet over medium heat for 4 minutes. Transfer to a slow cooker.
2.Combine all the remaining ingredients in the slow cooker.
3.Cover. Cook on low for 6 to 8 hours.
4.Serve over hot rice.

Texas-Style Pork Burritos

Prep time: 20 minutes | Cook time: 6½ to 8½ hours | Serves 10

1 boneless pork shoulder butt roast, cubed (3 to 4 pounds / 1.4 to 1.8 kg)
1 teaspoon salt
½ teaspoon pepper
2 tablespoons canola oil
2 (10-ounce / 284-g) cans green enchilada sauce
1 large onion, thinly sliced
2 medium carrots, thinly sliced
2 (2¼-ounce / 64-g) cans sliced ripe olives, drained
½ cup chicken broth
2 tablespoons ground cumin
3 garlic cloves, minced
2 teaspoons dried oregano
2 tablespoons all-purpose flour
1 cup sour cream
½ cup minced fresh cilantro
10 flour tortillas (8 inches), warmed
2 cups shredded Mexican cheese blend

1.Sprinkle the pork with salt and pepper. In a large skillet, brown the meat in the oil for 4 minutes, in batches. Transfer to a slow cooker.

Combine the enchilada sauce, onion, carrots, olives, broth, cumin, garlic and oregano in a bowl. Pour over the meat. Cover and cook on low for 6 to 8 hours or until meat is tender.
2.Combine the flour and sour cream. Stir into the meat mixture. Cover and cook on high for 30 minutes or until thickened. Stir in the cilantro.
3.Spoon ⅔ cup of the pork mixture onto each tortilla. Top with about 3 tablespoons cheese. Roll up tightly and serve.

Italian Pork Sausage Lasagna Soup

Prep time: 15 minutes | Cook time: 8 hours | Serves 6

1 tablespoon extra-virgin olive oil
¾ pound (340 g) hot or sweet Italian pork sausage, casings removed
1 medium onion, finely chopped
3 garlic cloves, minced
6 cups low-sodium chicken stock
1 (28-ounce / 794-g) can puréed tomatoes
¾ cup dry red wine
2 teaspoons dry Italian seasoning
½ teaspoon kosher salt, plus more for seasoning
½ teaspoon freshly ground black pepper, plus more for seasoning
¼ teaspoon red pepper flakes
8 ounces (227 g) dried elbow macaroni or ditalini
½ cup ricotta cheese, plus more for garnish
½ cup shredded Parmesan cheese

1.In a pan over medium-high heat, heat the oil until shimmering. Brown the Italian sausage for 10 minutes, breaking it up into small bits until no pink remains.
2.Put the Italian sausage in a slow cooker, along with the onion, garlic, chicken stock, tomatoes, wine, Italian seasoning, salt, pepper, and red pepper flakes. Cover and cook on low for 8 hours.
3.During the final hour of cooking, add the macaroni. Cover and continue cooking until tender.
4.In a small bowl, combine the ricotta and Parmesan. Season with salt and pepper and stir to combine. Season the soup with additional salt and pepper, as needed. Ladle the soup into bowls and top with a dollop of the ricotta mixture before serving.

Pork Wraps with Hoisin Sauce

Prep time: 10 minutes | Cook time: 7 to 8 hours | Serves 15

1 boneless pork loin roast (3 pounds / 1.4 kg)
1 cup hoisin sauce, divided
1 tablespoon minced fresh ginger
6 cups shredded red cabbage
1½ cups shredded carrots
¼ cup thinly sliced green onions
3 tablespoons rice vinegar
4½ teaspoons sugar
15 flour tortillas (8 inches), warmed

1.Cut the roast in half. Combine ⅓ cup of the hoisin sauce and ginger in a bowl. Rub over the pork. Transfer to a slow cooker. Cover and cook on low for 7 to 8 hours or until the pork is tender.
2.Meanwhile, in a large bowl, combine the cabbage, carrots, onions, vinegar and sugar. Chill until serving.
3.Shred the meat with two forks and return to the slow cooker. Heat through. Place 2 teaspoons of the hoisin sauce down the center of each tortilla. Top with ⅓ cup shredded pork and ⅓ cup coleslaw. Roll up and serve.

Sweet and Sour Pork

Prep time: 20 minutes | Cook time: 7½ to 8½ hours | Serves 6

1 (15-ounce / 425-g) can tomato sauce
1 medium onion, halved and sliced
1 medium green pepper, cut into strips
1 (4½-ounce / 128-g) can sliced mushrooms, drained
3 tablespoons brown sugar
4½ teaspoons white vinegar
2 teaspoons steak sauce
1 teaspoon salt
1½ pounds (680 g) pork tenderloin, cut into 1-inch cubes
1 tablespoon olive oil
1 (8-ounce / 227-g) can unsweetened pineapple chunks, drained
Hot cooked rice, for serving

1.In a large bowl, combine the first eight ingredients and set aside.
2.In a large skillet, brown the pork in the oil for 4 minutes, in batches. Transfer to a slow cooker. Pour the tomato sauce mixture over the pork. Cover and cook on low for 7 to 8 hours or until meat is tender.
3.Add the pineapple. Cover and cook for 30 minutes longer or until heated through. Serve with rice.

Lamb Tagine with Almonds

Prep time: 20 minutes | Cook time: 8 to 10 hours | Serves 8

3 pounds (1.4 kg) lamb stew meat, cut into 1½-inch cubes
1 teaspoon salt
1 teaspoon pepper
4 tablespoons olive oil, divided
6 medium carrots, sliced
2 medium onions, chopped
6 garlic cloves, minced
2 teaspoons grated lemon peel
¼ cup lemon juice
1 tablespoon minced fresh ginger
1½ teaspoons ground cinnamon
1½ teaspoons ground cumin
1½ teaspoons paprika
2½ cups reduced-sodium chicken broth
¼ cup sweet vermouth
¼ cup honey
½ cup pitted, chopped dates
½ cup toasted sliced almonds

1.Sprinkle the lamb with salt and pepper. In a Dutch oven, brown the meat in 2 tablespoons oil for 4 minutes, in batches. Using a slotted spoon, transfer to a slow cooker.
2.In the same skillet, sauté the carrots, onions, garlic and lemon peel in the remaining oil for 5 minutes, or until crisp-tender. Add the lemon juice, ginger, cinnamon, cumin and paprika. Cook and stir for 2 minutes longer. Add to the slow cooker.
3.Stir in the broth, vermouth, honey and dates. Cover and cook on low for 8 to 10 hours or until lamb is tender. Sprinkle with the almonds and serve warm.

Pork and Butternut Stew

Prep time: 20 minutes | Cook time: 8½ to 10½ hours | Serves 6

⅓ cup plus 1 tablespoon all-purpose flour, divided
1 tablespoon paprika
1 teaspoon salt
1 teaspoon ground coriander
1½ pounds (680 g) boneless pork shoulder butt roast, cut into 1-inch cubes
1 tablespoon canola oil
2¾ cups peeled, cubed butternut squash
1 (14½-ounce / 411-g) can diced tomatoes, undrained
1 cup frozen corn, thawed
1 medium onion, chopped
2 tablespoons cider vinegar
1 bay leaf
2½ cups reduced-sodium chicken broth
1⅔ cups frozen shelled edamame, thawed

1. In a large resealable plastic bag, combine ⅓ cup of the flour, paprika, salt and coriander. Add the pork, a few pieces at a time, and shake to coat.
2. In a large skillet, brown the pork in the oil for 4 minutes, in batches. Drain. Transfer to a slow cooker. Add the squash, tomatoes, corn, onion, vinegar and bay leaf. In a small bowl, combine the broth and remaining flour until smooth. Stir into the slow cooker.
3. Cover and cook on low for 8 to 10 hours or until pork and vegetables are tender. Stir in the edamame. Cover and cook for 30 minutes longer. Discard the bay leaf. Serve warm.

Pork Shoulder Chili Con Carne

Prep time: 15 minutes | Cook time: 10 hours | Serves 8

2 canned chipotle chiles en adobo, minced, plus 1 tablespoon adobo sauce
1 (28-ounce / 794-g) can puréed tomatoes
1 large onion, finely chopped
4 garlic cloves, minced
1½ tablespoons chili powder, preferably ancho
1 tablespoon ground cumin
2 teaspoons dried oregano
2 teaspoons ground paprika
½ teaspoon ground cinnamon
½ teaspoon kosher salt
½ teaspoon freshly ground black pepper

2 teaspoons apple cider vinegar
1 (4-pound / 1.8-kg) boneless pork shoulder
2 teaspoons coarse cornmeal
½ cup chopped fresh cilantro, for garnish

1. Put the chipotle chiles, adobo sauce, tomatoes, onion, garlic, chili powder, cumin, oregano, paprika, cinnamon, salt, pepper, and vinegar in a slow cooker and stir to combine. Place the pork shoulder in the slow cooker and spoon the sauce on top. Cover and cook on low for 10 hours.
2. About 30 minutes before serving, transfer the pork to a cutting board. Stir the cornmeal into the chili, cover with the lid, and continue cooking. Using two forks, shred the meat, discarding any undesirable bits of fat. Return the meat to the slow cooker and stir it into the sauce. Ladle the chili into bowls and garnish with the cilantro. Serve warm.

Hungarian Pork Paprikash

Prep time: 15 minutes | Cook time: 6 hours | Serves 6

3 pounds (1.4 kg) pork stew meat
1 large onion, finely chopped
1 large red or yellow bell pepper, deseeded and chopped
2 garlic cloves, minced
1 cup low-sodium chicken stock
3 tablespoons red wine vinegar
1 tablespoon Worcestershire sauce
¼ cup tomato paste
1 tablespoon paprika
½ teaspoon kosher salt, plus more for seasoning
½ teaspoon freshly ground black pepper, plus more for seasoning
¼ teaspoon ground caraway
½ cup sour cream
1 pound (454 g) egg noodles, cooked

1. To a slow cooker, add the pork, onion, bell pepper, garlic, chicken stock, vinegar, Worcestershire sauce, tomato paste, paprika, salt, pepper, and caraway. Stir to combine. Cover and cook on low for 6 hours.
2. About 20 minutes before the end of the cooking time, season with additional salt and pepper, if desired. Add the sour cream and stir to combine. Continue cooking until the ingredients are warmed through. Serve on top of the egg noodles.

Spiced Lamb Stew

Prep time: 15 minutes | Cook time: 5 to 6 hours | Serves 5

2 pounds (907 g) lamb stew meat, cut into ¾-inch cubes
3 tablespoons butter
1½ cups chopped sweet onion
¾ cup dried apricots
½ cup orange juice
½ cup chicken broth
2 teaspoons paprika
2 teaspoons ground allspice
2 teaspoons ground cinnamon
1½ teaspoons salt
1 teaspoon ground cardamom
Hot cooked couscous, for serving
Chopped dried apricots, for topping (optional)

1. In a large skillet, brown the lamb in the butter for 4 minutes, in batches. With a slotted spoon, transfer to a slow cooker. In the same skillet, sauté the onion in drippings until tender. Stir in the apricots, orange juice, broth and seasonings. Pour over the lamb.
2. Cover and cook on high for 5 to 6 hours or until meat is tender. Serve with the couscous. Sprinkle with the chopped apricots if desired.

Lemony Lamb with Orzo

Prep time: 10 minutes | Cook time: 8 to 10 hours | Serves 9

1 boneless lamb shoulder roast (3 pounds / 1.4 kg)
3 tablespoons lemon juice
3 garlic cloves, minced
2 teaspoons dried oregano
2 teaspoons grated lemon peel
¼ teaspoon salt
1 (16-ounce / 454-g) package orzo pasta
2 (9-ounce / 255-g) packages fresh spinach, torn, divided
1 cup crumbled feta cheese, divided

1. Cut the roast in half. Place in a slow cooker. Drizzle with the lemon juice. Sprinkle with the garlic, oregano, lemon peel and salt. Cover and cook on low for 8 to 10 hours or until meat is tender.
2. Bring a large pot of water to a boil and cook the orzo for 8 to 9 minutes.
3. Remove the lamb from the slow cooker. Shred the meat with two forks. Set aside and keep warm.
4. Skim fat from cooking juices if necessary and return 1 cup cooking juices to the slow cooker. Add one package of spinach. Cook on high for 5 to 10 minutes or until spinach is wilted. Drain the orzo and add to the spinach mixture. Stir in the reserved meat and ½ cup of the feta cheese.
5. To serve, arrange the remaining fresh spinach on nine individual plates. Top with the lamb mixture. Sprinkle each with the remaining feta cheese.

Leg of Lamb Braised in Zinfandel

Prep time: 5 minutes | Cook time: 3 to 4 hours | Serves 8

1 (3- to 4-pound / 1.4- to 1.8-kg) boneless leg of lamb, butterflied
4 cups Zinfandel wine
¼ cup olive oil
6 cloves garlic, sliced
1 tablespoon finely chopped fresh rosemary
¼ cup honey
1 teaspoon salt
½ teaspoon freshly ground black pepper
2 bay leaves

1. Put the lamb in a zipper-top plastic bag. Whisk the remaining ingredients together in a mixing bowl and pour over the lamb in the bag. Seal the bag and refrigerate for at least 8 hours or up to 24 hours.
2. Put the marinade in the insert of a slow cooker and tie the lamb at 1-inch intervals with kitchen string or silicone loops. Cover and cook on high for 3 to 4 hours, until the meat is tender.
3. Carefully remove the meat from the slow cooker, cover with aluminum foil, and allow to rest for 20 minutes. Strain the sauce through a fine-mesh sieve into a saucepan and remove any fat from the surface. Boil the sauce until reduced by half.
4. Slice the meat and serve with the sauce napped over the lamb.

Mediterranean Lamb with Green Beans

Prep time: 15 minutes | Cook time: 4 to 5 hours | Serves 8

½ cup extra-virgin olive oil, divided
2 to 2½ pounds (0.9 to 1.1 kg) small Yukon gold potatoes, cut in half
1 pound (454 g) green beans, ends snipped, cut into 1-inch lengths
6 cloves garlic, sliced
2 teaspoons salt, divided
1 teaspoon freshly ground black pepper, divided
2½ pounds (1.1 kg) lamb shoulder, fat trimmed, cut into 1-inch chunks
1 medium onion, finely chopped
¼ cup dry white wine or vermouth
¼ cup tomato paste
½ cup chicken broth
3 tablespoons finely chopped fresh mint

1. Toss together ¼ cup of the oil, the potatoes, green beans, garlic, 1 teaspoon of the salt, and ½ teaspoon of the pepper in the insert of a slow cooker. Sprinkle the lamb with the remaining salt and pepper.
2. Heat the remaining oil in a large skillet over high heat. Add the meat and brown on all sides for 4 minutes. Transfer the browned meat to the slow cooker insert. Add the onion to the same skillet and sauté until it is softened and beginning to turn translucent, for about 4 minutes. Add the wine, tomato paste, and broth to the skillet and heat, scraping up any of the browned bits from the bottom of the pan.
3. Transfer the contents of the skillet to the slow cooker. Don't stir up the vegetables on the bottom; just pour the liquids in and add the mint. Cover and cook on high for 4 to 5 hours or on low for 8 to 10 hours, until the potatoes are tender and the meat is fork tender.
4. Skim off any fat from the top of the stew. Using a slotted spoon, transfer the meat and vegetables to a serving bowl, then spoon the sauce over the top. Serve warm.

Lamb Meatballs in Tomato Sauce

Prep time: 15 minutes | Cook time: 3 to 4 hours | Serves 6 to 8

Sauce:
2 tablespoons vegetable oil
2 medium onions, finely chopped
2 cloves garlic, minced
1 teaspoon grated fresh ginger
1 teaspoon sweet curry powder
Pinch of cayenne pepper
1 (28- to 32-ounce / 794- to 907-g) can tomato purée
½ cup chicken broth

Meatballs:
2 pounds (907 g) ground lamb
½ cup finely chopped onion
½ teaspoon grated fresh ginger
1 clove garlic, minced
½ teaspoon ground coriander
¼ teaspoon ground cumin
½ teaspoon garam masala
½ teaspoon salt
½ cup soft fresh bread crumbs
½ cup chopped fresh cilantro

1. Heat the oil in a skillet over medium-high heat. Add the onions, garlic, ginger, curry powder, and cayenne and sauté for 2 minutes, until the mixture is fragrant.
2. Add the tomatoes and broth and heat, scraping up any of the spices that have stuck to the bottom of the pan.
3. Transfer the sauce to the insert of a slow cooker and keep warm while making the meatballs.
4. Combine all the meatball ingredients, except for the cilantro, in a large mixing bowl and mix until well blended. Shape into 2-inch meatballs and drop into the sauce in the slow cooker.
5. Cover and cook on high for 3 to 4 hours or on low for 6 to 8 hours, until the meatballs are cooked through. Skim off any fat from the sauce and stir in the cilantro.
6. Serve the meatballs with skewers from the cooker set on warm.

Spiced Lamb Shanks

Prep time: 10 minutes | Cook time: 8 to 10 hours | Serves 4 to 6

1 medium onion, thinly sliced
2 small carrots, cut in thin strips
1 rib celery, chopped
3 lamb shanks, cracked
1 to 2 cloves garlic, split
1½ teaspoons salt
¼ teaspoon pepper
1 teaspoon dried oregano
1 teaspoon dried thyme
2 bay leaves, crumbled
½ cup dry white wine
1 (8-ounce / 227-g) can tomato sauce

1. Place the onions, carrots, and celery in a slow cooker.
2. Rub the lamb with the garlic and season with salt and pepper. Add to the slow cooker.
3. Mix the remaining ingredients together in a separate bowl and add to the meat and vegetables.
4. Cover. Cook on low for 8 to 10 hours, or on high for 4 to 6 hours.
5. Serve warm.

Simple Braised Lamb Chops

Prep time: 10 minutes | Cook time: 4 to 6 hours | Serves 6 to 8

1 medium onion, sliced
1 teaspoon dried oregano
½ teaspoon dried thyme
½ teaspoon garlic powder
¼ teaspoon salt
⅛ teaspoon pepper
8 loin lamb chops (1¾ to 2 pounds / 794 to 907 g)
2 garlic cloves, minced
¼ cup water

1. Place the onion in a slow cooker.
2. Combine the oregano, thyme, garlic powder, salt, and pepper in a bowl. Rub over the lamb chops. Place in the slow cooker. Top with the garlic. Pour the water down alongside of the cooker, so as not to disturb the rub on the chops.
3. Cover. Cook on low for 4 to 6 hours.
4. Serve warm.

Traditional Irish Lamb Stew

Prep time: 10 minutes | Cook time: 8 hours | Serves 2

12 ounces (340 g) boneless lamb shoulder or stew meat, cut into 1-inch pieces
⅛ teaspoon sea salt
Freshly ground black pepper, to taste
1 cup diced and peeled parsnips
1 cup diced and peeled potatoes
½ cup diced onions
1 tablespoon minced garlic
1 cup low-sodium beef broth
½ cup dark beer, such as Guinness Stout
½ tablespoon tomato paste

1. Season the lamb with salt and black pepper. Put the lamb, parsnips, potatoes, onions, and garlic into a slow cooker.
2. In a measuring cup or small bowl, whisk together the beef broth, beer, and tomato paste. Pour this over the lamb and vegetables.
3. Cover and cook on low for 8 hours.
4. Serve warm.

Easy Lamb Goulash au Blanc

Prep time: 10 minutes | Cook time: 5 to 6 hours | Serves 4 to 6

3 tablespoons unsalted butter, softened
1 medium-size yellow onion, chopped
2 pounds (907 g) fresh spring lamb stew meat, such as shoulder, cut into 1½-inch cubes
1 lemon, deseeded and very thinly sliced
1 teaspoon caraway seeds
2 teaspoons dried marjoram
1 clove garlic, peeled
1 cup vegetable broth
Salt and freshly ground black pepper, to taste

1. Smear the bottom of a slow cooker with the butter and sprinkle with the onion. Put the lamb in the cooker and arrange the lemon slices over it.
2. In a mortar, mash together the caraway seeds, marjoram, and garlic with a pestle. Stir into the broth. Add the broth to the cooker, cover, and cook on low for 5 to 6 hours, until the lamb is fork-tender. Season with salt and pepper and serve.

Garlicky Braised Lamb Shanks

Prep time: 10 minutes | Cook time: 7 to 8 hours | Serves 2 to 3

1½ tablespoons olive oil
2 lamb shanks (about 2½ pounds / 1.1 kg total), trimmed of fat, and each cut crosswise into 3 pieces
¾ cup dry white wine
3 heads garlic, separated into cloves, unpeeled
2 medium-size fresh or canned tomatoes, coarsely chopped
1½ teaspoons chopped fresh rosemary
Salt and freshly ground black pepper, to taste
¼ cup chopped lemon zest, for garnish

1. In a large skillet, heat the oil over medium-high heat and cook the shanks until golden brown on all sides, for about 5 minutes total. As they brown, transfer the shanks to a slow cooker. Add the wine to the skillet and bring to a boil, scraping up any browned bits stuck to the pan. Add the garlic, tomatoes, and rosemary, bring to a boil, and pour over the lamb. Cover and cook on low for 7 to 8 hours, until the lamb is very tender and falling off the bone.
2. Season with salt and pepper, sprinkle with the lemon zest, and serve warm.

Soy-Honey Lamb and Brown Rice

Prep time: 10 minutes | Cook time: 8 hours | Serves

1 teaspoon extra-virgin olive oil
½ cup brown rice
1 cup low-sodium chicken broth or water
1 scallion, white and green parts, sliced thin on a bias
2 tablespoons low-sodium soy sauce
2 tablespoons honey
1 tablespoon freshly squeezed lime juice
Pinch of red pepper flakes
12 ounces (340 g) boneless lamb shoulder, cut into 1-inch cubes

1. Grease the inside of a slow cooker with the olive oil.
2. Put the brown rice, broth, and scallion in the slow cooker. Stir to mix the ingredients and make sure the rice is submerged in the liquid.
3. In a large bowl, whisk together the soy sauce, honey, lime juice, and red pepper flakes. Add the lamb cubes and toss to coat them in this mixture.
4. Place the lamb over the rice in the slow cooker.
5. Cover and cook on low for 8 hours.
6. Serve warm.

Chinese-Style Cumin Lamb

Prep time: 15 minutes | Cook time: 6 to 8 hours | Serves 6

1 tablespoon extra-virgin olive oil
½ tablespoon sesame oil
2 pounds (907 g) boneless lamb shoulder, cut into ½-inch-by-2-inch strips
Black pepper, to taste
1 large onion, sliced
2 garlic cloves, minced
½ cup low-sodium chicken stock
2 teaspoons soy sauce
2 tablespoons ground cumin
1 tablespoon packed brown sugar
1 tablespoon Chinese black vinegar, or white vinegar
½ teaspoon red pepper flakes
½ teaspoon kosher salt, plus more for seasoning
1½ teaspoons cornstarch
3 cups cooked white rice, for serving
3 scallions, white and green parts sliced, for garnish

1. In a pan over medium-high heat, heat the olive oil and the sesame oil until shimmering. Season the lamb shoulder with salt and pepper, and brown on all sides, for about 5 minutes total.
2. Put the lamb in a slow cooker, along with the onion and garlic. In a medium bowl, whisk together the chicken stock, soy sauce, cumin, brown sugar, vinegar, red pepper flakes, and salt. Pour over the lamb. Cover and cook on low for 6 to 8 hours.
3. Season with additional salt, as needed. About 30 minutes before serving, whisk in the cornstarch, taking care that there are no lumps. Cover and continue cooking until the sauce is thickened. Serve over the rice, garnished with the scallions.

Chapter 7 Fish and Seafood

Papaya Salsa Swordfish

Prep time: 15 minutes | Cook time: 1 to 2 hours | Serves 4

1 lime, sliced ¼ inch thick
2 tablespoons minced fresh cilantro, stems reserved
¼ cup dry white wine
¼ cup water
4 (6- to 8-ounce / 170- to 227-g) skinless swordfish steaks, 1 to 1½ inches thick
Salt and ground black pepper, to taste

Salsa:
1 papaya, peeled, deseeded, and cut into ½-inch pieces
1 jalapeño chile, stemmed, deseeded, and minced
1 tablespoon extra-virgin olive oil
½ teaspoon lime zest
2 tablespoons lime juice

1. Fold sheet of aluminum foil into sling and press widthwise into the slow cooker. Arrange lime slices in single layer in bottom of prepared slow cooker.
2. Scatter cilantro stems over lime slices. Add wine to slow cooker, then add water until liquid level is even with lime slices (about ¼ cup). Season swordfish with salt and pepper and arrange in even layer on top of cilantro stems.
3. Cover and cook until swordfish flakes apart when gently prodded with a paring knife and registers 140°F (60°C), 1 to 2 hours on low.
4. Combine papaya, jalapeño, oil, and lime zest and juice in a bowl. Season with salt and pepper to taste.
5. Using sling, transfer swordfish to baking sheet. Gently lift and tilt steaks with a spatula to remove cilantro stems and lime slices. Transfer to serving dish.
6. Discard poaching liquid and remove any white albumin from swordfish. Serve with salsa.

Hearty Cod Peperonata

Prep time: 15 minutes | Cook time: 1 to 2 hours | Serves 4

2 red or yellow bell peppers, stemmed, deseeded, and sliced thin
1 onion, halved and sliced thin
2 tablespoons extra-virgin olive oil, plus extra for drizzling
2 tablespoons tomato paste
4 garlic cloves, minced
1 tablespoon paprika
2 teaspoons minced fresh thyme or ½ teaspoon dried
¼ teaspoon red pepper flakes
Salt and ground black pepper, to taste
1 (14½-ounce / 411-g) can diced tomatoes, drained
¼ cup dry white wine
4 (6- to 8-ounce / 170- to 227-g) skinless cod fillets, 1 to 1½ inches thick
2 tablespoons coarsely chopped fresh basil
2 teaspoons balsamic vinegar

1. Microwave bell peppers, onion, oil, tomato paste, garlic, paprika, thyme, pepper flakes, ¼ teaspoon salt, and ¼ teaspoon pepper in a bowl, stirring occasionally, until vegetables are softened, about 8 minutes. Transfer to the slow cooker.
2. Stir tomatoes and wine into the slow cooker. Season cod with salt and pepper and nestle into the slow cooker. Spoon portion of sauce over cod.
3. Cover and cook until cod flakes apart when gently prodded with a paring knife and registers 140°F (60°C), 1 to 2 hours on low.
4. Using 2 metal spatulas, transfer cod to serving dish. Stir basil and vinegar into sauce and season with salt and pepper to taste. Spoon sauce over cod and drizzle with extra oil. Serve warm.

Veracruz Flavor Slow Cooked Tilapia

Prep time: 5 minutes | Cook time: 2 to 4 hours | Serves 6

6 (6-ounce / 170-g) tilapia fillets
1 tablespoon olive oil
¼ teaspoon sea salt
½ teaspoon freshly ground black pepper
2 large tomatoes, chopped
1 large onion, chopped
1 bell pepper (any color), deseeded and thinly sliced
½ cup sliced pimento-stuffed green olives
4 garlic cloves, sliced
1 medium pepperoncino, deseeded and diced
2 tablespoons drained capers
6 lime wedges
Cooking spray

1.Spray the slow cooker with cooking spray.
2.Brush the tilapia fillets with olive oil and sprinkle them lightly with salt and pepper. Lay the fillets on the bottom of the slow cooker.
3.In a medium bowl, combine the tomatoes, onion, bell pepper, olives, garlic, pepperoncino, and capers. Then spoon this mixture over the fillets.
4.Cover and cook on low for 2 to 4 hours, or until a meat thermometer inserted in the fish reads 145°F (63°C).
5.Carefully remove the fillets to warm plates and spoon some vegetables and sauce over each before serving. Garnish with lime wedges.

Salmon Fillets with Navy Beans

Prep time: 15 minutes | Cook time: 8 hours | Serves 2

1 cup dried navy beans
1 bulb fennel, chopped
3 garlic cloves, minced
3 cups chicken stock
1 bay leaf
½ teaspoon dried marjoram leaves
¼ teaspoon salt
1 cup chopped grape tomatoes
2 (6-ounce / 170-g) salmon fillets
½ teaspoon ground paprika

1.Sort the beans and rinse, then drain well.
2.In the slow cooker, top the beans with the fennel and garlic. Pour the stock over everything and add the bay leaf, marjoram, and salt.
3.Cover and cook on low for 7½ hours, or until the beans are tender.
4.Remove and discard the bay leaf. Stir in the tomatoes.
5.Sprinkle the salmon with the paprika and place it on top of the beans.
6.Cover and cook on high for 25 to 30 minutes, or until the salmon flakes when tested with a fork, and serve.

Tuscan Grouper with Vegetables

Prep time: 20 minutes | Cook time: 7½ hours | Serves 2

1 red bell pepper, cut into strips
1 orange bell pepper, cut into strips
1 onion, chopped
1 small eggplant, peeled and cubed
1 cup sliced mushrooms
2 cups creamer potatoes
3 garlic cloves, minced
1 tablespoon extra-virgin olive oil
1 teaspoon minced fresh rosemary leaves
½ teaspoon dried thyme leaves
½ teaspoon salt
⅛ teaspoon freshly ground black pepper
½ cup chicken stock or vegetable broth
2 (6-ounce / 170-g) grouper or arctic char fillets
Nonstick cooking spray

1.Spray the slow cooker with the nonstick cooking spray.
2.In the slow cooker, combine the red and orange bell peppers, onion, eggplant, mushrooms, potatoes, and garlic, and drizzle with the olive oil. Sprinkle with the rosemary, thyme, salt, and pepper.
3.Pour the stock over the mixture in the slow cooker.
4.Cover and cook on low for 7 hours, or until the vegetables are tender.
5.Place the fish on top of the vegetables. Cover and cook on high for 20 to 30 minutes, or until the fish flakes when tested with a fork, and serve.

Herbed Salmon Creole

Prep time: 15 minutes | Cook time: 7¾ hours | Serves 2

1 (14-ounce / 397-g) can diced tomatoes, undrained
3 tablespoons tomato paste
1 onion, chopped
1 cup sliced cremini mushrooms
3 celery stalks and their leaves, sliced
1 green bell pepper, chopped
3 garlic cloves, minced
1 cup chicken stock
1 teaspoon ground sweet paprika
½ teaspoon dried oregano leaves
½ teaspoon dried basil leaves
¼ teaspoon dried thyme leaves
½ teaspoon salt
¼ teaspoon freshly ground black pepper
¼ teaspoon crushed red pepper flakes
2 (6-ounce / 170-g) salmon fillets, cubed

1.In the slow cooker, combine all the ingredients except the salmon.
2.Cover and cook on low for 7½ hours, or until the vegetables are tender.
3.Add the salmon to the slow cooker and stir.
4.Cover and cook on high for 15 to 20 minutes, or until the salmon flakes when tested with a fork, and serve.

Shrimp and Grouper Jambalaya

Prep time: 20 minutes | Cook time: 8 hours | Serves 2

1 onion, chopped
1 green bell pepper, chopped
2 celery stalks, sliced
4 garlic cloves, minced
1 (14-ounce / 397-g) can diced tomatoes, undrained
2 tablespoons tomato paste
1 teaspoon jerk rub
½ teaspoon dried thyme leaves
½ teaspoon dried oregano leaves
½ teaspoon salt
¼ teaspoon freshly ground black pepper
⅛ teaspoon crushed red pepper flakes
1 cup clam juice
¾ cup chicken stock
½ pound (227 g) raw shrimp, peeled and deveined

2 grouper fillets, cut into 1-inch pieces

1.In the slow cooker, combine all the ingredients except the shrimp and grouper.
2.Cover and cook on low for 7½ hours.
3.Add the shrimp and grouper fillets, cover, and cook on high for 15 to 20 minutes, or until the shrimp curl and turn pink and the fish is firm, and serve.

Sumptuous Seafood Chowder

Prep time: 15 minutes | Cook time: 7 hours | Serves 2

3 slices bacon
1 onion, chopped
2 garlic cloves, minced
3 Yukon Gold potatoes, peeled and cubed
1 cup frozen corn
1 cup clam juice
2 cups chicken stock
½ teaspoon salt
⅛ teaspoon freshly ground black pepper
4 ounces (113 g) cod, cut into 1-inch pieces
4 ounces (113 g) bay scallops
4 ounces (113 g) medium shrimp, peeled and deveined
½ cup light cream
1 tablespoon cornstarch
1 tablespoon minced fresh chives

1.In a small skillet over medium-high heat, cook the bacon until crisp, about 10 minutes. Drain on paper towels, crumble, and set aside in the refrigerator.
2.In the same skillet over medium heat, cook the onion and garlic in the bacon drippings for 5 minutes, or until crisp-tender.
3.In the slow cooker, combine the onion-garlic mixture, potatoes, corn, clam juice, stock, salt, and pepper.
4.Cover and cook on low for 6½ hours, or until the vegetables are tender.
5.Add the cod, cover, and cook on low for 5 minutes.
6.Add the scallops and shrimp.
7.In a small bowl, mix the cream and cornstarch well. Stir the mixture into the slow cooker.
8.Cover and cook on low for 10 minutes, or until the shrimp curl and turn pink and all the seafood is cooked.
9.Garnish with the bacon crumbles and chives and serve.

Cod au Gratin

Prep time: 15 minutes | Cook time: 1 to 1½ hours | Serves 6

6 tablespoons olive oil
3 tablespoons all-purpose flour
1½ teaspoons sea salt
½ tablespoon dry mustard
1 teaspoon rosemary
¼ tablespoon ground nutmeg
1¼ cups milk
2 teaspoons lemon juice
⅓ cup grated Parmesan cheese
⅓ cup grated asiago cheese
⅓ cup grated romano cheese
3 pounds (1.4 kg) Pacific cod fillets

1.Heat the olive oil in a small saucepan over medium heat. Stir in the flour, salt, mustard, rosemary, and nutmeg.
2.Gradually add the milk, stirring constantly until thickened.
3.Add the lemon juice, and the Parmesan, Asiago, and Romano cheeses to the saucepan. Stir until the cheeses are melted.
4.Place the fish into the slow cooker, and spoon the cheese sauce over the fish. Cover and cook on high for 1 to 1½ hours or until the fish flakes. Serve hot.

Tuna and Pea Casserole

Prep time: 10 minutes | Cook time: 4 hours | Serves 6

2 cups uncooked, dry egg noodles
1 medium onion, finely chopped
½ cup sliced mushrooms
¾ cup chicken stock
¾ cup heavy (whipping) cream
½ teaspoon kosher salt, plus more for seasoning
½ teaspoon freshly ground black pepper, plus more for seasoning
2 (5-ounce / 142-g) cans tuna in water, drained
½ cup shredded Swiss cheese
1 cup frozen peas
Cooking spray or 1 tablespoon extra-virgin olive oil

1.Use the cooking spray or olive oil to coat the inside (bottom and sides) of the slow cooker.
2.Add the noodles, onion, mushrooms, chicken stock, heavy cream, salt, pepper, and tuna. Stir to combine.
3.Cover and cook on low for 4 hours, stirring every hour to prevent sticking.
4.During the last 20 minutes of cooking, add the cheese and peas. Cover and continue cooking until the cheese has melted. Season with additional salt and pepper, as needed. Serve immediately.

Tuna with White Beans and Tomatoes

Prep time: 10 minutes | Cook time: 8 to 10 hours | Serves 6

1 pound (454 g) small white beans, such as cannellini, soaked overnight, drained, and rinsed
1 medium onion, finely chopped
2 garlic cloves, minced
2 bay leaves
1¼ teaspoons kosher salt, plus more for seasoning
½ teaspoon freshly ground black pepper, plus more for seasoning
½ teaspoon Italian seasoning
6 to 8 cups chicken stock
1 pound (454 g) cherry tomatoes
2 tablespoons pepperoncini, chopped
2 (5-ounce / 142-g) cans tuna in water, drained

1.To the slow cooker, add the beans, onion, garlic, bay leaves, salt, pepper, Italian seasoning, and 6 cups of chicken stock. Stir to combine, cover, and cook on low for 8 to 10 hours, adding additional stock as needed.
2.About 30 minutes before serving, add the tomatoes, pepperoncini, and tuna. Stir to combine. Cover and continue cooking until warmed through and the beans are tender when pierced with a fork.
3.Discard the bay leaves. Season with additional salt and pepper, as needed. Spoon into bowls and serve immediately.

Super Citrus Swordfish Fillets

Prep time: 15 minutes | Cook time: 1½ hours | Serves 2

1½ pounds (680 g) swordfish fillets
Sea salt and black pepper, to taste
1 yellow onion, chopped
5 tablespoons chopped fresh flat-leaf parsley
1 tablespoon olive oil
2 teaspoons lemon zest
2 teaspoons orange zest
Orange and lemon slices, for garnish
Fresh parsley sprigs, for garnish
Nonstick cooking spray

1.Spritz the slow cooker with nonstick cooking spray.
2.Season the fish fillets with salt and pepper. Place the fish in the slow cooker.
3.Distribute the onion, parsley, olive oil, lemon zest, and orange zest over fish.
4.Cover and cook on low for 1½ hours.
5.Serve hot, garnished with orange and lemon slices and sprigs of fresh parsley.

Lemony and Creamy Herbed Salmon

Prep time: 15 minutes | Cook time: 1¼ hours | Serves 4

2 cups water
1 cup dry white wine
1 lemon, thinly sliced
2 tablespoons minced onion
2 garlic cloves, thinly sliced
3 fresh thyme sprigs
3 fresh tarragon sprigs
1 teaspoon peppercorns
2 pounds (907 g) skin-on salmon or 4 skin-on fillets
1 teaspoon kosher salt, plus more for seasoning
1 cup sour cream
¾ cup mayonnaise
2 tablespoons chopped fresh chives
2 tablespoons chopped fresh dill
2 tablespoons freshly squeezed lemon juice
Freshly ground black pepper, to taste
Extra-virgin olive oil, for garnish
Lemon wedges, for garnish

1.To the slow cooker, add the water, wine, lemon, onion, garlic, thyme, tarragon, and peppercorns. Stir to combine. Cover and cook on high for 30 minutes.
2.Season the salmon with the salt and place it in the slow cooker. Reduce the heat to low. Cover and cook for 45 minutes or until the fish flakes easily and is no longer opaque.
3.While the salmon is cooking, combine the sour cream, mayonnaise, chives, dill, and lemon juice in a medium bowl. Season with additional salt and pepper, as needed. Stir to combine and set aside.
4.Remove the salmon from the poaching liquid and discard the liquid. Serve the salmon drizzled with olive oil, a sprinkle of coarse salt, lemon wedges, and the reserved dill cream sauce.

Italian Seafood and Vegetable Stew

Prep time: 20 minutes | Cook time: 7½ hours | Serves 2

1 onion, chopped
1 fennel bulb, chopped
2 carrots, sliced
1 celery stalk, sliced
1 large tomato, deseeded and chopped
2 cups small red potatoes
1½ cups chicken stock or vegetable broth
¼ cup dry white wine
½ teaspoon dried thyme leaves
½ teaspoon dried marjoram leaves
½ teaspoon salt
⅛ teaspoon freshly ground black pepper
1 cod fillet, cut into 1-inch pieces
1 cup medium raw shrimp, peeled and deveined
8 clams, scrubbed

1.In the slow cooker, combine the onion, fennel, carrots, celery, tomato, and potatoes. Pour the stock and wine over. Add the thyme, marjoram, salt, and pepper, and stir well.
2.Cover and cook on low for 7 hours, or until the vegetables are tender.
3.Add the cod, cover, and cook on high for 10 minutes.
4.Add the shrimp and clams, cover, and cook on high for 15 to 20 minutes more, or until the shrimp curl and turn pink and the clams open, and serve.

Super Seafood Pot-Au-Feu

Prep time: 10 minutes | Cook time: 6 hours | Serves 6

1 small leek (white and light green parts), thinly sliced and washed
1 small fennel bulb, trimmed and thinly sliced
12 baby carrots
1 medium onion, finely chopped
2 garlic cloves, thinly sliced
7 cups fish stock
¼ cup dry white wine
1 (15-ounce / 425-g) can diced tomatoes, undrained
¾ teaspoon kosher salt, plus more for seasoning
½ teaspoon freshly ground black pepper, plus more for seasoning
¼ teaspoon red pepper flakes
1 bay leaf
⅛ teaspoon ground turmeric
¾ pound (340 g) boneless, skinless, firm-fleshed white fish, such as cod, cut into 1-inch cubes
½ pound (227 g) boneless, skinless salmon, cut into 1-inch cubes
12 small mussels, scrubbed and debearded
½ pound (227 g) medium shrimp, shelled and deveined
¼ cup mixed chopped fresh herbs, for garnish

1.To the slow cooker, add the leek, fennel, carrots, onion, garlic, fish stock, wine, tomatoes, salt, pepper, red pepper flakes, bay leaf, and turmeric. Stir to combine. Cover and cook on low for 6 hours.
2.About 45 minutes before serving, add the white fish, salmon, mussels, and shrimp. Cover and cook until the fish flakes easily and is opaque, and the mussels have all opened. Discard the bay leaf, along with any mussels that have not opened. Season with additional salt and pepper, as needed.
3.Ladle the soup into bowls, garnish with the chopped herbs, such as thyme, parsley, and tarragon, and serve immediately.

Moroccan Sea Bass with Bell Pepper

Prep time: 20 minutes | Cook time: 2 hours | Serves 8

2 tablespoons extra-virgin olive oil
1 large yellow onion, finely chopped
1 medium red bell pepper, cut into ½-inch strips
1 medium yellow bell pepper, cut into ½-inch strips
4 garlic cloves, minced
1 teaspoon saffron threads, crushed
1½ teaspoons sweet paprika
¼ teaspoon hot paprika or ¼ teaspoon smoked paprika (or pimentón)
½ teaspoon ground ginger
1 (15-ounce / 425-g) can diced tomatoes, with the juice
¼ cup fresh orange juice
2 pounds (907 g) fresh sea bass fillets
¼ cup finely chopped fresh flat-leaf parsley
¼ cup finely chopped fresh cilantro
Sea salt and black pepper, to taste
1 navel orange, thinly sliced, for garnish

1.In a large skillet, heat the olive oil over medium-high heat. Add the onion, red and yellow bell peppers, garlic, saffron, sweet paprika, hot or smoked paprika, and ginger and cook, stirring often, for 3 minutes, or until the onion begins to soften.
2.Add the tomatoes and stir for another 2 minutes to blend the flavors.
3.Transfer the mixture to the slow cooker and stir in the orange juice.
4.Place the sea bass fillets on top of the tomato mixture, and spoon some mixture over the fish. Cover and cook on high for 2 hours, or on low for 3 to 4 hours. At the end of the cooking time, the sea bass should be opaque in the center.
5.Carefully lift the fish out of the slow cooker with a spatula and transfer to a serving platter. Cover loosely with aluminum foil.
6.Skim off any excess fat from the sauce, stir in the parsley and cilantro, and season with salt and pepper.
7.Spoon some sauce over the fish and garnish with the orange slices. Serve hot, passing the remaining sauce on the side.

Fruit Salsa Mahi-mahi with Lentils

Prep time: 15 minutes | Cook time: 5½ to 6 hours | Serves 6

1¼ cups vegetable or chicken stock
1 cup orange juice
¾ cup orange lentils
½ cup finely diced carrot
¼ cup finely diced red onion
¼ cup finely diced celery
1 tablespoon honey
6 (4- to 5-ounce / 113- to 142-g) mahimahi fillets
Sea salt and black pepper, to taste
1 teaspoon lemon juice
Salsa:
¾ cup finely diced pineapple
¾ cup finely diced mango
½ cup finely diced strawberries
¼ cup finely diced red onion
2 tablespoons chopped fresh mint (or 2 teaspoons dried)
2 tablespoons orange juice
1 tablespoon lime juice
¼ teaspoon salt

1.Combine the stock, orange juice, lentils, carrot, onion, celery, and honey in the slow cooker.
2.Cover and cook on low for 5 to 5½ hours, or until the lentils are tender.
3.Place 1 sheet of parchment paper over the lentils in the slow cooker. Season mahimahi lightly with salt and black pepper and place it on the parchment (skin-side down, if you have not removed the skin).
4.Replace the lid and continue to cook on low for 25 minutes or until the mahimahi is opaque in the center. Remove the fish by lifting out the parchment paper and putting it on a plate.
5.Stir the lemon juice into the lentils and season with salt and pepper.
To make the salsa
1.While the fish is cooking, combine the pineapple, mango, strawberries, red onion, mint, orange juice, lime juice, and salt into a big jar. Combine and chill to give the flavors a chance to blend.
2.To serve, place about ½ cup of hot lentils on a plate and top with a mahimahi fillet and ⅓ cup of salsa.

Lime Buttered Salmon

Prep time: 5 minutes | Cook time: 2 hours | Serves 2

2 (6-ounce / 170-g) salmon fillets
1 tablespoon olive oil
½ tablespoon lime juice
2 cloves garlic, minced
1 teaspoon finely chopped fresh parsley
¼ teaspoon black pepper

1.Spread a length of foil onto the countertop and put the salmon fillets directly in the middle.
2.In a small bowl, combine the olive oil, lime juice, garlic, parsley, and black pepper. Brush the mixture over the fillets. Fold the foil over and crimp the sides to make a packet.
3.Place the packet into the slow cooker. Cover and cook on high for 2 hours.
4.Salmon is finished when it flakes easily with a fork. Serve hot.

Poached Tuna with Olives

Prep time: 15 minutes | Cook time: 1 hours | Serves 2

2 (1-inch-thick) tuna steaks (about 1¼ pounds / 567 g in total)
2 teaspoons coarse salt
6 (1-inch) strips orange zest
4 garlic cloves, smashed and peeled
2 dried bay leaves
1 serrano chile, halved
1 rosemary sprig
¼ cup pitted green olives, smashed
2 cups canola, safflower, or extra-virgin olive oil

1.Rub tuna all over with the salt and let sit at room temperature for 30 minutes.
2.Place the tuna (do not rinse) in the slow cooker. Add orange zest, garlic, bay leaves, chile, rosemary, olives, and oil.
3.Cover and cook on high until tuna is just firm, 1 hour (flip to check underside). Remove the tuna and let sit in oil for 30 minutes.
4.Transfer tuna to a wide bowl and strain oil through a sieve over tuna, then discard solids, but reserve olives, if desired. Serve warm.

Garlicky Tilapia

Prep time: 5 minutes | Cook time: 2 hours | Serves 3 to 4

2 tablespoons butter, at room temperature
2 cloves garlic, minced
2 teaspoons minced fresh flat-leaf parsley
4 tilapia fillets
Sea salt and black pepper, to taste

1. In a small bowl, mix the butter, garlic, and parsley to combine.
2. Pull out a large sheet of aluminum foil and put it on the counter. Place the fillets in the middle of the foil.
3. Season the fish generously with salt and pepper.
4. Evenly divide the butter mixture among the fillets and place on top.
5. Wrap the foil around the fish, sealing all sides and crimping the edges to make a packet. Place in the slow cooker, cover, and cook on high for 2 hours. Serve hot.

Lemon-Dijon Salmon

Prep time: 15 minutes | Cook time: 2 hours | Serves 6

1 medium yellow onion, diced
2 teaspoons garlic, minced
2 teaspoons olive oil
2 cups vegetable or chicken stock
1 cup quick-cooking barley
1 tablespoon minced fresh dill weed
1½ pounds (680 g) salmon fillets
Sea salt and black pepper, to taste
Lemon-Dijon **Sauce:**
⅓ cup Dijon mustard
3 tablespoons olive oil
3 tablespoons fresh lemon juice
⅓ cup plain Greek yogurt
1 clove garlic, minced

1. Combine the onion, garlic, and oil in a microwave-safe bowl. Heat in the microwave on medium-high for 4 to 5 minutes, stirring occasionally. Put into the slow cooker.
2. Add the stock, barley, and dill weed to the slow cooker and stir.
3. Season the salmon fillets with salt and pepper,

and gently place them on top of the barley mixture.
4. Cover and cook on low for about 2 hours, until the salmon and barley are cooked through.
To make the lemon-Dijon sauce
1. In a small bowl, whisk together the Dijon mustard, olive oil, lemon juice, Greek yogurt, and garlic. Set aside and allow the flavors to blend.
2. To serve, place some barley on a plate and top with a salmon fillet. Spoon the lemon-Dijon sauce over of the salmon.

Branzino and Potato Bake

Prep time: 15 minutes | Cook time: 4 hours | Serves 4

1 lemon, thinly sliced
½ bunch fresh thyme
½ fennel bulb, cored and thinly sliced
1 small garlic clove, thinly sliced
2 whole branzino (about 2 pounds / 907 g in total), scaled, gutted, and cleaned (head left on, if desired)
1 (3-pound / 1.4-kg) box kosher salt
2 pounds (907 g) small (1 to 1¼ inches) white potatoes, such as Honey Gold, scrubbed
1 tablespoon extra-virgin olive oil, plus more for drizzling

1. Divide lemon, thyme, fennel, and garlic between fish, stuffing each cavity.
2. Cover bottom of the slow cooker with a ½-inch layer of salt. Toss potatoes with oil and arrange over salt layer. Bury potatoes in salt, adding more salt, as necessary, to cover. Cover slow cooker and cook on high for 1 hour.
3. Wrap fish well in a parchment, tucking ends under, and place on top of potato-salt layer. Sprinkle about 1 cup more salt on top. Cover and cook on high until fish is cooked through, about 3 hours.
4. Carefully lift parchment package out of slow cooker, brushing off salt layer. Open parchment packet and transfer fish to a serving platter.
5. Arrange potatoes around fish, drizzle fish and potatoes with oil, and top with lemon slices. Serve warm.

Honeyed Worcestershire Salmon

Prep time: 10 minutes | Cook time: 1 hours | Serves 6

6 (6-ounce / 170-g) salmon fillets
½ cup honey
2 tablespoons lime juice
3 tablespoons Worcestershire sauce
1 tablespoon water
2 cloves garlic, minced
1 teaspoon ground ginger
½ teaspoon black pepper

1.Place the salmon fillets in the slow cooker.
2.In a medium bowl, whisk the honey, lime juice, Worcestershire sauce, water, garlic, ginger, and pepper. Pour the sauce mixture over the salmon.
3.Cover and cook on high for 1 hour.
4.Serve warm.

Crayfish Creole

Prep time: 15 minutes | Cook time: 3 to 4 hours | Serves 2

1½ cups diced celery
1 large yellow onion, chopped
2 small bell peppers, any colors, chopped
1 (8-ounce / 227-g) can tomato sauce
1 (28-ounce / 794-g) can whole tomatoes, broken up, with the juice
1 clove garlic, minced
1 teaspoon sea salt
¼ teaspoon black pepper
6 drops hot pepper sauce (such as tabasco)
1 pound (454 g) precooked crayfish meat

1.Place the celery, onion, and bell peppers in the slow cooker. Add the tomato sauce, tomatoes, and garlic. Sprinkle with the salt and pepper and add the hot sauce.
2.Cover and cook on high for 3 to 4 hours or on low for 6 to 8 hours.
3.About 30 minutes before the cooking time is completed, add the crayfish.
4.Serve hot.

Coconut Halibut with Eggplant Relish

Prep time: 15 minutes | Cook time: 2½ hours | Serves 4

4 medium Japanese eggplants (or 2 large eggplants), cut into ½-inch cubes
¼ cup coarse salt
¼ cup extra-virgin olive oil, divided
2 onions, diced
3 garlic cloves, minced
1 (1-inch) piece fresh ginger, peeled and finely grated
2 kaffir lime leaves
1 teaspoon brown sugar
1 tablespoon rice vinegar
¼ cup fresh lime juice
1 cup packed fresh cilantro, finely chopped
1 pound (454 g) halibut, cut into 1-inch pieces
½ cup unsweetened flaked coconut, toasted, for garnish

1.Combine eggplant and salt in a colander set over a bowl, then let stand about 1 hour. Rinse well and pat dry.
2.Heat 2 tablespoons oil in a large skillet over medium. Add onions and sauté until deeply golden, about 15 minutes. Add garlic and ginger, and cook for 2 more minutes. Add eggplants and cook just until hot. Transfer vegetables to the slow cooker.
3.Add remaining 2 tablespoons oil, the lime leaves, brown sugar, vinegar, and lime juice to the slow cooker. Cover and cook on low until soft but not mushy, about 4 hours or on high for 2 hours.
4.Stir in cilantro. Nestle fish on top of eggplant mixture and cook on low until cooked through, about 20 minutes or on high for 10 minutes. Serve relish topped with halibut and sprinkled with toasted coconut.

Parmesan Shrimp Risotto

Prep time: 10 minutes | Cook time: 5¾ hours | Serves 2

1 onion, chopped
2 garlic cloves, minced
1⅓ cups Arborio rice
½ teaspoon salt
4 cups chicken stock
¼ cup white wine
¾ pound (340 g) medium raw shrimp, peeled and deveined
¼ cup grated Parmesan cheese
2 tablespoons butter

1. In the slow cooker, combine the onion, garlic, rice, and salt. Stir in the stock and wine.
2. Cover and cook on low for 5½ hours, or until the rice is tender.
3. Add the shrimp and stir gently. Cover and cook on high for 15 minutes, or until the shrimp curl and turn pink.
4. Stir in the cheese and butter, and turn off the slow cooker. Cover and let stand for 10 minutes.
5. Stir again and serve.

White Fish Curry

Prep time: 15 minutes | Cook time: 2½ hours | Serves 4 to 6

½ cup flaked unsweetened coconut
2 serrano chiles, sliced
1 teaspoon coriander seeds
½ onion, coarsely chopped
1 (1-inch) piece fresh turmeric, peeled and coarsely chopped
1 (1-inch) piece fresh ginger, peeled and coarsely chopped
2 garlic cloves, thinly sliced
2 tablespoons tamarind paste
1 teaspoon ground cumin
¼ teaspoon fenugreek seeds
1 tablespoon mild curry powder
Coarse salt, to taste
2 (13½-ounce / 383-g) cans unsweetened coconut milk
2 pounds (907 g) firm white fish fillets, such as cod or halibut, cut into 2- to 3-inch pieces
Fresh cilantro, for garnish

1. Combine coconut, chiles, coriander seeds, onion, turmeric, ginger, garlic, tamarind, cumin, fenugreek, curry powder, and 1 teaspoon salt in a food processor, then purée to form a paste.
2. Transfer paste to a saucepan, add coconut milk, and bring to a boil. Transfer coconut mixture to the slow cooker. Cover and cook on high until slightly thickened, 2 hours or on low for 4 hours.
3. Season fish with salt and transfer to the slow cooker, then submerge fish in coconut mixture. Reduce slow cooker to low and cook until fish is flaky but does not fall apart, about 20 minutes.
4. Serve fish curry sprinkled with cilantro.

Shrimp and Tomato Creole

Prep time: 15 minutes | Cook time: 6 hours | Serves 4

2 large onions, finely chopped
2 celery stalks, finely chopped
1 green bell pepper, deseeded and finely chopped
4 garlic cloves, minced
1 (28-ounce / 794-g) can diced tomatoes, undrained
1 tablespoon Worcestershire sauce
1 tablespoon hot sauce, such as Tabasco
1 teaspoon kosher salt, plus more for seasoning
½ teaspoon freshly ground black pepper, plus more for seasoning
½ teaspoon cayenne pepper
½ teaspoon Cajun or Creole seasoning
2 bay leaves
1½ pounds (680 g) large shrimp, shelled and deveined
4 scallions, sliced, for garnish

1. To the slow cooker, add the onions, celery, bell pepper, garlic, tomatoes, Worcestershire sauce, hot sauce, salt, pepper, cayenne, Cajun seasoning, and bay leaves. Stir to combine. Cover and cook on low for 6 hours.
2. About 25 minutes before serving, add the shrimp. Cover and continue cooking until the shrimp are pink and no longer translucent.
3. Discard the bay leaves. Season with additional salt and pepper, as needed. Serve garnished with the scallions.

Poached Turbot

Prep time: 5 minutes | Cook time: 40 to 50 minutes | Serves 4

1 cup vegetable or chicken stock
½ cup dry white wine
1 yellow onion, sliced
1 lemon, sliced
4 sprigs fresh dill
½ teaspoon sea salt
4 (6-ounce / 170-g) turbot fillets

1.Combine the stock and wine in the slow cooker. Cover and cook on high for 20 to 30 minutes.
2.Add the onion, lemon, dill, salt, and turbot to the slow cooker. Cover and cook on high for about 20 minutes, until the turbot is opaque and cooked through according to taste. Serve hot.

Shrimp, Quinoa, and Corn Salad

Prep time: 15 minutes | Cook time: 2 to 3 hours | Serves 4

1 cup white quinoa, rinsed
2 scallions, white parts minced, green parts cut into ½-inch pieces
2 jalapeño chiles, stemmed, deseeded, and minced
5 teaspoons extra-virgin olive oil, divided
1 teaspoon chili powder
1⅓ cups water
Salt and ground black pepper, to taste
1 pound (454 g) medium-large shrimp (31 to 40 per pound), peeled, deveined, and tails removed
¾ cup frozen corn, thawed
3 tomatoes, cored and chopped
⅓ cup minced fresh cilantro
1 tablespoon lime juice
2 ounces (57 g) Cotija cheese, crumbled (½ cup)
Cooking spray

1.Spritz the slow cooker with cooking spray. Microwave quinoa, scallion whites, jalapeños, 2 teaspoons oil, and chili powder in a bowl, stirring occasionally, until vegetables are softened, about 2 minutes. Transfer to the prepared slow cooker. Stir in water and ½ teaspoon salt. Cover and cook until water is absorbed and quinoa is tender, 3 to 4 hours on low or 2 to 3 hours on high.
2.Season shrimp with pepper. Fluff quinoa with fork, then nestle shrimp into quinoa and sprinkle with corn. Cover and cook on high until shrimp are opaque throughout, 30 to 40 minutes.
3.Combine tomatoes, cilantro, lime juice, scallion greens, remaining 1 tablespoon oil, ¼ teaspoon salt, and ¼ teaspoon pepper in a separate bowl. Sprinkle quinoa and shrimp with Cotija and serve, passing salsa separately.

Barbecue Shrimp and Scallops

Prep time: 15 minutes | Cook time: 1 hours | Serves 2

½ teaspoon paprika
½ teaspoon garlic powder
¼ teaspoon onion powder
¼ teaspoon cayenne pepper
¼ teaspoon dried oregano
¼ teaspoon dried thyme
½ teaspoon sea salt
½ teaspoon black pepper
2 cloves garlic, minced
½ cup olive oil
¼ cup Worcestershire sauce
1 tablespoon hot pepper sauce (such as tabasco)
Juice of 1 lemon
1 pound (454 g) scallops
1 pound (454 g) large shrimp, unpeeled
1 green onion, finely chopped

1.Combine the paprika, garlic powder, onion powder, cayenne pepper, oregano, thyme, ½ teaspoon salt, and ¼ teaspoon black pepper.
2.Combine the paprika blend, garlic, olive oil, Worcestershire sauce, hot pepper sauce, and lemon juice in the slow cooker. Season with salt and pepper.
3.Cover and cook on high for 30 minutes or until hot.
4.Rinse the scallops and shrimp, and drain.
5.Spoon one-half of the sauce from the slow cooker into a glass measuring cup.
6.Place the scallops and shrimp in the slow cooker with the remaining sauce. Drizzle with the sauce in the measuring cup and stir to coat.
7.Cover and cook on high for 30 minutes, until the scallops and shrimp are opaque.
8.Turn the heat to warm for serving. Sprinkle with the chopped green onion to serve.

Marinara Shrimp

Prep time: 15 minutes | Cook time: 6¼ to 7¼ hours | Serves 4

1 (15-ounce / 425-g) can diced tomatoes, with the juice one
1 (6-ounce / 170-g) can tomato paste
1 clove garlic, minced
2 tablespoons minced fresh flat-leaf parsley
½ teaspoon dried basil
1 teaspoon dried oregano
1 teaspoon garlic powder
1½ teaspoons sea salt
¼ teaspoon black pepper
1 pound (454 g) cooked shrimp, peeled and deveined
2 cups hot cooked spaghetti or linguine, for serving
½ cup grated Parmesan cheese, for serving

1.Combine the tomatoes, tomato paste, and minced garlic in the slow cooker. Sprinkle with the parsley, basil, oregano, garlic powder, salt, and pepper.
2.Cover and cook on low for 6 to 7 hours.
3.Turn up the heat to high, stir in the cooked shrimp, and cover and cook on high for about 15 minutes longer.
4.Serve hot over the cooked pasta. Top with Parmesan cheese.

Cajun Shrimp with Sausage

Prep time: 15 minutes | Cook time: 4 hours | Serves 6

¾ pound (340 g) andouille sausage, cut into ½-inch rounds
1 red onion, sliced into wedges
2 garlic cloves, minced
2 celery stalks, coarsely chopped
1 red or green bell pepper, coarsely chopped
2 tablespoons all-purpose flour
1 (28-ounce / 794-g) can diced tomatoes, with their juice
½ cup water
¼ teaspoon cayenne pepper
Coarse sea salt, to taste
½ pound (227 g) large shrimp, peeled and deveined
2 cups fresh okra, sliced

1.Put the sausage, onion, garlic, celery, and bell pepper into the slow cooker. Sprinkle with the flour and toss to coat.
2.Add the tomatoes and water. Sprinkle with the cayenne pepper and season with salt.
3.Cover and cook on high for 3½ hours or on low for 7 hours, until the vegetables are tender.
4.Add the shrimp and okra. Cover and cook until the shrimp are opaque throughout, on high for 30 minutes or on low for 1 hour. Serve hot.

Shrimp with Sausage and Potatoes

Prep time: 15 minutes | Cook time: 4 to 5 hours | Serves 6

8 ounces (227 g) andouille sausage, cut into 1-inch lengths
2 celery ribs, cut into 2-inch lengths
2 tablespoons tomato paste
4 teaspoons Old Bay seasoning
¼ teaspoon red pepper flakes
4 cups water
1½ pounds (680 g) small red potatoes, unpeeled, halved
1 (8-ounce / 227-g) bottle clam juice
3 ears corn, husks and silk removed, halved
3 bay leaves
1½ pounds (680 g) extra-large shrimp (21 to 25 per pound), peeled, deveined, and tails removed
Salt and ground black pepper, to taste

1.Microwave andouille, celery, tomato paste, Old Bay seasoning, and pepper flakes in a bowl, stirring occasionally, until celery is softened, about 5 minutes. Transfer to the slow cooker.
2.Stir in the water, potatoes, clam juice, corn, and bay leaves. Cover and cook until potatoes are tender, 7 to 8 hours on low or 4 to 5 hours on high.
3.Season shrimp with salt and pepper and stir into the slow cooker. Cover and cook on high until shrimp are opaque throughout, 30 to 40 minutes. Strain shrimp boil and discard bay leaves. Serve warm.

Spanish Shrimp and Chorizo Braise

Prep time: 15 minutes | Cook time: 4 to 5 hours | Serves 4

12 ounces (340 g) chorizo sausage, halved lengthwise and sliced ¼ inch thick
1 onion, chopped fine
2 serrano chiles, stemmed and sliced thin
3 tablespoons tomato paste
3 garlic cloves, minced
1 tablespoon extra-virgin olive oil
1 (28-ounce / 794-g) can fire-roasted diced tomatoes, drained
½ cup mild lager, such as Budweiser
1 pound (454 g) extra-large shrimp (21 to 25 per pound), peeled, deveined, and tails removed
Salt and ground black pepper, to taste
2 tablespoons minced fresh cilantro
Lime wedges

1. Microwave chorizo, onion, serranos, tomato paste, garlic, and oil in a bowl, stirring occasionally, until onion is softened, about 5 minutes. Transfer to the slow cooker.
2. Stir in tomatoes and beer, cover, and cook until flavors meld, 7 to 8 hours on low or 4 to 5 hours on high.
3. Season shrimp with salt and pepper and stir into the slow cooker. Cover and cook on high until shrimp are opaque throughout, 30 to 40 minutes. Sprinkle with cilantro and serve with lime wedges.

Shrimp Polenta

Prep time: 15 minutes | Cook time: 2 to 3 hours | Serves 4

3 scallions, white parts minced, green parts sliced thin on bias
1 tablespoon unsalted butter
2 garlic cloves, minced
1 teaspoon minced canned chipotle chile in adobo sauce
½ teaspoon dry mustard
4 cups water
1 cup coarse-ground cornmeal
½ cup whole milk
Salt and ground black pepper, to taste
1 cup Cheddar cheese, shredded
1 pound (454 g) extra-large shrimp (21 to 25 per pound), peeled, deveined, and tails removed
Cooking spray

1. Spritz the slow cooker with cooking spray. Microwave scallion whites, butter, garlic, chipotle, and mustard in a bowl, stirring occasionally, until scallions are softened, about 2 minutes. Transfer to the prepared slow cooker.
2. Whisk in water, cornmeal, milk, and ¼ teaspoon salt. Cover and cook until polenta is tender, 3 to 4 hours on low or 2 to 3 hours on high.
3. Stir Cheddar into polenta until melted, and season with salt and pepper to taste. Season shrimp with pepper and nestle into polenta.
4. Cover and cook on high until shrimp are opaque throughout, 30 to 40 minutes. Sprinkle with scallion greens and serve.

Crab and Scallop Cioppino

Prep time: 15 minutes | Cook time: 6 hours | Serves 4

1 medium yellow onion, finely chopped
4 cloves garlic, minced
1 (15-ounce / 425-g) can diced tomatoes, with the juice
1 (10-ounce / 283-g) can diced tomatoes with green chiles
2 cups seafood stock
1 cup red wine
3 tablespoons chopped fresh basil
2 bay leaves
1 pound (454 g) cooked crabmeat, shredded
1½ pounds (680 g) scallops
Sea salt and black pepper, to taste
¼ cup fresh flat-leaf parsley, for garnish
Cooking spray

1. Spritz a large sauté pan with cooking spray and heat over medium-high heat. Add the onion and sauté for about 5 minutes, until softened.
2. Add the garlic and sauté until golden and fragrant, about 2 minutes.
3. Transfer the onion and garlic to the slow cooker, and add the tomatoes, tomatoes with green chiles, stock, wine, basil, and bay leaves. Cover and cook on low for 6 hours.
4. About 30 minutes before the cooking time is completed, add the crabmeat and scallops. Cover and cook on high for 30 minutes. The seafood will turn opaque. Season to taste with salt and pepper. Serve hot, garnished with parsley.

Mushroom and Tomato Mussels

Prep time: 15 minutes | Cook time: 2½ to 3½ hours | Serves 4

3 tablespoons olive oil
4 cloves garlic, minced
3 shallot cloves, minced
8 ounces (227 g) mushrooms, diced
1 (28-ounce / 794-g) can diced tomatoes, with the juice
¾ cup white wine
2 tablespoons dried oregano
½ tablespoon dried basil
½ teaspoon black pepper
1 teaspoon paprika
¼ teaspoon red pepper flakes
3 pounds (1.4 kg) mussels

1. In a large sauté pan, heat the olive oil over medium-high heat. Cook the garlic, shallots, and mushrooms for 2 to 3 minutes, until the garlic is brown and fragrant. Scrape the entire contents of the pan into the slow cooker.
2. Add the tomatoes and white wine to the slow cooker. Sprinkle with the oregano, basil, black pepper, paprika, and red pepper flakes.
3. Cover and cook on low for 4 to 5 hours, or on high for 2 to 3 hours. The mixture is done cooking when mushrooms are fork tender.
4. Clean and debeard the mussels. Discard any open mussels.
5. Increase the heat on the slow cooker to high once the mushroom mixture is done. Add the cleaned mussels to the slow cooker and secure the lid tightly. Cook for 30 more minutes.
6. To serve, ladle the mussels into bowls with plenty of broth. Discard any mussels that didn't open up during cooking. Serve hot, with crusty bread for sopping up the sauce.

Spanish Herbed Octopus

Prep time: 15 minutes | Cook time: 1¼ hours | Serves 6

2 pounds (907 g) octopus, cleaned
1 small fennel, trimmed, bulb and fronds coarsely chopped
2 small onions, thickly sliced
1 bunch fresh flat-leaf parsley
1 bunch fresh oregano
2 dried bay leaves
¼ cup plus 2 tablespoons extra-virgin olive oil
Coarse salt, to taste
2 garlic cloves, minced
¼ cup capers, drained, rinsed, and coarsely chopped
Juice of 2 lemons (about ⅓ cup)
¼ teaspoon hot smoked paprika
¼ teaspoon sweet smoked paprika

1. Bring a large stockpot of water to a boil. Add octopus and boil briefly to tenderize, about 2 minutes. Drain and let cool, then slice octopus into 2-inch pieces.
2. Place fennel, onions, parsley, oregano, and bay leaves in the slow cooker. Arrange octopus over vegetables. Drizzle with 1 tablespoon oil and ½ teaspoon salt. Cover and cook on low until octopus is tender, 2 hours, or on high for 1 hour.
3. Heat a grill or grill pan to high. Remove octopus and half the vegetables from the slow cooker (discard remaining vegetables and liquid). Toss with 1 tablespoon oil and grill until charred, about 6 minutes. Transfer to a bowl.
4. Meanwhile, gently heat remaining ¼ cup oil in a small skillet. Add garlic and cook until just fragrant, about 2 minutes. Stir in capers and lemon juice.
5. Remove from heat and stir in both paprikas. Pour over octopus, toss, season with salt, and serve.

Chapter 8 Soups, Stews, and Chilies

Chicken Noodle Soup

Prep time: 15 minutes | Cook time: 3½ to 4½ hours | Serves 8

1 pound (454 g) boneless, skinless chicken breasts, cubed
2 medium carrots, shredded
3 tablespoons sherry or reduced-sodium chicken broth
2 tablespoons rice vinegar
1 tablespoon reduced-sodium soy sauce
2 to 3 teaspoons minced fresh ginger
¼ teaspoon pepper
6 cups reduced-sodium chicken broth
1 cup water
2 cups fresh snow peas, halved
2 ounces (57 g) uncooked angel hair pasta, broken into thirds

1.In a slow cooker, combine the first seven ingredients. Stir in the broth and water. Cook, covered, on low for 3 to 4 hours or until chicken is tender.
2.Stir in the snow peas and pasta. Cook, covered, on low for 30 minutes longer or until snow peas and pasta are tender.
3.Serve warm.

Lemony Chicken and Rice Soup

Prep time: 15 minutes | Cook time: 4 to 5 hours | Serves 12

2 tablespoons olive oil, divided
2 pounds (907 g) boneless, skinless chicken breasts, cut into ½-inch pieces
5 (14½-ounce / 411-g) cans reduced-sodium chicken broth
8 cups coarsely chopped Swiss chard, kale or spinach
2 large carrots, finely chopped
1 small onion, chopped
1 medium lemon, halved and thinly sliced
¼ cup lemon juice
4 teaspoons grated lemon peel

½ teaspoon pepper
4 cups cooked brown rice

1.In a large skillet, heat 1 tablespoon of the oil over medium-high heat. Add half of the chicken. Cook and stir until browned, for 10 to 12 minutes. Transfer to a slow cooker. Repeat with the remaining oil and chicken.
2.Stir the broth, vegetables, lemon slices, lemon juice, peel and pepper into chicken. Cook, covered, on low for 4 to 5 hours or until chicken is tender. Stir in the rice and heat through.
3.Serve warm.

Spinach and Chicken Soup

Prep time: 20 minutes | Cook time: 4½ to 5½ hours | Serves 4

1 pound (454 g) boneless, skinless chicken thighs, cut into ½-inch pieces
1 (16-ounce / 454-g) can kidney beans, rinsed and drained
1 (14½-ounce / 411-g) can chicken broth
1 medium onion, chopped
1 medium sweet red pepper, chopped
1 celery rib, chopped
2 tablespoons tomato paste
3 garlic cloves, minced
½ teaspoon minced fresh rosemary or ¼ teaspoon crushed dried rosemary
½ teaspoon minced fresh thyme or ¼ teaspoon dried thyme
½ teaspoon dried oregano
¼ teaspoon salt
¼ teaspoon pepper
3 cups fresh baby spinach
¼ cup shredded Parmesan cheese

1.In a slow cooker, combine the first 13 ingredients. Cover and cook on low for 4 to 5 hours or until chicken is tender.
2.Stir in the spinach and cook for 30 minutes longer or until spinach is wilted.
3.Top with the cheese. Serve warm.

Mushroom and Chicken Soup

Prep time: 15 minutes | Cook time: 6 to 7 hours | Serves 8

3 tablespoons olive oil
2 leeks, chopped, using the white and some of the tender green parts
3 stalks celery with leaves, chopped
3 medium carrots, chopped
1 pound (454 g) cremini mushrooms, sliced
1 teaspoon dried thyme
1 bay leaf
1 cup pearl barley
6 cups chicken broth
¼ cup dried porcini mushrooms
¼ cup dry sherry
2 cups bite-size pieces cooked chicken

1.Heat the oil in a large skillet over medium-high heat. Add the leeks, celery, carrots, cremini mushrooms, thyme, and bay leaf and sauté until the vegetables are softened, for about 3 minutes.
2.Transfer the contents of the skillet to the insert of a slow cooker and stir in the barley, broth, dried mushrooms, sherry, and chicken.
3.Cover the slow cooker and cook on low for 6 to 7 hours, until the barley is tender.
4.Remove the bay leaf before serving.

Veggie-Chicken Soup

Prep time: 15 minutes | Cook time: 3 hours | Serves 8

¼ cup vegetable oil
1 medium onion, coarsely chopped
2 stalks celery, coarsely chopped
4 medium carrots, coarsely chopped
1 large Granny Smith apple, peeled, cored, and coarsely chopped
1 teaspoon sweet curry powder
2 tablespoons all-purpose flour
8 cups chicken broth
2 tablespoons honey
2 cups shredded cooked chicken or turkey
2 cups diced small new potatoes or Yukon gold potatoes
Salt and freshly ground black pepper, to taste
1 cup toasted sliced almonds, for garnish

1.Heat the oil in a large skillet over medium-high heat. Add the onion, celery, carrots, apple, curry powder, and flour. Sauté until the vegetables are softened, for 5 to 7 minutes.
2.Transfer the mixture to the insert of a slow cooker. Stir in the chicken broth, honey, chicken, and potatoes, stirring to distribute the ingredients.
3.Cover the slow cooker and cook on high for 3 hours or on low for 5½ to 6 hours. Season with salt and pepper.
4.Serve the soup garnished with the toasted almonds.

Lush Seafood Cioppino

Prep time: 20 minutes | Cook time: 4½ to 5½ hours | Serves 8

1 (28-ounce / 794-g) can diced tomatoes, undrained
2 medium onions, chopped
3 celery ribs, chopped
1 (8-ounce / 227-g) bottle clam juice
1 (6-ounce / 170-g) can tomato paste
½ cup white wine or vegetable broth
5 garlic cloves, minced
1 tablespoon red wine vinegar
1 tablespoon olive oil
1 to 2 teaspoons Italian seasoning
½ teaspoon sugar
1 bay leaf
1 pound (454 g) haddock fillets, cut into 1-inch pieces
1 pound (454 g) uncooked small shrimp, peeled and deveined
1 (6-ounce / 170-g) can lump crab meat, drained
1 (6-ounce / 170-g) can chopped clams
2 tablespoons minced fresh parsley or 2 teaspoons dried parsley flakes

1.In a slow cooker, combine the first 12 ingredients. Cover and cook on low for 4 to 5 hours.
2.Stir in the haddock, shrimp, crab meat and clams. Cover and cook for 30 minutes longer or until fish flakes easily with a fork and shrimp turn pink.
3.Stir in the parsley. Discard the bay leaf. Serve warm.

Lima Bean and Chicken Soup

Prep time: 20 minutes | Cook time: 6 to 8 hours | Serves 6

4 bone-in chicken thighs (1½ pounds / 680 g), skin removed
2 cups frozen lima beans, thawed
2 cups frozen corn, thawed
1 large green pepper, chopped
1 large onion, chopped
2 (14-ounce / 397-g) cans fire-roasted diced tomatoes, undrained
¼ cup tomato paste
3 tablespoons Worcestershire sauce
3 garlic cloves, minced
1½ teaspoons ground cumin
1½ teaspoons dried oregano
¼ teaspoon salt
¼ teaspoon pepper
Chopped fresh cilantro or parsley, for garnish

1. Place the first five ingredients in a slow cooker. In a large bowl, combine the tomatoes, tomato paste, Worcestershire sauce, garlic and dry seasonings. Pour over top.
2. Cook, covered, on low for 6 to 8 hours or until chicken is tender. Remove the chicken from the slow cooker. When cool enough to handle, remove meat from bones and discard bones. Shred the meat with two forks. Return to the slow cooker and heat through. Sprinkle with cilantro and serve.

Spicy Hominy and Chicken Soup

Prep time: 15 minutes | Cook time: 4 to 5 hours | Serves 4

1 pound (454 g) boneless, skinless chicken breasts, cubed
2 tablespoons olive oil
1 medium onion, chopped
3 garlic cloves, minced
2 chipotle peppers in adobo sauce
2 (14½-ounce / 411-g) cans chicken broth, divided
1 (15-ounce / 425-g) can hominy, rinsed and drained

1 (4-ounce / 113-g) can chopped green chilies
1 teaspoon dried oregano
1 teaspoon ground cumin
¼ teaspoon pepper

1. In a large skillet, brown the chicken in the oil for 10 to 12 minutes. With a slotted spoon, transfer the chicken to a slow cooker. In the same skillet, sauté the onion and garlic in drippings for 4 minutes, until tender. Add to the chicken.
2. Place chipotle peppers and ¼ cup of the broth in a blender or food processor. Cover and process until blended. Add to the chicken mixture. Stir in the hominy, chilies, seasonings and the remaining broth. Cover and cook on low for 4 to 5 hours or until chicken is tender.
3. Serve warm.

Cheesy Sausage-Veggie Soup

Prep time: 20 minutes | Cook time: 9½ to 10½ hours | Serves 15

1 pound (454 g) bulk pork sausage
4 cups water
1 (10¾-ounce / 305-g) can condensed cream of mushroom soup, undiluted
1 (10¾-ounce / 305-g) can condensed Cheddar cheese soup, undiluted
5 medium red potatoes, cubed
4 cups chopped cabbage
3 large carrots, thinly sliced
4 celery ribs, chopped
1 medium zucchini, chopped
1 large onion, chopped
5 chicken bouillon cubes
1 tablespoon dried parsley flakes
¾ teaspoon pepper
1 (12-ounce / 340-g) can evaporated milk

1. In a large skillet, cook the sausage over medium heat for 8 minutes, or until no longer pink. Drain. Transfer to a slow cooker. Stir in the water and soups until blended. Add the vegetables, bouillon, parsley and pepper.
2. Cover and cook on low for 9 to 10 hours or until vegetables are tender. Stir in the milk. Cover and cook for 30 minutes longer.
3. Serve warm.

Creamy Chicken Tortilla Soup

Prep time: 25 minutes | Cook time: 5 to 6 hours | Serves 4 to 5

1 (28-ounce / 794-g) can diced tomatoes, with their juice
1 (10-ounce / 284-g) can red or green enchilada sauce
2 medium-size yellow or white onions, chopped
1 (4-ounce / 113-g) can chopped green chiles, drained
1 clove garlic, minced
3 tablespoons chopped fresh cilantro
2 cups water
1 (14½-ounce / 411-g) can chicken or vegetable broth
1 teaspoon ground cumin
1 teaspoon chili powder
½ teaspoon salt
Pinch of black pepper
1 bay leaf
¾ teaspoon dried oregano
1½ pounds (680 g) boneless, skinless chicken breasts, cooked through in gently simmering water, drained, and shredded
1 (10-ounce / 284-g) can Mexican corn, drained
8 yellow or white soft corn tortillas
3 tablespoons light olive oil
For Serving:
Finely shredded sharp Cheddar cheese
Sour cream, thinned with a few tablespoons milk, or crema Mexicana
Sliced avocado
Fresh cilantro sprigs

1. Combine the tomatoes, enchilada sauce, onions, chiles, garlic, cilantro, water, broth, cumin, chili powder, salt, pepper, bay leaf, and oregano in a slow cooker. Cover and cook on low for 5 to 6 hours or on high for 2 to 2 ½ hours.
2. Add the shredded chicken and corn. Cover and continue to cook on low for another hour. Discard the bay leaf.
3. Meanwhile, preheat the oven to 400°F (205°C). Lightly brush both sides of each tortilla with some of the oil. With a knife, cut the tortillas into 2½ × 1-inch strips. Spread out the tortilla strips on a parchment paper-lined baking sheet. Bake

until crisp but not browned, turning once halfway through baking, for 8 to 12 minutes.
4. To serve, ladle the soup into bowls. Sprinkle each serving with tortilla strips and grated cheese. Top with a tablespoon of sour cream or crema Mexicana, then with a few slices of avocado and cilantro sprigs. Serve immediately.

Beef and Parsnip Soup

Prep time: 15 minutes | Cook time: 4 to 5 hours | Serves 8

2 tablespoons olive oil
¼ cup all-purpose flour
Salt and freshly ground black pepper, to taste
2 pounds (907 g) beef chuck or short ribs, fat trimmed and cut into 1-inch pieces
2 medium onions, coarsely chopped
3 cloves garlic, sliced
1 teaspoon dried thyme
1 (12-ounce / 340-g) bottle dark ale
3 cups beef broth
4 cups baby carrots
4 medium parsnips, cut into 1-inch lengths
2 cups red, Yukon gold, or new white potatoes

1. Heat the oil in a large skillet over high heat. Combine the flour, 1½ teaspoons salt and ½ teaspoon pepper in a zipper top plastic bag. Toss the meat in the flour, a few pieces at a time.
2. Add the meat, a few pieces at a time, to the oil and brown on all sides for 4 minutes. Transfer the browned meat to the insert of a slow cooker.
3. When all the beef is browned, add the onions, garlic, and thyme to the same skillet over medium-high heat and sauté for 3 minutes, or until the onions begin to soften and become translucent. Add the ale to the pan and scrape up any browned bits from the bottom of the pan.
4. Transfer the contents of the skillet to the slow cooker insert and add the broth, carrots, parsnips, and potatoes. Cover the slow cooker and cook on high for 4 to 5 hours or on low for 8 to 10 hours, until the vegetables are tender and the beef is fork tender.
5. Season with salt and pepper before serving.

Creamy Butternut Squash Soup

Prep time: 10 minutes | Cook time: 6⅓ to 8⅓ hours | Serves 14

1 medium onion, chopped
2 tablespoons butter
1 medium butternut squash (about 4 pounds / 1.8 kg), peeled and cubed
3 (14½-ounce / 411-g) cans vegetable broth
1 tablespoon brown sugar
1 tablespoon minced fresh ginger
1 garlic clove, minced
1 cinnamon stick (3 inches)
1 (8-ounce / 227-g) package cream cheese, softened and cubed

1. In a small skillet, sauté the onion in the butter for 5 minutes, or until tender. Transfer to a slow cooker and add the squash. Combine the broth, brown sugar, ginger, garlic and cinnamon and pour over the squash. Cover and cook on low for 6 to 8 hours or until squash is tender.
2. Cool slightly. Discard the cinnamon stick. In a blender, process soup in batches until smooth. Return all to the slow cooker. Whisk in the cream cheese. Cover and cook for 15 minutes longer or until cheese is melted.
3. Serve warm.

Creamy Beef and Potato Soup

Prep time: 15 minutes | Cook time: 6½ to 8½ hours | Serves 10

1½ pounds (680 g) lean ground beef (90% lean)
¾ cup chopped onion
½ cup all-purpose flour
2 (14½-ounce / 411-g) cans reduced-sodium chicken broth, divided
5 medium potatoes, peeled and cubed
5 medium carrots, chopped
3 celery ribs, chopped
3 teaspoons dried basil
2 teaspoons dried parsley flakes
1 teaspoon garlic powder
½ teaspoon pepper
12 ounces (340 g) reduced-fat process cheese, cubed
1½ cups 2% milk
½ cup reduced-fat sour cream

1. In a large skillet, cook the beef and onion over medium heat for 4 minutes, or until meat is no longer pink. Drain. Combine the flour and 1 can broth until smooth. Add to the beef mixture. Bring to a boil. Cook and stir for 2 minutes or until thickened.
2. Transfer to a slow cooker. Stir in the potatoes, carrots, celery, seasonings and the remaining broth. Cover and cook on low for 6 to 8 hours or until vegetables are tender.
3. Stir in the cheese and milk. Cover and cook for 30 minutes longer or until cheese is melted. Just before serving, stir in the sour cream. Serve warm.

Vegetable Beef Soup

Prep time: 15 minutes | Cook time: 5¾ to 6¾ hours | Serves 6 to 8

1½ pounds (680 g) beef sirloin, cut into ½-inch pieces
1½ teaspoons salt
½ teaspoon freshly ground black pepper
2 tablespoons vegetable oil
1 medium onion, finely chopped
3 medium carrots, finely chopped
1 (15-ounce / 425-g) can tomato sauce
3 cups beef broth
2 cups chicken broth
4 ounces (113 g) green beans, ends snipped, cut into 1-inch lengths
2 cups frozen petite peas, thawed
2 cups frozen corn, thawed
2 cups cooked alphabet noodles or other small pasta shapes

1. Sprinkle the beef with the salt and pepper. Heat the oil in a large skillet over high heat. Add the beef a few pieces at a time and brown on all sides for 4 minutes.
2. Transfer the browned beef to the insert of a slow cooker. Add the onion and carrots to the same skillet and sauté until the onion is softened, for about 3 minutes.
3. Transfer the contents of the skillet to the slow cooker insert and add the tomato sauce, beef broth, chicken broth, and green beans. Cover and cook on low for 5 to 6 hours. Remove the cover and add the peas, corn, and noodles.
4. Cover and cook for an additional 45 minutes before serving.

Bean and Spinach Rice Soup

Prep time: 10 minutes | Cook time: 6¼ to 7¼ hours | Serves 8

3 (14½-ounce / 411-g) cans vegetable broth
1 (15½-ounce / 439-g) can great northern beans, rinsed and drained
1 (15-ounce / 425-g) can tomato purée
½ cup finely chopped onion
½ cup uncooked converted long grain rice
2 garlic cloves, minced
1 teaspoon dried basil
½ teaspoon salt
¼ teaspoon pepper
1 (6-ounce / 170-g) package fresh baby spinach, coarsely chopped
¼ cup shredded Parmesan cheese

1. In a slow cooker, combine the first nine ingredients. Cover and cook on low for 6 to 7 hours or until heated through.
2. Stir in the spinach. Cover and cook for 15 minutes or until spinach is wilted. Sprinkle with the cheese and serve.

Onion Meatball Soup

Prep time: 15 minutes | Cook time: 8 to 10 hours | Serves 6

1 (12-ounce / 340-g) package frozen fully cooked Italian meatballs, thawed
2 large sweet onions, sliced
2 garlic cloves, minced
1 teaspoon beef bouillon granules
½ teaspoon dried thyme
¼ teaspoon salt
¼ teaspoon pepper
5 cups beef broth
1 (12-ounce / 340-g) bottle pale ale or additional beef broth
18 slices French bread baguette, ¼ inch thick
12 slices Muenster or Cheddar cheese

1. In a slow cooker, combine the first nine ingredients. Cook, covered, on low for 8 to 10 hours or until the onions are tender.
2. Ladle the soup into six broiler-safe ramekins. Top each with three slices of bread and two slices of cheese. Broil for 2 to 3 minutes or until the cheese is melted. Serve the soup immediately.

Braised Potato and Ham Soup

Prep time: 10 minutes | Cook time: 6¼ to 8⅓ hours | Serves 8

1 (32-ounce / 907-g) carton chicken broth
1 (30-ounce / 850-g) package frozen shredded hash brown potatoes, thawed
1 small onion, finely chopped
¼ teaspoon pepper
4 ounces (113 g) cream cheese, softened and cubed
1 cup cubed deli ham
1 (5-ounce / 142-g) can evaporated milk
Sour cream and chopped green onions, for serving (optional)

1. In a slow cooker, combine the broth, potatoes, onion and pepper. Cook, covered, on low for 6 to 8 hours or until vegetables are tender.
2. Mash the potatoes to desired consistency. Whisk in the cream cheese until melted. Stir in the ham and milk. Cook, covered, on low for 15 to 20 minutes longer or until heated through. Serve with the sour cream and green onions, if desired.

Pepperoni Mushroom Soup

Prep time: 10 minutes | Cook time: 8¼ to 9½ hours | Serves 6

2 (14½-ounce / 411-g) cans Italian stewed tomatoes, undrained
2 (14½-ounce / 411-g) cans reduced-sodium beef broth
1 small onion, chopped
1 small green pepper, chopped
½ cup sliced fresh mushrooms
½ cup sliced pepperoni, halved
1½ teaspoons dried oregano
⅛ teaspoon pepper
1 (9-ounce / 255-g) package refrigerated cheese ravioli
Toppings:
Shredded part-skim Mozzarella cheese
Sliced ripe olives

1. In a slow cooker, combine the first eight ingredients. Cook, covered, on low for 8 to 9 hours.
2. Stir in the ravioli. Cook, covered, on low for 15 to 30 minutes or until the pasta is tender. Serve topped with the cheese and olives.

Braised Turkey Bean Soup

Prep time: 10 minutes | Cook time: 5 to 6 hours | Serves 4

2 (15-ounce / 425-g) cans white kidney or cannellini beans, rinsed and drained
2 cups cubed cooked turkey
1 (14½-ounce / 411-g) can chicken broth
1 (10-ounce / 284-g) can diced tomatoes and green chilies, undrained
1 cup salsa
½ teaspoon ground cumin
¼ teaspoon curry powder
¼ teaspoon ground ginger
¼ teaspoon paprika

1.In a slow cooker, combine all the ingredients. Cover and cook on low for 5 to 6 hours or until heated through.
2.Serve warm.

Pork Veggie Soup

Prep time: 20 minutes | Cook time: 7 to 8 hours | Serves 6

1 pork tenderloin (1 pound / 454 g), cut into 1-inch pieces
1 teaspoon garlic powder
2 teaspoons canola oil
1 (28-ounce / 794-g) can diced tomatoes
4 medium carrots, cut into ½-inch pieces
2 medium potatoes, cubed
1 (12-ounce / 340-g) can light or nonalcoholic beer
¼ cup quick-cooking tapioca
2 bay leaves
1 tablespoon Worcestershire sauce
1 tablespoon honey
1 teaspoon dried thyme
¼ teaspoon salt
¼ teaspoon pepper
⅛ teaspoon ground nutmeg

1.Sprinkle the pork with the garlic powder. In a large skillet, brown the pork in the oil for 4 minutes. Drain.
2.Transfer to a slow cooker. Add the remaining ingredients. Cover and cook on low for 7 to 8 hours or until meat is tender.
3.Discard the bay leaves. Serve warm.

Hearty Split Pea and Bacon Soup

Prep time: 15 minutes | Cook time: 7 to 8 hours | Serves 6

1 large onion, chopped
1 cup chopped celery
1 cup chopped fresh carrots
2 tablespoons olive oil
1 teaspoon dried thyme
1 (16-ounce / 454-g) package dried green split peas, rinsed
4 cups vegetable broth
2 cups water
6 ounces (170 g) Canadian bacon, chopped
¼ teaspoon pepper

1.In a large skillet, sauté the onion, celery and carrots in the oil for 5 minutes, or until tender. Add the thyme and cook for 1 minute longer.
2.Transfer to a slow cooker. Add the peas, broth and water. Cover and cook on low for 7 to 8 hours or until peas are tender.
3.Cool slightly. In a blender, process half of the soup until smooth. Return all to the slow cooker. Add the bacon and pepper and heat through.
4.Serve warm.

Classic Mulligatawny Soup

Prep time: 20 minutes | Cook time: 6 to 8 hours | Serves 8

1 (32-ounce / 907-g) carton chicken broth
1 (14½-ounce / 411-g) can diced tomatoes
2 cups cubed cooked chicken
1 large tart apple, peeled and chopped
¼ cup finely chopped onion
¼ cup chopped carrot
¼ cup chopped green pepper
1 tablespoon minced fresh parsley
2 teaspoons lemon juice
1 teaspoon salt
1 teaspoon curry powder
½ teaspoon sugar
¼ teaspoon pepper
2 whole cloves

1.In a slow cooker, combine all the ingredients. Cover and cook on low for 6 to 8 hours or until vegetables are tender.
2.Discard the cloves. Serve warm.

Creamy Sausage Cabbage Soup

Prep time: 10 minutes | Cook time: 5¼ to 6¼ hours | Serves 8

4 cups low-fat, low-sodium chicken broth
1 medium head of cabbage, chopped
2 medium onions, chopped
½ pound (227 g) fully cooked smoked turkey sausage, halved lengthwise and sliced
½ cup all-purpose flour
¼ teaspoon black pepper
1 cup skim milk

1.Combine the chicken broth, cabbage, onions, and sausage in a slow cooker.
2.Cover. Cook on high for 5 to 6 hours, or until the cabbage is tender.
3.Mix the flour and black pepper in a bowl. Gradually add the milk, stirring until smooth.
4.Gradually stir the milk mixture into the hot soup.
5.Cook, stirring occasionally for about 15 minutes, until soup is thickened. Serve.

Turkey Chili with Beans

Prep time: 25 minutes | Cook time: 7⅓ to 9½ hours | Serves 8

2 tablespoons olive oil
1½ pounds (680 g) ground turkey
1 medium onion, chopped
2 tablespoons ground ancho chili pepper
1 tablespoon chili powder
1½ teaspoons salt
1½ teaspoons ground cumin
1½ teaspoons paprika
2 (14½-ounce / 411-g) cans fire-roasted diced tomatoes, undrained
1 medium sweet yellow pepper, chopped
1 medium sweet red pepper, chopped
1 (4-ounce / 113-g) can chopped green chilies
1 garlic clove, minced
1 cup brewed coffee
¾ cup dry red wine or chicken broth
1 (16-ounce / 454-g) can kidney beans, rinsed and drained
1 (15-ounce / 425-g) can white kidney or cannellini beans, rinsed and drained
Sliced avocado, for topping

Chopped green onions, for topping

1.In a large skillet, heat the oil over medium heat. Add the turkey and onion. Cook for 8 to 10 minutes or until meat is no longer pink, breaking up turkey into crumbles.
2.Transfer to a slow cooker and stir in the seasonings. Add the tomatoes, sweet peppers, chilies and garlic. Stir in the coffee and wine.
3.Cook, covered, on low for 7 to 9 hours. Stir in the beans and cook for 15 to 20 minutes longer or until heated through. Serve topped with the avocado and green onions.

Red Pepper and Lentil Soup

Prep time: 10 minutes | Cook time: 7 to 9 hours | Serves 4 to 6

2 tablespoons extra-virgin olive oil, divided
1 small onion, finely chopped
4 to 6 cloves garlic, finely chopped
1 teaspoon sweet paprika or smoked paprika
1 large or 2 medium-size red bell peppers, deseeded and finely chopped
1 cup dried brown lentils, picked over and rinsed
5 cups water
2 teaspoons salt
½ teaspoon freshly ground black pepper
1 to 2 tablespoons sherry vinegar or red or white wine vinegar

1.In a medium-size skillet, heat 1 tablespoon of the oil over medium heat. Add the onion and garlic and cook, stirring a few times, until they begin to soften, for about 3 minutes. Reduce the heat if they begin to brown.
2.Stir in the paprika and allow it to cook for about a minute more. Add the bell pepper and cook for 2 to 3 minutes, stirring a few times, until it just begins to soften. Use a heat-resistant rubber spatula to scrape the vegetables and oil into a slow cooker. Add the lentils and water and stir to combine. Cover and cook on low until the lentils are completely soft, for 7 to 9 hours.
3.Season the soup with the salt and pepper and the remaining 1 tablespoon of olive oil. Stir in 1 tablespoon of the vinegar, adding more if needed. Serve hot ladled into soup bowls.

Classic Gyro Soup

Prep time: 10 minutes | Cook time: 6 to 8 hours | Serves 6

2 pounds (907 g) ground lamb
2 tablespoons extra-virgin olive oil
5 cups water
1 (14½-ounce / 411-g) can diced tomatoes, undrained
1 medium onion, chopped
¼ cup red wine
3 tablespoons minced fresh mint or 1 tablespoon dried mint
6 garlic cloves, minced
1 tablespoon dried marjoram
1 tablespoon crushed dried rosemary
2 teaspoons salt
½ teaspoon pepper

Optional Toppings:
Plain Greek yogurt
Crumbled feta cheese

1. In a large skillet, cook the lamb in the oil for 4 minutes, or until no longer pink. Drain. Transfer to a slow cooker. Add the water, tomatoes, onion, wine, mint, garlic, marjoram, rosemary, salt and pepper. Cover and cook on low for 6 to 8 hours or until flavors are blended.
2. Serve with the yogurt and feta cheese, if desired.

Mushroom Tofu Soup

Prep time: 10 minutes | Cook time: 2½ to 3 hours | Serves 6 to 8

2 tablespoons vegetable oil
1 clove garlic, minced
1 teaspoon freshly grated ginger
8 ounces (227 g) shiitake mushrooms, stems removed, caps sliced
4 small baby bok choy, stem ends removed and chopped into ½-inch pieces
¼ cup light miso paste
6 cups vegetable or chicken broth
2 teaspoons soy sauce
6 green onions, white and tender green parts only, finely chopped
1 pound (454 g) firm tofu, drained and cut into

½-inch cubes

1. Heat the oil in a medium skillet over medium-high heat.
2. Add the garlic and ginger and sauté for about 1 minute until fragrant. Add the mushrooms and toss to combine.
3. Transfer the contents of the skillet to the insert of a slow cooker and add the bok choy. Stir in the miso paste, broth, and soy sauce.
4. Cover the slow cooker and cook on high for 2½ to 3 hours.
5. Remove the cover and stir in the green onions and tofu.
6. Serve the soup from the slow cooker.

Kale and White Bean Soup

Prep time: 20 minutes | Cook time: 5½ to 7½ hours | Serves 4 to 6

3 (14-ounce / 397-g) cans vegetable broth
1 (15-ounce / 425-g) can tomato purée
1 (15-ounce / 425-g) can white, cannellini, or great northern beans, rinsed and drained
½ cup converted rice
1 medium-size yellow onion, chopped
2 cloves garlic, minced
2 teaspoons dried basil
Salt and freshly ground black pepper, to taste
1 pound (454 g) kale, stems removed and leaves coarsely cut on the diagonal into wide ribbons and coarsely chopped
1 pound (454 g) sweet Italian sausage, cooked, cooled, and thickly sliced (optional)
For Serving:
Finely shredded Parmesan cheese
Extra-virgin olive oil

1. Combine the broth, tomato purée, beans, rice, onion, garlic, and basil in a slow cooker. Season with salt and pepper, and stir to blend. Cover and cook on low for 5 to 7 hours.
2. Stir in the kale and sausage (if using), cover, and continue to cook on low for another 20 to 30 minutes, or until the kale is limp and tender.
3. Ladle the soup into bowls and serve hot with the Parmesan cheese and a drizzle of olive oil.

Spiced Veggie and Chicken Stew

Prep time: 15 minutes | Cook time: 8 to 10 hours | Serves 5

1 pound (454 g) boneless, skinless chicken breasts, cubed
1 (14½-ounce / 411-g) can low-sodium Italian diced tomatoes, undrained
2 potatoes, peeled and cubed
5 carrots, chopped
3 celery ribs, chopped
1 onion, chopped
2 (4-ounce / 113-g) cans mushroom stems and pieces, drained
3 chicken bouillon cubes
2 teaspoons sugar
½ teaspoon dried basil
½ teaspoon dill weed
1 teaspoon chili powder
¼ teaspoon black pepper
1 tablespoon cornstarch
1 cup water

1. Combine all the ingredients, except for the cornstarch and water, in a slow cooker.
2. Combine the water and cornstarch in a bowl. Stir into the slow cooker.
3. Cover. Cook on low for 8 to 10 hours until the vegetables are tender.
4. Serve warm.

Simple Oyster Stew

Prep time: 5 minutes | Cook time: 2 hours | Serves 4

1 pint oysters, with liquor
¼ cup butter
1 pint milk
1 pint half-and-half
Salt and pepper, to taste

1. In a large nonstick skillet, heat the oysters slowly in their own juice until edges begin to curl (do not boil).
2. Place the oysters and their liquor in a slow cooker.
3. Add the butter, milk, and half-and-half. Season with salt and pepper.
4. Cook on low for about 2 hours, or until heated through.
5. Serve hot.

Spanish Beef and Rice Soup

Prep time: 10 minutes | Cook time: 4 to 5 hours | Serves 8

1 pound (454 g) lean ground beef (90% lean)
1 medium onion, chopped
3 cups water
1 (16-ounce / 454-g) jar salsa
1 (14½-ounce / 411-g) can diced tomatoes, undrained
1 (7-ounce / 198-g) jar roasted sweet red peppers, drained and chopped
1 (4-ounce / 113-g) can chopped green chilies
1 envelope taco seasoning
1 tablespoon dried cilantro flakes
½ cup uncooked converted rice

1. In a large skillet, cook the beef and onion over medium heat for 4 minutes, or until meat is no longer pink. Drain.
2. Transfer to a slow cooker. Add the water, salsa, tomatoes, red peppers, chilies, taco seasoning and cilantro. Stir in the rice. Cover and cook on low for 4 to 5 hours or until rice is tender.
3. Serve warm.

Leek and Potato Soup

Prep time: 10 minutes | Cook time: 5 to 7 hours | Serves 6

4 medium-size leeks (white part only), washed well and thinly sliced
4 medium-size to large russet potatoes, peeled and diced
4 to 6 cups water or vegetable or chicken broth
Salt, to taste
2 tablespoons unsalted butter
French bread, for serving

1. Put the leeks and potatoes in a slow cooker. Add enough of the water or broth to just cover them. Cover and cook on low, until the potatoes are tender, for 5 to 7 hours.
2. Purée the soup with a handheld immersion blender or transfer to a food processor or blender and purée in batches. Add the salt and butter, swirling until it is melted. Ladle the hot soup into bowls and serve immediately with French bread.

Sausage and Kale Soup

Prep time: 10 minutes | Cook time: 5 to 6 hours | Serves 8

2 tablespoons olive oil
1 pound (454 g) smoked linguiça, chorizo, or andouille sausage, cut into ½-inch rounds
2 medium onions, finely chopped
4 medium carrots, finely chopped
1 pound (454 g) kale, chopped into 1-inch pieces
5 medium red potatoes, peeled (or unpeeled) and cut into ½-inch pieces
6 cups chicken broth
2 bay leaves
¼ cup finely chopped fresh cilantro

1.Heat the oil in a large skillet over high heat. Add the sausage, onions, and carrots and sauté for 4 minutes, or until the onions are translucent.
2.Transfer the contents of the skillet to the insert of a slow cooker. Add the kale, potatoes, broth, and bay leaves to the cooker and stir to combine. Cover and cook on low for 5 to 6 hours, until the potatoes are tender.
3.Remove the bay leaves and stir in the cilantro before serving.

Creamy Onion and Tomato Soup

Prep time: 10 minutes | Cook time: 5 to 6 hours | Serves 4

½ cup unsalted butter
1 large or 2 medium-size yellow onions, chopped
1 (28-ounce / 794-g) can imported Italian whole or chopped plum tomatoes, with their juice
½ cup dry vermouth or dry white wine
1 tablespoon sugar
1 heaping teaspoon dried tarragon
Sea salt, to taste
Cold sour cream, for serving

1.In a large skillet over medium heat, melt the butter. Add the onion and cook until golden, for about 15 minutes, stirring often to cook evenly.
2.Combine the tomatoes, vermouth, sugar, and tarragon in a slow cooker. Add the onion and butter, scraping out the pan. Cover and cook on low for 5 to 6 hours.
3.Purée in batches in a food processor or with a handheld immersion blender. Season with salt. Ladle the hot soup into bowls and top with a spoonful of cold sour cream.

Ham and Vegetable Soup

Prep time: 10 minutes | Cook time: 9 to 10 hours | Serves 12

4 medium carrots, thinly sliced
2 celery ribs, chopped
1 medium onion, chopped
2 cups fully cooked ham cubes, trimmed of fat
1½ cups dried navy beans
1 (68-ounce / 1.9-kg) package dry vegetable soup mix
1 envelope dry onion soup mix
1 bay leaf
½ teaspoon black pepper
8 cups water
1 teaspoon salt (optional)

1.Combine all the ingredients in a slow cooker.
2.Cover. Cook on low for 9 to 10 hours.
3.Discard the bay leaf before serving.

Authentic Zuppa Bastarda

Prep time: 10 minutes | Cook time: 7 to 9 hours | Serves 8

1 pound (454 g) dried borlotti beans, picked over, soaked overnight in cold water to cover, and drained
1 large white onion, coarsely chopped
3 cloves garlic, minced
2 tablespoons finely chopped fresh sage, plus a few whole leaves
Salt and freshly ground black pepper, to taste
8 thin slices stale or toasted chewy whole grain country bread
For Serving:
Extra-virgin olive oil
Shredded or shaved Parmesan or Asiago cheese

1.Put the drained beans in a slow cooker and add the water to cover by 4 inches. Add the onion and garlic. Cover and cook on low for 5 to 7 hours.
2.Stir in the sage, cover, and continue to cook on low for another 2 hours, until the beans are tender.
3.Season with salt and pepper. The soup will be very thick. Place a toasted slice of bread in each of 8 shallow soup bowls and drizzle liberally with the olive oil. Ladle the soup over the bread, sprinkle with the Parmesan cheese. Serve hot.

Tangy Carrot Bisque

Prep time: 10 minutes | Cook time: 8 hours | Serves 2

½ cup diced onion
¼ cup diced celery
1 tablespoon minced ginger
2 cups low-sodium chicken broth
2 cups diced carrots
1 white potato, peeled and diced
1 teaspoon curry powder
⅛ teaspoon sea salt
1 tablespoon freshly squeezed lime juice
2 tablespoons heavy cream (optional)
¼ cup roughly chopped fresh cilantro

1.Put the onion, celery, ginger, broth, carrots, potato, curry powder, and salt in a slow cooker and stir to combine. Cover and cook on low for 8 hours.
2.Add the lime juice to the slow cooker and purée the bisque with an immersion blender.
3.Swirl in the heavy cream (if using) just before serving. Garnish each bowl with the cilantro and serve.

Fennel and Leek Soup

Prep time: 10 minutes | Cook time: 8 hours | Serves 2

1 teaspoon freshly ground fennel seed
1 fennel bulb, cored and chopped
1 leek, white and pale green parts only, sliced thin
1 white potato, peeled and diced
⅛ teaspoon sea salt
2 cups low-sodium chicken broth
1 teaspoon white wine vinegar or lemon juice
2 tablespoons heavy cream
1 sprig fresh tarragon, roughly chopped (optional)

1.Put the fennel seed, fennel bulb, leek, potato, salt, and broth in a slow cooker and stir to combine. Cover and cook on low for 8 hours.
2.Just before serving, add the vinegar to the crock and then purée the soup with an immersion blender. Stir in the heavy cream.
3.Serve garnished with fresh tarragon (if using).

Curried Vegetable Soup

Prep time: 10 minutes | Cook time: 6 to 8 hours | Serves 2

1 small eggplant, cut into 1-inch cubes
1 teaspoon sea salt
1 cup quartered button mushrooms
1 onion, halved and sliced into thick half-circles
1 red bell pepper, cut into long strips
1 cup coconut milk
2 cups low-sodium chicken broth
1 tablespoon Thai red curry paste
1 tablespoon freshly squeezed lime juice
¼ cup fresh cilantro, for garnish

1.Put the eggplant in a colander over the sink. Sprinkle it with the salt and allow it to rest for 10 minutes, or up to 30 minutes.
2.Put the mushrooms, onion, red bell pepper, coconut milk, broth, and red curry paste into a slow cooker.
3.Rinse the eggplant in the colander and gently press to squeeze out any excess moisture from each cube. Add the eggplant to the slow cooker. Stir the ingredients to combine.
4.Cover and cook on low for 6 to 8 hours.
5.Just before serving, stir in the lime juice and garnish each serving with the cilantro.

Creamy Butternut Squash Soup

Prep time: 10 minutes | Cook time: 8 hours | Serves 2

2 cups peeled, diced butternut squash
1 cup peeled, diced parsnip
1 Granny Smith apple, cored, peeled, and diced
½ cup diced onion
⅛ teaspoon sea salt
2 cups low-sodium vegetable broth
1 sprig fresh thyme
1 tablespoon heavy cream

1.Put the butternut squash, parsnip, apple, onion, salt, vegetable broth, and thyme into a slow cooker and stir to combine.
2.Cover and cook on low for 8 hours. Remove the thyme sprig and stir in the heavy cream.
3.Use an immersion blender to purée the soup until smooth.

Chickpea and Lentil Stew

Prep time: 10 minutes | Cook time: 6 to 8 hours | Serves 2

½ cup canned chickpeas, drained and rinsed
½ cup canned white beans, drained and rinsed
½ cup lentils, rinsed and sorted
½ cup white rice
½ cup diced carrots
½ cup diced red bell pepper
¼ cup parsley
1 ounce (28 g) pancetta, diced
2 cups low-sodium vegetable broth
⅛ teaspoon sea salt

1.Put all the ingredients into a slow cooker and stir to mix thoroughly.
2.Cover and cook on low for 6 to 8 hours.
3.Serve hot.

Mushroom Chicken Stew

Prep time: 15 minutes | Cook time: 4¼ hours | Serves 6

6 boneless, skinless chicken breast halves (about 1½ pounds / 680 g), cut in 1-inch cubes
2 tablespoons cooking oil, divided
8 ounces (227 g) sliced fresh mushrooms
1 medium onion, diced
3 cups diced zucchini
1 cup diced green bell peppers
4 garlic cloves, diced
3 medium tomatoes, diced
1 (6-ounce / 170-g) can tomato paste
¾ cup water
2 teaspoons salt (optional)
1 teaspoon dried thyme
1 teaspoon dried oregano
1 teaspoon dried marjoram
1 teaspoon dried basil

1.Brown the chicken in 1 tablespoon of the oil in a large skillet, for 12 to 15 minutes.
2.Transfer to a slow cooker, reserving the drippings. In the same skillet, sauté the mushrooms, onion, zucchini, green peppers, and garlic in drippings and remaining 1 tablespoon oil, for 5 minutes, or until crisp-tender. Place in the slow cooker.
3.Add the tomatoes, tomato paste, water, and seasonings.
4.Cover. Cook on low for 4 hours, or until vegetables are tender.

Easy Beef and Barley Soup

Prep time: 10 minutes | Cook time: 8 hours | Serves 2

8 ounces (227 g) beef stew meat, trimmed of fat and cut into 1-inch cubes
¼ cup pearl barley
1 cup diced onion
1 cup diced carrot
1 teaspoon fresh thyme
½ teaspoon dried oregano
2 cups low-sodium beef stock
⅛ teaspoon sea salt

1.Put all the ingredients in a slow cooker and stir to combine.
2.Cover and cook on low for 8 hours. The meat should be tender and the barley soft.
3.Serve hot.

Teriyaki Pork Stew

Prep time: 15 minutes | Cook time: 8 t0 10 hours | Serves 6

1 boneless pork shoulder butt roast (3 to 4 pounds / 1.4 to 1.8 kg), cut into 1½-inch cubes
2 medium parsnips, peeled and sliced
1 small sweet red pepper, thinly sliced
1 cup chicken broth
¼ cup reduced-sodium teriyaki sauce
2 tablespoons rice vinegar
1 tablespoon minced fresh ginger
1 tablespoon honey
2 garlic cloves, minced
½ teaspoon crushed red pepper flakes
¼ cup creamy peanut butter
Hot cooked rice, for serving (optional)
2 green onions, chopped
2 tablespoons chopped dry roasted peanuts

1.In a slow cooker, combine the first 10 ingredients. Cover and cook on low for 8 to 10 hours or until the pork is tender. Skim fat and stir in the peanut butter. Serve with the rice, if desired. Top with the onions and peanuts. Serve hot.

Traditional Trail Chili

Prep time: 15 minutes | Cook time: 4½ to 6½ hours | Serves 8 to 10

2 pounds (907 g) ground beef
1 large onion, diced
1 (28-ounce / 794-g) can diced tomatoes
2 (8-ounce / 227-g) cans tomato purée
1 to 2 (16-ounce / 454-g) cans kidney beans, undrained
1 (4-ounce / 113-g) can diced green chilies
1 cup water
2 garlic cloves, minced
2 tablespoons mild chili powder
2 teaspoons salt
2 teaspoons ground cumin
1 teaspoon pepper

1.Brown the beef and onion in a skillet for 4 minutes. Drain. Place in a slow cooker.
2.Stir in the remaining ingredients. Cook on high for 30 minutes.
3.Reduce the heat to low. Cook for 4 to 6 hours.
4.Serve warm.

Beef Chili with Cilantro Cream

Prep time: 15 minutes | Cook time: 7 to 8 hours | Serves 4

1 pound (454 g) boneless beef chuck, tri tip (a triangular sirloin cut), or round steak, trimmed of excess fat and cut into bite-size pieces
1 large yellow onion, chopped
2 cloves garlic, finely chopped
1 tablespoon chili powder
2 teaspoons ground cumin
2 (16-ounce / 454-g) jars thick-and-chunky salsa, mild or hot
1 (14½-ounce / 411-g) can diced tomatoes, with their juice
1 medium-size red or green bell pepper, deseeded and chopped
1 (15-ounce / 425-g) can pinto beans, rinsed and drained
Salt, to taste
Warm cornbread, for serving
Cilantro Cream:
⅔ cup sour cream

¼ cup minced fresh cilantro
2 tablespoons fresh lime juice

1.Put the meat, onion, garlic, chili powder, cumin, salsa, and tomatoes in a slow cooker and stir to combine. Cover and cook on low for 5 to 6 hours.
2.Add the bell pepper and pinto beans, season with salt, and continue to cook on low for another 2 hours.
3.Combine all the ingredients for the cilantro cream in a small bowl, and stir until well combined. Cover and chill until serving. Serve the chili in bowls with a dollop of the cilantro cream and cornbread.

Beef and Pearl Barley Stew

Prep time: 10 minutes | Cook time: 8 hours | Serves 2

¼ cup pearl barley
½ cup water
½ teaspoon ground cinnamon
½ teaspoon ground coriander
Freshly ground black pepper, to taste
⅛ teaspoon sea salt
1 tablespoon tomato paste
¼ cup red wine vinegar
1 cup dry red wine
12 ounces (340 g) beef brisket, cut into 1-inch cubes
½ cup minced onions
¼ cup minced celery
2 garlic cloves, minced
2 tablespoons minced fresh flat-leaf parsley

1.Put the pearl barley and water in a slow cooker and give it a stir to make sure all the barley is submerged.
2.In a large bowl, combine the cinnamon, coriander, black pepper, salt, tomato paste, vinegar, and red wine. Add the beef, onions, celery, garlic, and parsley to the bowl and stir together. Gently pour this mixture over the barley. Do not stir.
3.Cover and cook on low for 8 hours.
4.Serve hot.

Sweet Potato and Sirloin Stew

Prep time: 20 minutes | Cook time: 7 to 9 hours | Serves 8

2 pounds (907 g) sirloin tip, cut into 2-inch pieces
2 onions, chopped
3 garlic cloves, minced
2 large sweet potatoes, peeled and cubed
⅔ cup chopped dried apricots
⅔ cup golden raisins
5 large tomatoes, deseeded and chopped
9 cups beef stock
2 teaspoons curry powder
1 cup cooked whole-wheat couscous

1.In a slow cooker, mix the sirloin, onions, garlic, sweet potatoes, apricots, raisins, tomatoes, beef stock, and curry powder. Cover and cook on low for 7 to 9 hours, or until the sweet potatoes are tender.
2.Stir in the couscous. Cover and let stand for 5 to 10 minutes, or until the couscous has softened.
3.Stir the stew and serve.

Hominy and Turkey Thigh Chili

Prep time: 20 minutes | Cook time: 6 to 8 hours | Serves 6

1 medium-size yellow onion, chopped
1 medium-size red bell pepper, deseeded and chopped
1 jalapeño, deseeded and minced
2 ribs celery, chopped
3 cloves garlic, minced
1 cup chicken broth
1 tablespoon chili powder
1½ teaspoons ground cumin
½ teaspoon pure ancho chile powder
1½ teaspoons dried oregano
3 pounds (1.4 kg) turkey thighs (about 3), skin and excess fat removed and rinsed
1 (15-ounce / 425-g) can golden or white hominy, rinsed and drained
2 (15-ounce / 425-g) cans chopped golden tomatoes, drained; or 1 (28-ounce / 794-g) can chopped plum tomatoes, drained
Salt, to taste
For Serving:
Shredded Monterey Jack cheese
Sliced ripe California black olives
Minced red onion
Chopped fresh cilantro

1.Combine the onion, bell pepper, jalapeño, celery, garlic, broth, chili powder, cumin, ancho powder, and oregano in a slow cooker. Arrange the turkey thighs on top and pour the hominy and tomatoes over them. Cover and cook on low until the turkey meat pulls away easily from the bone, for 6 to 7 hours.
2.Remove the turkey from the cooker and shred the meat, discarding the bones. Return the meat to the chili. Season with salt. Serve the chili in shallow bowls with the toppings.

Lush Brown Lentil Chili

Prep time: 20 minutes | Cook time: 6 to 8 hours | Serves 4 to 6

1 medium-size yellow onion, diced
1 medium-size red bell pepper, deseeded and chopped
1 jalapeño, deseeded and finely chopped
2 ribs celery, chopped
1 medium-size carrot, chopped
3 cloves garlic, minced
2 tablespoons light or dark brown sugar
2 tablespoons chili powder
1 tablespoon ground cumin
½ teaspoon cayenne pepper or 1 teaspoon pure New Mexico chile powder
2 teaspoons dried oregano
1 teaspoon dried thyme
1 teaspoon dry mustard
2½ cups dried brown lentils, rinsed and picked over
8 cups chicken broth
3 tablespoons olive oil
Salt, to taste
For Serving:
Sour cream or crema Mexicana
Chopped fresh tomatoes
Chopped green onions, white part and some of the green
Chopped fresh cilantro

1.Combine all the ingredients in a slow cooker, except for the olive oil and salt. Cover and cook on low for 6 to 8 hours, stirring occasionally, until the lentils are soft. During the last hour, add the olive oil and season with salt. Continue cooking.
2.Serve the chili in bowls with the toppings.

Mexican Chili Bean and Turkey Chili

Prep time: 15 minutes | Cook time: 6¼ to 8¼ hours | Serves 8

2 pounds (907 g) 99% fat-free ground turkey
2 medium onions, diced
2 garlic cloves, minced
1 green bell pepper, diced
⅔ tablespoon chili powder
1 teaspoon salt
1 teaspoon black pepper
1 teaspoon ground cumin
1 (16-ounce / 454-g) can low-sodium stewed or diced tomatoes
2 (12-ounce / 340-g) cans low-sodium tomato sauce
2 (16-ounce / 454-g) cans Mexican chili beans

1. Brown the turkey with the onions, garlic, and green pepper in a nonstick skillet, for about 15 minutes. Drain and transfer to a slow cooker.
2. Combine all the remaining ingredients in the slow cooker.
3. Cover. Cook on low for 6 to 8 hours.
4. Serve warm.

Southern Brunswick Stew

Prep time: 10 minutes | Cook time: 6½ to 8½ hours | Serves 10 to 12

2 to 3 pounds (0.9 to 1.4 kg) pork butt
1 (17-ounce / 482-g) can white corn
1 (14-ounce / 397-g) bottle ketchup
2 cups diced potatoes, cooked
1 (10-ounce / 284-g) package frozen peas, thawed
2 (10¾-ounce / 305-g) cans tomato soup
Hot sauce, as needed
Salt and pepper, to taste

1. Place the pork in a slow cooker.
2. Cover. Cook on low for 6 to 8 hours. Remove the meat from bone and shred.
3. Combine all the ingredients in the slow cooker.
4. Cover. Bring to a boil on high. Reduce heat to low and simmer for 30 minutes.
5. Serve hot.

Hoisin Turkey and Bean Chili

Prep time: 20 minutes | Cook time: 6 hours | Serves 6

2 cups yellow onions, diced
1 small red bell pepper, diced
1 pound (454 g) ground turkey, browned
2 tablespoons minced ginger
3 cloves garlic, minced
¼ cup dry sherry
¼ cup hoisin sauce
2 tablespoons chili powder
1 tablespoon corn oil
2 tablespoons soy sauce
1 teaspoon sugar
2 cups canned whole tomatoes
1 (16-ounce / 454-g) can dark red kidney beans, undrained

1. Combine all the ingredients in a slow cooker.
2. Cover. Cook on low for 6 hours.
3. Serve hot.

Spiced Sausage and Beef Chili

Prep time: 20 minutes | Cook time: 2 to 3 hours | Serves 4 to 6

½ pound (227 g) sausage, either cut in thin slices or removed from casings
½ pound (227 g) ground beef
½ cup chopped onions
½ pound (227 g) fresh mushrooms, sliced
⅛ cup chopped celery
⅛ cup chopped green peppers
1 cup salsa
1 (16-ounce / 454-g) can tomato juice
1 (6-ounce / 170-g) can tomato paste
½ teaspoon sugar
½ teaspoon salt
½ teaspoon dried oregano
½ teaspoon Worcestershire sauce
¼ teaspoon dried basil
¼ teaspoon pepper

1. Brown the sausage, ground beef, and onion in a skillet for 6 minutes. During last 3 minutes of browning, add the mushrooms, celery, and green peppers. Continue cooking and drain.
2. Add the remaining ingredients. Pour into a slow cooker.
3. Cover. Cook on high for 2 to 3 hours.
4. Serve warm.

Peppery Chicken Chili

Prep time: 15 minutes | Cook time: 8 to 10 hours | Serves 8

3 (15-ounce / 425-g) cans Great Northern beans, drained
8 ounces (227 g) cooked chicken breasts, shredded
1 cup chopped onions
1½ cups chopped yellow, red, or green bell peppers
2 jalapeño chili peppers, stemmed, deseeded, and chopped (optional)
2 garlic cloves, minced
2 teaspoons ground cumin
½ teaspoon salt
½ teaspoon dried oregano
3½ cups chicken broth
Toppings:
Sour cream
Shredded Cheddar cheese
Tortilla chips

1. Combine all the ingredients, except for the sour cream, Cheddar cheese, and chips, in a slow cooker.
2. Cover. Cook on low for 8 to 10 hours, or on high for 4 to 5 hours.
3. Ladle into bowls and top each bowl with the sour cream, Cheddar cheese, and chips. Serve hot.

Veggie Bulgur Wheat Chili

Prep time: 25 minutes | Cook time: 5 to 7 hours | Serves 4

⅓ cup bulgur wheat
⅔ cup boiling water
2 tablespoons olive oil
2 medium-size yellow onions, chopped
1 medium-size green, yellow, or red bell pepper, deseeded and chopped
2 to 3 cloves garlic, minced
1 (28-ounce / 794-g) can diced tomatoes, drained
1 (15-ounce / 425-g) can tomato purée
2 (15-ounce / 425-g) cans red kidney or pinto beans, rinsed and drained
2 tablespoons chopped canned jalapeño
2 tablespoons chili powder or pure New Mexican chile powder
1½ tablespoons ground cumin

2 tablespoons light or dark brown sugar
2 teaspoons dried oregano or marjoram
½ teaspoon ground coriander
¼ teaspoon ground cloves
Pinch of ground allspice
Salt, to taste
For Serving:
Shredded Monterey Jack cheese
Sliced ripe California black olives
Sliced avocado
Extra-firm tofu, rinsed, blotted dry, and cut into cubes
Chopped fresh cilantro

1. Put the bulgur in a slow cooker and add the boiling water. Let stand for 15 minutes.
2. Heat the olive oil in a large skillet over medium-high heat and cook the onions, bell pepper, and garlic, stirring, until softened, for 5 to 10 minutes. Transfer the mixture to the slow cooker. Add the drained tomatoes, tomato purée, beans, jalapeño, chili powder, cumin, brown sugar, oregano, coriander, cloves, and allspice, and stir to combine. Cover and cook on high for 1 hour.
3. Turn the cooker to low and cook for 4 to 6 hours. During the last hour, season with salt.
4. Serve the chili in bowls topped with the cheese, olives, avocado slices, tofu, and lots of cilantro.

Brown Rice and Black Bean Chili

Prep time: 10 minutes | Cook time: 6 to 8 hours | Serves 4

2 (15-ounce / 425-g) cans black beans
1 (14½- to 16-ounce / 411- to 454-g) can crushed or chopped tomatoes, with their liquid
½ cup brown rice
1 teaspoon onion powder
⅛ teaspoon garlic powder
¼ teaspoon ground cumin
½ teaspoon dried oregano
½ to 1 whole canned chipotle chile, cut into small pieces
Plain yogurt or warm flour tortillas, for serving

1. Pour the beans with their liquid and the tomatoes with their liquid into a slow cooker. Add the brown rice, onion powder, garlic powder, cumin, oregano, and chipotle. Stir to combine. Cover and cook on low for 6 to 8 hours.
2. Serve the chili in bowls, topped with a spoonful of yogurt, or wrap some in a warm tortilla.

Chapter 9 Classic Comfort Foods

Super Cheesy Macaroni

Prep time: 25 minutes | Cook time: 2 to 3 hours | Serves 16

3 cups cooked elbow macaroni, drained
1 pound (454 g) process cheese (Velveeta), cubed
2 cups shredded white Cheddar cheese
2 cups shredded Mexican cheese blend
3 eggs, lightly beaten
1 (12-ounce / 340-g) can evaporated milk
1¾ cups milk
¾ cup butter, melted

1.Combine all the ingredients in the slow cooker. Stir to mix well.
2.Cover and cook on low for 2 to 3 hours or until a thermometer inserted in the mixture reads 160ºF (71ºC), stirring once.
3.Serve warm.

Mustard-Herb Chicken and Vegetables

Prep time: 20 minutes | Cook time: 6 hours | Serves 4

4 medium red potatoes, quartered
3 medium parsnips, cut into 1-inch pieces
2 medium leeks (white portion only), thinly sliced
¾ cup fresh baby carrots
4 chicken leg quarters, skin removed
1 (10¾-ounce / 305-g) can condensed cream of chicken soup with herbs, undiluted
2 tablespoons minced fresh parsley
1 tablespoon snipped fresh dill or 1 teaspoon dill weed
1 tablespoon Dijon mustard

1.In the slow cooker, place the potatoes, parsnips, leeks, carrots and chicken, then pour the soup over.
2.Cover and cook on low for 6 to 8 hours or until chicken is tender.
3.Remove chicken and vegetables, then cover and keep warm. Stir in the parsley, dill and mustard, then serve with chicken and vegetables.

Salsa Beef

Prep time: 15 minutes | Cook time: 8 hours | Serves 8

1½ pounds (680 g) beef stew meat, cut into ¾-inch cubes
2 cups salsa
1 tablespoon brown sugar
1 tablespoon soy sauce
1 garlic clove, minced
4 cups hot cooked brown rice

1.In the slow cooker, combine the beef, salsa, brown sugar, soy sauce and garlic.
2.Cover and cook on low for 8 to 10 hours or until meat is tender. Using a slotted spoon to remove the beef from the slow cooker and serve with rice.

Pork and Black Bean Cubano

Prep time: 30 minutes | Cook time: 7 to 9 hours | Serves 8

3 pounds (1.4 kg) boneless pork shoulder butt roast
2 tablespoons olive oil
1 (15-ounce / 425-g) can black beans, rinsed and drained
1 medium sweet potato, cut into ½-inch cubes
1 small sweet red pepper, cubed
1 (14-ounce / 397-g) can light coconut milk
½ cup salsa verde
1 teaspoon minced fresh gingerroot
2 green onions, thinly sliced
Sliced papaya, for serving

1.In a large skillet, brown the butt roast in oil on all sides. Transfer to the slow cooker. Add black beans, sweet potato, and red pepper.
2.In a small bowl, mix coconut milk, salsa and ginger, then pour the mixture over the butt roast in the slow cooker.
3.Cook, covered, on low for 7 to 9 hours or until pork is tender. Sprinkle with green onions, then serve with papaya.

Caribbean Fruit Bread Pudding

Prep time: 30 minutes | Cook time: 4 to 5 hours | Serves 16

1 cup raisins
1 (8-ounce / 227-g) can crushed pineapple, undrained
2 large firm bananas, halved
1 (12-ounce / 340-g) can evaporated milk
1 (10-ounce / 283-g) can frozen non-alcoholic pina colada mix
1 (6-ounce / 170-g) can unsweetened pineapple juice
3 eggs
½ cup cream of coconut
¼ cup light rum, optional
1 (1-pound / 454-g) loaf French bread, cut into 1-inch cubes, divided

1. In a small bowl, combine raisins and pineapple, then set aside. In a blender, combine bananas, milk, pina colada mix, pineapple juice, eggs, cream of coconut and rum if desired. Cover and process until smooth.
2. Place two-thirds of the bread in a greased slow cooker. Top with 1 cup raisin mixture. Layer with remaining bread and raisin mixture. Pour the banana mixture into the slow cooker.
3. Cover and cook on low for 4 to 5 hours or until a knife inserted near the center comes out clean. Serve warm.

Super Bean Soup

Prep time: 20 minutes | Cook time: 7 hours | Serves 8 to 10

¼ cup dried red beans
¼ cup dried small white beans
¼ cup dried pinto beans
¼ cup dried kidney beans
¼ cup dried cranberry beans
¼ cup dried baby lima beans
¼ cup dried black-eyed peas
¼ cup dried yellow split peas
¼ cup dried green split peas
¼ cup dried brown lentils
¼ cup dried red lentils
1 (15-ounce / 425-g) can chopped plum tomatoes, with their juice
1 smoked ham hock or ham bone
3 medium carrots, chopped
3 stalks celery, finely chopped
1 large onion, finely chopped
8 cups chicken or vegetable broth
2 teaspoons dried thyme
1 bay leaf
Salt and freshly ground black pepper, to taste

1. Soak the red, white, pinto, kidney, cranberry, lima beans, and black-eyed peas overnight in water to cover. Drain and rinse thoroughly.
2. Add the soaked beans, split peas, and lentils to the slow cooker. Add the remaining ingredients and stir to combine.
3. Cook on low for 8 to 10 hours, until the beans are tender and the ham is falling off the bone.
4. Remove the ham hock or bone from the soup, chop any meat, removing the fat, and return the meat to the slow cooker.
5. Season with salt and pepper. Remove the bay leaf before serving.

Chicken and Red Potato Stew

Prep time: 15 minutes | Cook time: 7 to 9 hours | Serves 4

1 pound (454 g) small red potatoes, halved
1 large onion, finely chopped
¾ cup shredded carrots
3 tablespoons all-purpose flour
6 garlic cloves, minced
2 teaspoons lemon zest
2 teaspoons dried thyme
½ teaspoon salt
¼ teaspoon pepper
1½ pounds (680 g) boneless skinless chicken thighs, halved
2 cups chicken broth
2 bay leaves
2 tablespoons minced fresh parsley

1. Place the potatoes, onion and carrots in the slow cooker. Sprinkle with flour, garlic, lemon zest, thyme, salt and pepper, then toss to coat. Place the chicken over. Add broth and bay leaves.
2. Cook, covered, on low for 7 to 9 hours or until chicken and vegetables are tender. Remove the bay leaves. Sprinkle with parsley and serve.

Scalloped Potatoes

Prep time: 15 minutes | Cook time: 7 to 9 hours | Serves 8

4 cups thinly sliced peeled potatoes
1 (10¾-ounce / 305-g) can condensed cream of celery soup or mushroom soup, undiluted
1 (12-ounce / 340-g) can evaporated milk
1 large onion, sliced
2 tablespoons butter
½ teaspoon salt
¼ teaspoon pepper
1½ cups chopped fully cooked ham

1. In the slow cooker, combine all the ingredients except for the ham.
2. Cover and cook on high for 1 hour. Stir in ham. Reduce heat to low, then cook 6 to 8 hours longer or until potatoes are tender.
3. Serve warm.

Creamy Cheddar Potato Soup

Prep time: 25 minutes | Cook time: 7½ to 9½ hours | Serves 11

8 medium Yukon Gold potatoes, peeled and cubed
1 celery rib, chopped
1 large red onion, chopped
1 teaspoon garlic powder
½ teaspoon white pepper
2 (14½-ounce / 411-g) cans chicken broth
1 (10¾-ounce / 305-g) can condensed cream of celery soup, undiluted
1½ cups shredded sharp Cheddar cheese, plus more for topping, if desired
1 cup half-and-half cream
Toppings:
Salad croutons
Crumbled cooked bacon

1. Combine the potatoes, celery, onion, garlic powder, and white pepper in the slow cooker. Pour in the chicken broth and celery soup.
2. Cover and cook on low for 7 to 9 hours or until potatoes are tender.
3. Stir in the cheese and cream. Cover and cook for 30 minutes longer or until cheese is melted. Garnish with croutons and bacon before serving.

Super Cheesy Sausage Lasagna

Prep time: 15 minutes | Cook time: 4 to 5 hours | Serves 6 to 8

8 curly-edged lasagna noodles, broken in half
Salt and ground black pepper, to taste
1 pound (454 g) whole-milk ricotta cheese
1¼ cups Parmesan cheese, grated, divided
½ cup chopped fresh basil
1 large egg
3 cups jarred pasta sauce, divided
1 pound (454 g) hot or sweet Italian sausage, casings removed, divided
4 cups Mozzarella cheese, shredded, divided
Cooking spray

1. Line slow cooker with aluminum foil, then press 2 large sheets of foil into slow cooker perpendicular to one another, with extra foil hanging over edges. Lightly spritz the prepared slow cooker with cooking spray.
2. Bring 4 quarts water to boil in a large pot. Add noodles and 1 tablespoon salt and cook, stirring often, until al dente. Drain noodles, rinse under cold water, then spread out in a single layer over clean dish towels and let dry. (Do not use paper towels, then they will stick to noodles.)
3. Combine ricotta, 1 cup Parmesan, basil, egg, ½ teaspoon salt, and ½ teaspoon pepper in a bowl. Spread ½ cup pasta sauce into the prepared slow cooker.
4. Arrange 4 noodle pieces in the slow cooker (they may overlap), then dollop 10 rounded tablespoons of ricotta mixture over noodles. Pinch off one-third of sausage into tablespoon-size pieces and scatter over ricotta. Sprinkle with 1 cup Mozzarella, then spoon ½ cup sauce over. Repeat layering of noodles, ricotta mixture, sausage, Mozzarella, and sauce twice more.
5. For the final layer, arrange remaining 4 noodles in the slow cooker, then top with remaining 1 cup sauce and sprinkle with remaining 1 cup Mozzarella and remaining ¼ cup Parmesan. Cover and cook until lasagna is heated through, 4 to 5 hours on low.
6. Let lasagna cool for 20 minutes. Serve warm.

Creamy Grape-Nuts Custard Pudding

Prep time: 10 minutes | Cook time: 2 hours | Serves 8

1½ cups grape-nuts cereal (nuggets, not flakes)
6 large eggs
4 cups milk
1⅓ cups sugar
1 tablespoon vanilla bean paste
1 teaspoon ground cinnamon
2½ cups heavy cream
Nonstick cooking spray

1. Spray the slow cooker with nonstick cooking spray. Pour the cereal in the slow cooker.
2. Whisk together the eggs, milk, sugar, vanilla bean paste, and cinnamon in a large mixing bowl. Gently pour over the cereal.
3. Cover and cook on high for 2 hours, until the custard is just set. It may seem a little jiggly in the center, but will firm while the custard cools. Allow the pudding to cool to room temperature. Cover with plastic wrap and chill.
4. Whip the cream in a mixing bowl until it forms stiff peaks.
5. Scoop the pudding into bowls and top each serving with a dollop of the cream.

Hearty Chicken and Wild Rice Soup

Prep time: 20 minutes | Cook time: 4 to 5 hours | Serves 6 to 8

4 tablespoons (½ stick) unsalted butter
1 medium onion, finely chopped
4 medium carrots, finely chopped
4 medium stalks celery with leaves, finely chopped
1 pound (454 g) cremini mushrooms, cut into ½-inch slices
1 teaspoon dried thyme
1 teaspoon dried sage, crushed
1½ teaspoons salt
1 teaspoon freshly ground black pepper
8 cups chicken broth
3 cups bite-size pieces cooked chicken or turkey, either shredded or diced
2 cups wild rice, rinsed several times with cold water
1 cup heavy cream

1. Heat the butter in a large skillet over medium-high heat.
2. Add the onion, carrots, and celery and sauté until the vegetables are softened, about 3 minutes.
3. Add the mushrooms, thyme, and sage to the pan and season with the salt and pepper.
4. Transfer the contents of the skillet to the slow cooker. Stir in the chicken broth, chicken, and wild rice.
5. Cover the slow cooker and cook on low for 4 to 5 hours, until the wild rice is tender and the soup is thickened.
6. Stir in the cream, turn the cooker to warm, and serve the soup.

Smothered Pork

Prep time: 20 minutes | Cook time: 4 to 6 hours | Serves 6

1 tablespoon extra-virgin olive oil
6 (1-inch-thick) sirloin pork chops
½ teaspoon kosher salt, plus more for seasoning
½ teaspoon freshly ground black pepper, plus more for seasoning
1 onion, finely chopped
4 garlic cloves, minced
½ cup dry white wine
2 cups chicken stock
⅓ cup all-purpose flour
½ teaspoon garlic powder
2 bay leaves
1 tablespoon browning sauce

1. In a saucepan over medium-high heat, heat the oil until shimmering. Season the chops with salt and pepper, and brown, about 3 minutes per side. Remove and set aside.
2. In the same saucepan, add the onion and garlic. Sauté until tender, about 5 minutes. Add the wine and bring to a boil. Simmer for a minute before adding the chicken stock. Whisk in the flour, stirring until no lumps remain.
3. Place the pork chops and the sauce mixture in the slow cooker. Add the garlic powder, salt, pepper, bay leaves, and browning sauce. Stir to combine. Cover and cook on low for 4 to 6 hours.
4. Discard the bay leaves. Season with additional salt and pepper, as needed. Serve, spooning the sauce on top of the chops.

Thai Red Curry Chicken with Vegetables

Prep time: 15 minutes | Cook time: 6 to 8 hours | Serves 4

¼ cup creamy peanut butter
2 tablespoons red curry paste
2 tablespoons packed brown sugar
2 tablespoons fish sauce
½ teaspoon kosher salt, plus more for seasoning
2 tablespoons freshly squeezed lime juice
1 (14-ounce / 397-g) can coconut milk
½ cup chicken stock
1 pound (454 g) boneless, skinless chicken thighs
3 garlic cloves, minced
3 cups mixed vegetables, such as sliced red pepper, sliced red onion, and snap peas
¼ cup finely chopped fresh cilantro, for garnish

1. In a medium bowl, whisk together the peanut butter, curry paste, brown sugar, fish sauce, salt, lime juice, coconut milk, and chicken stock until thoroughly combined.
2. Put the chicken and garlic in the slow cooker, then spoon the sauce on top. Cover and cook on low for 6 to 8 hours.
3. During the last hour of cooking, add the vegetables. Cover and continue cooking until the vegetables are crisp-tender. Season with additional salt, as needed. Garnish with the cilantro before serving.

Chicken and Carrot Fricassee

Prep time: 15 minutes | Cook time: 6 to 8 hours | Serves 6

3½ pounds (1.6 kg) chicken drumsticks and thighs, skinned
4 medium carrots, cut into matchsticks (about 2 cups)
1 small onion, diced
2 garlic cloves, minced
1½ cups chicken stock
½ cup dry white wine
¼ cup heavy (whipping) cream
1 teaspoon poultry seasoning
½ teaspoon kosher salt, plus more for seasoning
½ teaspoon freshly ground black pepper
2 tablespoons all-purpose flour
2 tablespoons freshly squeezed lemon juice
3 tablespoons chopped fresh tarragon leaves, for garnish

1. Put the chicken in the slow cooker, along with the carrots, onion, garlic, chicken stock, wine, heavy cream, poultry seasoning, salt, and pepper. Stir to combine. Cover and cook on low for 6 to 8 hours.
2. About 30 minutes before serving, spoon out ¼ cup of cooking liquid from the slow cooker and whisk it in a small bowl with the flour.
3. Pour the mixture back into the slow cooker, add the lemon juice, and whisk to combine. Cover and continue cooking until the sauce is slightly thickened.
4. Season with additional salt, as needed. Serve garnished with the tarragon.

Chapter 10 Desserts

Poached Pears with Amaretto

Prep time: 10 minutes | Cook time: 4 hours | Serves 6 to 8

½ cup amaretto liqueur
1 cup pear nectar
1½ cups firmly packed light brown sugar
½ cup (1 stick) unsalted butter, melted
6 firm red pears, peeled and cored
½ cup crushed amaretti cookies (about 6)
½ cup chopped almonds, toasted

1. Combine the amaretto, nectar, sugar, and butter in the slow cooker and stir until the sugar is dissolved.
2. Stand the pears in the liquid, stem-ends up. Cover and cook on low for 4 hours until the pears are tender.
3. Combine the cookie crumbs and almonds in a small bowl and set aside. Uncover the pears and allow to cool.
4. Serve each pear in sauce and sprinkled with almond mixture.

Blueberry and Pear Granola

Prep time: 15 minutes | Cook time: 3 to 4 hours | Serves 10

2 cups fresh or frozen unsweetened blueberries
5 medium pears, peeled and thinly sliced
½ cup packed brown sugar
⅓ cup apple cider or unsweetened apple juice
1 tablespoon all-purpose flour
1 tablespoon lemon juice
2 teaspoons ground cinnamon
2 tablespoons butter
3 cups granola without raisins

1. In the slow cooker, combine the first seven ingredients. Dot with butter. Sprinkle granola with raisins over.
2. Cover and cook on low for 3 to 4 hours or until fruit is tender.
3. Serve warm.

Caramel Pear Cake

Prep time: 15 minutes | Cook time: 2 to 3 hours | Serves 6

6 medium pears, peeled and sliced
¼ cup heavy whipping cream
¾ cup packed brown sugar
1 teaspoon cornstarch
1 tablespoon chopped crystallized ginger
2 teaspoons lemon juice
½ teaspoon ground cinnamon
2 tablespoons butter, melted
Grilled pound cake, whipped topping and sliced almonds

1. In the slow cooker, combine all the ingredients except for the cake. Stir to mix well. Cover and cook on low for 2 to 3 hours or until heated through.
2. Serve warm over pound cake. Top with whipped topping, then sprinkle with almonds.

Rice and Raisin Pudding

Prep time: 15 minutes | Cook time: 3 to 4 hours | Serves 4

1¼ cups 2% milk
½ cup sugar
½ cup uncooked converted rice
½ cup raisins
2 eggs, lightly beaten
1 teaspoon ground cinnamon, plus more for garnish
1 teaspoon butter, melted
1 teaspoon vanilla extract
¾ teaspoon lemon extract
1 cup heavy whipping cream, whipped

1. In the slow cooker, combine the first nine ingredients. Cover and cook on low for 2 hours, then stir. Cover and cook for 1 to 2 hours longer or until rice is tender. Transfer to a small bowl, then cool. Refrigerate until chilled.
2. Fold in the whipped cream and garnish with more cinnamon before serving.

Apple Granola

Prep time: 10 minutes | Cook time: 6 to 8 hours | Serves 4 to 6

4 medium tart apples, peeled and sliced
2 cups granola cereal with fruit and nuts
¼ cup honey
2 tablespoons butter, melted
1 teaspoon ground cinnamon
½ teaspoon ground nutmeg

1.In the slow cooker, combine the apples and cereal. In a small bowl, combine the honey, butter, cinnamon and nutmeg.
2.Pour the honey mixture over apple mixture and mix well. Cover and cook on low for 6 to 8 hours.
3.Serve warm..

Bread and Raisin Pudding

Prep time: 20 minutes | Cook time: 4 to 5 hours | Serves 6

8 slices bread, cubed
4 eggs
2 cups milk
¼ cup sugar
¼ cup butter, melted
¼ cup raisins
½ teaspoon ground cinnamon
Cooking spray
Sauce:
2 tablespoons butter
2 tablespoons all-purpose flour
1 cup water
¾ cup sugar
1 teaspoon vanilla extract

1.Place the bread cubes in the slow cooker spritzed with cooking spray. In a large bowl, beat the eggs and milk, then stir in the sugar, butter, raisins and cinnamon. Pour over bread, then stir.
2.Cover and cook on high for 1 hour. Reduce heat to low, then cook for 3 to 4 hours or until a thermometer inserted in the mixture reads 160°F (71°C).
3.Meanwhile, melt the butter in a small saucepan. Stir in the flour until smooth. Gradually add the water, sugar and vanilla. Bring to a boil, then cook and stir for 2 minutes or until thickened. Serve with warm bread pudding.

Baked Raisin Stuffed Apples

Prep time: 25 minutes | Cook time: 4 to 5 hours | Serves 6

6 medium tart apples
½ cup raisins
⅓ cup packed brown sugar
1 tablespoon orange zest
1 cup water
3 tablespoons thawed orange juice concentrate
2 tablespoons butter

1.Core apples and peel top third of each if desired. Combine the raisins, brown sugar and orange zest, then spoon into apples. Place in the slow cooker.
2.Pour the water around apples. Drizzle with orange juice concentrate. Dot with butter. Cover and cook on low for 4 to 5 hours or until apples are tender.
3.Serve warm.

Banana and Peanut Butter Pudding Cake

Prep time: 10 minutes | Cook time: 3 to 3½ hours | Serves 12

3 cups cold 2% milk
1 (3½-ounce / 99-g) package instant banana cream pudding mix
1 package banana cake mix (regular size)
½ cup creamy peanut butter
2 cups peanut butter chips
1 cup chopped dried banana chips
Cooking spray

1.In a small bowl, whisk milk and pudding mix for 2 minutes. Let stand for 2 minutes or until soft. Transfer to the slow cooker spritzed with cooking spray.
2.Prepare the cake mix batter according to package directions, adding peanut butter before mixing. Pour over pudding.
3.Cover and cook on low for 3 to 3½ hours or until a toothpick inserted near the center comes out with moist crumbs.
4.Sprinkle with peanut butter chips, then cover and let stand for 15 to 20 minutes or until partially melted. Top with banana chips before serving.

Pecan and Caramel Stuffed Apples

Prep time: 20 minutes | Cook time: 3 to 4hours | Serves 6

6 large tart apples
2 teaspoons lemon juice
⅓ cup chopped pecans
¼ cup chopped dried apricots
¼ cup packed brown sugar
3 tablespoons butter, melted
¾ teaspoon ground cinnamon
2 cups water
¼ teaspoon ground nutmeg

1.Core apples and peel top third of each, then brush the peeled portions with lemon juice. Place in the slow cooker.
2.Combine the pecans, apricots, brown sugar, butter, cinnamon and nutmeg. Place a heaping tablespoonful of mixture in each apple. Pour the water around apples.
3.Cover and cook on low for 3 to 4 hours or until apples are tender. Serve warm.

Chocolate and Raspberry Bread Pudding

Prep time: 10 minutes | Cook time: 2¼ to 2½ hours | Serves 6 to 8

6 cups cubed day-old bread (¾-inch cubes), divided
1½ cups semisweet chocolate chips, divided
1 cup fresh raspberries, divided
4 eggs
½ cup heavy whipping cream
½ cup milk
¼ cup sugar
1 teaspoon vanilla extract
Cooking spray

1.In the slow cooker spritzed with cooking spray, layer half of the bread cubes, chocolate chips and raspberries. Repeat layers.
2.In a bowl, whisk the eggs, cream, milk, sugar and vanilla. Pour over the bread mixture.
3.Cover and cook on high for 2¼ to 2½ hours or until a thermometer inserted in the mixture reads 160ºF (71ºC). Let stand for 5 to 10 minutes. Serve warm.

Butterscotch Crispy Apples

Prep time: 10 minutes | Cook time: 2½ to 3½ hours | Serves 3

3 cups thinly sliced peeled tart apples (about 3 medium)
⅓ cup packed brown sugar
¼ cup all-purpose flour
¼ cup quick-cooking oats
⅓ cup cook-and-serve butterscotch pudding mix
½ teaspoon ground cinnamon
¼ cup cold butter, cubed

1.Place the apples in the slow cooker. In a small bowl, combine the brown sugar, flour, oats, pudding mix and cinnamon. Cut in butter until the mixture resembles coarse crumbs. Sprinkle the mixture over apples.
2.Cover and cook on low for 2½ to 3½ hours or until apples are tender. Serve warm.

Apple and Pecan Bread Pudding

Prep time: 15 minutes | Cook time: 3 to 4 hours | Serves 6 to 8

8 slices raisin bread, cubed
2 to 3 medium tart apples, peeled and sliced
1 cup chopped pecans, toasted
1 cup sugar
1 teaspoon ground cinnamon
½ teaspoon ground nutmeg
3 eggs, lightly beaten
2 cups half-and-half
¼ cup apple juice
¼ cup butter, melted
Cooking spray

1.Place the bread cubes, apples, and pecans in the slow cooker spritzed with cooking spray and mix gently.
2.Combine the sugar, cinnamon, and nutmeg in a small bowl. Add the remaining ingredients. Mix well. Pour over the bread mixture.
3.Cover. Cook on low for 3 to 4 hours, or until a knife inserted in center comes out clean. Allow to cool under room temperature before serving.
4.Serve warm or refrigerate for 2 hours and serve chilled.

Peanut Butter Cake

Prep time: 10 minutes | Cook time: 1½ to 2 hours | Serves 4

⅓ cup milk
¼ cup peanut butter
1 tablespoon canola oil
½ teaspoon vanilla extract
¾ cup sugar, divided
½ cup all-purpose flour
¾ teaspoon baking powder
2 tablespoons baking cocoa
1 cup boiling water
Vanilla ice cream, for serving
Cooking spray

1. In a large bowl, beat the milk, peanut butter, oil and vanilla until well blended.
2. In a small bowl, combine ¼ cup sugar, flour and baking powder, then gradually beat into milk mixture until blended. Spread into the slow cooker coated with cooking spray.
3. In a separate small bowl, combine cocoa and remaining sugar, then stir in boiling water. Pour into the slow cooker (do not stir).
4. Cover and cook on high for 1½ to 2 hours or until a toothpick inserted near the center comes out clean. Serve warm with ice cream.

Pumpkin Bread Pudding

Prep time: 15 minutes | Cook time: 3 to 4 hours | Serves 8

8 slices cinnamon bread, cut into 1-inch cubes
4 eggs, beaten
2 cups 2% milk
1 cup canned pumpkin
¼ cup packed brown sugar
¼ cup butter, melted
1 teaspoon vanilla extract
½ teaspoon ground cinnamon
¼ teaspoon ground nutmeg
½ cup dried cranberries
Cooking spray
Sauce:
1 cup sugar
⅔ cup water
1 cup heavy whipping cream
2 teaspoons vanilla extract

1. Place the bread in the slow cooker spritzed with cooking spray. In a large bowl, combine the eggs, milk, pumpkin, brown sugar, butter, vanilla, cinnamon and nutmeg, then stir in cranberries. Pour over bread cubes.
2. Cover and cook on low for 3 to 4 hours or until a knife inserted near the center comes out clean.
3. Meanwhile, in a large saucepan, bring sugar and water to a boil over medium heat. Cook until sugar is dissolved and mixture turns a golden amber color, about 20 minutes. Gradually stir in cream until smooth. Remove from the heat, then stir in vanilla. Serve warm with bread pudding.

Chocolate and Cream Cheese Pudding Cake

Prep time: 25 minutes | Cook time: 2 to 3 hours | Serves 8

½ cup 2% milk
2 tablespoons canola oil
½ teaspoon almond extract
1 cup all-purpose flour
½ cup packed brown sugar
2 tablespoons baking cocoa
1½ teaspoons baking powder
½ cup coarsely chopped malted milk balls
½ cup semisweet chocolate chips
¾ cup sugar
¼ cup malted milk powder
1¼ cups boiling water
4 ounces (113 g) cream cheese, softened and cubed
Vanilla ice cream and sliced almonds, for serving
Cooking spray

1. In a large bowl, combine the milk, oil and almond extract. Combine the flour, brown sugar, cocoa and baking powder in a separate bowl, then gradually beat into the milk mixture until blended. Stir in the malted milk balls and chocolate chips.
2. Spoon the mixture into the slow cooker spritzed with cooking spray. In a small bowl, combine the sugar and milk powder, then stir in the boiling water and cream cheese. Pour over the batter (do not stir).
3. Cover and cook on high for 2 to 3 hours or until a toothpick inserted in center of cake comes out clean. Turn off heat. Let stand 15 minutes.
4. Serve warm with ice cream, then sprinkle with almonds.

Hot Fudge Sundae Cake

Prep time: 15 minutes | Cook time: 4 to 4½ hours | Serves 12

1¾ cups packed brown sugar, divided
1 cup all-purpose flour
5 tablespoons baking cocoa, divided
2 teaspoons baking powder
½ teaspoon salt
½ cup evaporated milk
2 tablespoons butter, melted
½ teaspoon vanilla extract
⅛ teaspoon almond extract
1 (5-ounce / 142-g) package mint Andes candies
1¾ cups boiling water
4 teaspoons instant coffee granules
Vanilla ice cream, whipped cream and maraschino cherries, for serving
Cooking spray

1.In a large bowl, combine 1 cup brown sugar, flour, 3 tablespoons cocoa, baking powder and salt. In another bowl, combine the milk, butter and extracts. Stir into dry ingredients just until moistened. Transfer to the slow cooker spritzed with cooking spray. Sprinkle with candies.
2.Combine the water, instant coffee granules and remaining brown sugar and cocoa, then pour over batter (do not stir). Cover and cook on high for 4 to 4½ hours or until a toothpick inserted near the center of the cake comes out clean. Serve with ice cream, whipped cream and cherries.

Sweet Cherry Grunt

Prep time: 15 minutes | Cook time: 2 to 3 hours | Serves 8

2¼ pounds (1.0 kg) frozen sweet cherries, thawed
2 cups all-purpose flour, divided
1 cup plus 3 tablespoons sugar, divided
1 tablespoon lemon juice
1¼ teaspoons ground cinnamon, divided
1 teaspoon almond extract
1 tablespoon baking powder
½ teaspoon salt
½ cup plus 2 tablespoons milk
4 tablespoons unsalted butter, melted and cooled

1.Combine the cherries, ¼ cup flour, 1 cup sugar, lemon juice, 1 teaspoon cinnamon, and almond extract in a medium bowl. Microwave

until cherries release their liquid, about 5 minutes, stirring halfway through microwaving. Stir cherry mixture well, transfer to the slow cooker, and spread into an even layer.
2.In a large bowl, combine the remaining 1¾ cups of flour, 2 tablespoons sugar, baking powder, and salt. Stir in the milk and melted butter until just combined, then do not over-mix.
3.In a small bowl, combine the remaining 1 tablespoon sugar and remaining ¼ teaspoon cinnamon.
4.Using greased ¼ cup measure, drop 8 dumplings around the perimeter of the slow cooker on top of cherries, leaving center empty. Sprinkle dumplings with cinnamon-sugar mixture.
5.Cover and cook until toothpick inserted in center of dumplings comes out clean, 3 to 4 hours on low or 2 to 3 hours on high. Turn off slow cooker and let cool for 20 minutes before serving.

Hot Chocolate Fudge Cake

Prep time: 20 minutes | Cook time: 4 to 4½ hours | Serves 8

1¾ cups packed brown sugar, divided
1 cup all-purpose flour
6 tablespoons baking cocoa, divided
2 teaspoons baking powder
½ teaspoon salt
½ cup 2% milk
2 tablespoons butter, melted
½ teaspoon vanilla extract
1½ cups semisweet chocolate chips
1¾ cups boiling water
Vanilla ice cream, for serving
Cooking spray

1.In a bowl, combine 1 cup brown sugar, flour, 3 tablespoons cocoa, baking powder and salt.
2.Combine the milk, butter and vanilla in a separate bowl, then stir into dry ingredients just until combined.
3.Pour the mixture into the slow cooker coated with cooking spray. Sprinkle with chocolate chips.
4.In a third bowl, combine the remaining brown sugar and cocoa, then stir in boiling water. Pour over batter (do not stir).
5.Cover and cook on high for 4 to 4½ hours or until a toothpick inserted near center of cake comes out clean. Serve warm with ice cream.

Self-Frosting Chocolate Cake

Prep time: 10 minutes | Cook time: 2 to 3 hours | Serves 8 to 10

2½ cups chocolate fudge pudding cake mix
2 eggs
1 cup water, divided
3 tablespoons olive oil
⅓ cup pecan halves
¼ cup chocolate syrup
3 tablespoons sugar

1. Combine the cake mix, eggs, ¾ cup water, and oil in a blender. Pulse to mix well.
2. Pour into buttered and floured cake pan that will fit into the slow cooker.
3. Sprinkle the pecans over the mixture.
4. Blend chocolate syrup, ¼ cup water, and sugar. Spoon over batter.
5. Cover. Bake on high for 2 to 3 hours.
6. Serve warm.

Apple Cake with Walnuts

Prep time: 15 minutes | Cook time: 3½ to 4 hours | Serves 8 to 10

2 cups sugar
1 cup olive oil
2 eggs
1 teaspoon vanilla
2 cups chopped apples
2 cups flour
1 teaspoon salt
1 teaspoon baking soda
1 teaspoon nutmeg
1 cup chopped walnuts

1. Beat together the sugar, oil, and eggs in a large bowl. Add vanilla and apples. Mix well.
2. Sift together flour, salt, baking soda, and nutmeg in a bowl. Add dry ingredients and nuts to the apple mixture. Stir well.
3. Pour batter into greased and floured cake pan that fits into the slow cooker. Cover with pan's lid, or greased foil. Place pan in the slow cooker. Cover cooker.
4. Bake on high for 3½ to 4 hours. Let cake stand in pan for 5 minutes after removing from the slow cooker.
5. Remove cake from pan, slice, and serve.

Lush Fruity Cake

Prep time: 10 minutes | Cook time: 2 to 3 hours | Serves 8 to 10

1 (20-ounce / 567-g) can crushed pineapple
1 (21-ounce / 595-g) can blueberry or cherry pie filling
1 (18½-ounce / 524-g) package yellow cake mix
Cinnamon, to taste
½ cup butter
1 cup chopped nuts
Vanilla ice cream, for serving
Cooking spray

1. Spritz the slow cooker with cooking spray.
2. Spread layers of pineapple, blueberry pie filling, and dry cake mix. Be careful not to mix the layers. Sprinkle with cinnamon.
3. Top with thin layers of butter and nuts.
4. Cover. Cook on high for 2 to 3 hours.
5. Serve with vanilla ice cream.

Tropical Compote

Prep time: 15 minutes | Cook time: 2¼ hours | Serves 6

1 (23½-ounce / 666-g) jar mixed tropical fruit
1 jalapeño pepper, deseeded and chopped
¼ cup sugar
1 tablespoon chopped crystallized ginger
¼ teaspoon ground cinnamon
1 (15-ounce / 425-g) can mandarin oranges, drained
1 (6-ounce / 170-g) jar maraschino cherries, drained
1 medium firm banana, sliced
6 individual round sponge cakes
6 tablespoons flaked coconut, toasted

1. Drain the tropical fruit, reserving ¼ cup liquid.
2. Combine the tropical fruit and jalapeño in the slow cooker. Mix in the sugar, ginger, cinnamon and reserved juice, then pour over fruit.
3. Cover and cook on low for 2 hours. Stir in the mandarin oranges, cherries and banana, then cook 15 minutes longer.
4. Place sponge cakes on dessert plates, then top with the compote. Sprinkle with coconut and serve.

Posh Fruit Compote

Prep time: 20 minutes | Cook time: 3¼ to 4¼ hours | Makes 8 cups

5 medium apples, peeled and chopped
3 medium pears, chopped
1 medium orange, thinly sliced
½ cup dried cranberries
½ cup packed brown sugar
½ cup maple syrup
⅓ cup butter, cubed
2 tablespoons lemon juice
2 teaspoons ground cinnamon
1 teaspoon ground ginger
5 tablespoons orange juice, divided
4 teaspoons cornstarch
Sweetened whipped cream and toasted chopped pecans, optional

1. In the slow cooker, combine the first 10 ingredients. Stir in 2 tablespoons orange juice.
2. Cook, covered, on low for 3 to 4 hours or until fruit is tender.
3. In a small bowl, mix cornstarch and remaining orange juice until smooth, then gradually stir into fruit mixture.
4. Cook, covered, on high for 15 to 20 minutes longer or until sauce is thickened. If desired, top with whipped cream and pecans before serving.

Berry Cobbler

Prep time: 15 minutes | Cook time: 2 to 2½ hours | Serves 8

1¼ cups all-purpose flour, divided
2 tablespoons plus 1 cup sugar, divided
1 teaspoon baking powder
¼ teaspoon ground cinnamon
1 egg, lightly beaten
¼ cup fat-free milk
2 tablespoons canola oil
⅛ teaspoon salt
2 cups fresh or frozen blueberries, thawed
2 cups fresh or frozen raspberries, thawed
Low-fat vanilla frozen yogurt, optional
Cooking spray

1. In a large bowl, combine 1 cup flour, 2 tablespoons sugar, baking powder and cinnamon.

2. Combine the egg, milk and oil in a medium bowl, then stir into dry ingredients just until moistened (batter will be thick). Spread the batter evenly into the slow cooker coated with cooking spray.
3. In a separate large bowl, combine the salt and remaining flour and sugar, then add the berries and toss to coat. Spread over the batter.
4. Cover and cook on high for 2 to 2½ hours or until a toothpick inserted into cobbler comes out clean.
5. Serve with frozen yogurt if desired.

Flan

Prep time: 10 minutes | Cook time: 4 hours | Serves 6

3 tablespoons unsalted butter
¾ cup sugar
5 eggs
1 (12-ounce / 340-g) can evaporated milk
1 (14-ounce / 397-g) can dulce de leche
4 ounces (113 g) cream cheese, cut into 1-inch cubes
1 teaspoon pure vanilla extract
Vanilla sea salt, to taste

1. Grease 6 ramekins with the butter.
2. In a blender, add the sugar, eggs, evaporated milk, dulce de leche, cream cheese, and vanilla, and blend until smooth.
3. On the bottom of the slow cooker, place a folded tea towel.
4. Pour the flan mixture into the ramekins and arrange the ramekins on the towel in the slow cooker. Cover the ramekins tightly with foil.
5. Pour warm water into the slow cooker until it reaches halfway up the sides of the ramekins. (Make sure the water reaches no more than halfway up the sides—it will ruin the flans if it splashes into the ramekins.)
6. Cook on high for 4 hours. Then remove the ramekins from the slow cooker, take off the aluminum foil, and let them cool for at least an hour in the refrigerator.
7. Sprinkle with the vanilla sea salt before serving.

Simple Applesauce

Prep time: 5 minutes | Cook time: 6 to 8 hours | Makes 5 cups

8 to 10 large tart apples, peeled and cut into chunks
½ to 1 cup sugar
½ cup water
1 teaspoon ground cinnamon

1.Combine apples, sugar, water and cinnamon in the slow cooker, then stir gently.
2.Cover and cook on low for 6 to 8 hours or until apples are tender.
3.Serve warm.

Vanilla Chocolate Cake

Prep time: 15 minutes | Cook time: 3 hours | Serves 2

1 cup all-purpose flour
⅓ cup granulated sugar
⅓ cup brown sugar
1 teaspoon baking powder
½ teaspoon baking soda
Pinch salt
¼ cup cocoa powder
¼ cup semisweet chocolate chips, finely chopped
3 tablespoons butter
¼ cup boiling water
½ cup light cream
1 egg
2 teaspoons vanilla
½ cup water
Nonstick baking spray containing flour

1.Spray a loaf pan with the nonstick baking spray containing flour.
2.In a medium bowl, mix the flour, granulated sugar, brown sugar, baking powder, baking soda, and salt.
3.In a small saucepan over low heat, heat the cocoa powder, chocolate chips, butter, and boiling water, stirring frequently, until the chocolate chips melt, about 5 minutes.
4.Add the cocoa mixture to the flour mixture. Add the cream, egg, and vanilla, and beat for 1 minute.
5.Pour the mixture into the loaf pan.
6.Place the loaf pan in the slow cooker and pour

½ cup of water around the pan. Place a double layer of paper towels on top of the slow cooker and add the cover.
7.Cook on low for 3 hours, or until the cake springs back when lightly touched with a finger.
8.Remove the pan from the slow cooker and cool for 5 minutes, then invert onto a cooling rack, cool completely, and serve.

Hearty Apricot Cheesecake

Prep time: 20 minutes | Cook time: 4 hours | Serves 2

⅓ cup graham cracker crumbs
1 tablespoon melted butter
8 ounces (227 g) cream cheese, at room temperature
2 teaspoons cornstarch
⅓ cup granulated sugar
Pinch salt
1 egg
¼ cup Mascarpone cheese
1 cup canned sliced apricots, drained, divided
½ cup water
2 tablespoons honey
1 tablespoon orange juice
Nonstick cooking spray

1.Spray a springform pan with the nonstick cooking spray.
2.In a small bowl, combine the graham cracker crumbs and butter and mix well. Press the mixture into the bottom of the pan.
3.In a medium bowl, beat the cream cheese until smooth.
4.Add the cornstarch, sugar, salt, and egg, and beat until smooth. Beat in the Mascarpone cheese.
5.Chop the apricots and stir ⅓ cup into the cream cheese mixture.
6.Spoon the cream cheese mixture on top of the crust in the springform pan.
7.Place a small rack in the slow cooker and add the water. Place the springform pan on the rack.
8.Cover and cook on low for 4 hours. Remove the pan from the slow cooker and cool for 1 hour.
9.In a small pan over low heat, bring the remaining ⅓ cup chopped apricots and the honey and orange juice to a simmer. Simmer for 5 minutes, until thickened. Spoon the mixture over the cheesecake, and then chill until cold, about 3 to 4 hours, and serve.

Autumn Apple and Pecan Cake

Prep time: 15 minutes | Cook time: 3 to 5 hours | Serves 8

2 (1-pound / 454-g) cans sliced apples, undrained (not pie filling)
1 (18¼-ounce / 517-g) package spice cake mix
½ cup butter, melted
½ cup pecans, chopped
Nonstick cooking spray

1. Spray the slow cooker with nonstick cooking spray.
2. Spoon the apples and their juice into the slow cooker, spreading evenly over the bottom. Sprinkle with spice cake mix.
3. Pour the melted butter over the spice cake mix. Top with chopped pecans.
4. Cook on low for 3 to 5 hours, or until a toothpick inserted into topping comes out dry.
5. Serve warm.

Simple Lemony Pudding Cake

Prep time: 15 minutes | Cook time: 2 to 3 hours | Serves 5 to 6

3 eggs, whites and yolks separated
1 teaspoon lemon zest
¼ cup lemon juice
3 tablespoons butter, melted
1½ cups milk
¾ cup sugar
¼ cup flour
⅛ teaspoon salt

1. Beat the eggs whites until stiff peaks form in a bowl. Set aside.
2. Beat the eggs yolks in a separate bowl. Blend in the lemon zest, lemon juice, butter, and milk.
3. In a third bowl, combine the sugar, flour, and salt. Add to the egg-lemon mixture, beating until smooth.
4. Fold them into the beaten egg whites. Spoon the mixture into the slow cooker.
5. Cover and cook on high for 2 to 3 hours.
6. Serve warm.

Apple Betty

Prep time: 15 minutes | Cook time: 3 to 4 hours | Serves 8

3 pounds (1.8 kg) tart apples, peeled and sliced
10 slices cinnamon-raisin bread, cubed
¾ cup packed brown sugar
½ cup butter, melted
1 teaspoon almond extract
½ teaspoon ground cinnamon
¼ teaspoon ground cardamom
⅛ teaspoon salt
Whipped Cream:
1 cup heavy whipping cream
2 tablespoons sugar
1 teaspoon lemon zest
½ teaspoon almond extract

1. Place the apples in the slow cooker.
2. In a large bowl, combine the bread, brown sugar, butter, extract, cinnamon, cardamom and salt, then spoon over the apples.
3. Cover and cook on low for 3 to 4 hours or until apples are tender.
4. In a small bowl, beat the cream until it begins to thicken. Add the sugar, lemon zest and extract, then beat until soft peaks form. Serve with apple mixture.

Candy Clusters

Prep time: 15 minutes | Cook time: 1 hour | Makes 6½ dozen

2 pounds (907 g) white candy coating, coarsely chopped
1½ cups peanut butter
½ teaspoon almond extract, optional
4 cups crisp rice cereal
4 cups Cap'n Crunch cereal
4 cups miniature marshmallows

1. Place the candy coating in the slow cooker. Cover and cook on high for 1 hour. Add peanut butter. Stir in extract if desired.
2. In a large bowl, combine the cereals and marshmallows. Stir into the peanut butter mixture until well coated. Drop by tablespoonfuls onto waxed paper.
3. Let stand until set. Store at room temperature or serve immediately.

Apple Caramel

Prep time: 15 minutes | Cook time: 6 hours | Serves 7

½ cup apple juice
7 ounces (198 g) caramel candies
1 teaspoon vanilla
½ teaspoon ground cinnamon
⅛ teaspoon ground cardamom
⅓ cup creamy peanut butter
2 medium apples, peeled, cored, and cut in wedges
7 slices angel food cake
4 cups vanilla ice cream

1.Combine the apple juice, caramel candies, vanilla, and spices. Place in the slow cooker.
2.Drop peanut butter, 1 teaspoon at a time, into the slow cooker. Stir. Add apple wedges.
3.Cover. Cook on low for 5 hours. Stir well.
4.Cover. Then cook for 1 more hour on low.
5.Serve ⅓ cup warm mixture over each slice of angel food cake and top with ice cream.

Almond and Sour Cream Cheesecake

Prep time: 15 minutes | Cook time: 5 to 6 hours | Serves 10

¼ cup butter, melted, divided
1 cup ground almonds
¾ cup plus 1 tablespoon granulated erythritol, divided
¼ teaspoon ground cinnamon
12 ounces (340 g) cream cheese, at room temperature
2 eggs
2 teaspoons pure vanilla extract
1 cup sour cream

1.Lightly grease a springform pan with 1 tablespoon of the butter.
2.In a small bowl, stir together the almonds, 1 tablespoon of the erythritol, and cinnamon until blended.
3.Add the remaining 3 tablespoons of the butter and stir until coarse crumbs form.
4.Press the crust mixture into the springform pan along the bottom and about 2 inches up the sides.
5.In a large bowl, using a handheld mixer, beat together the cream cheese, eggs, vanilla, and remaining ¾ cup of the erythritol. Beat the sour cream into the cream-cheese mixture until smooth.
6.Spoon the batter into the springform pan and smooth out the top.
7.Place a wire rack in the slow cooker and place the springform pan on top.
8.Cover and cook on low for 5 to 6 hours, or until the cheesecake doesn't jiggle when shaken.
9.Cool completely before removing from pan.
10.Chill the cheesecake completely before serving.

Almond and Peanut Butter Cheesecake

Prep time: 15 minutes | Cook time: 5 to 6 hours | Serves 10

¼ cup butter, melted, divided
1 cup ground almonds
2 tablespoons cocoa powder
1 cup granulated erythritol, divided
12 ounces (340 g) cream cheese, room temperature
½ cup natural peanut butter
2 eggs, room temperature
1 teaspoon pure vanilla extract

1.Lightly grease a springform pan with 1 tablespoon butter.
2.In a small bowl, stir together the almonds, cocoa powder, and ¼ cup erythritol until blended. Add the remaining 3 tablespoons of the butter and stir until coarse crumbs form.
3.Press the crust mixture into the springform pan along the bottom and about 2 inches up the sides.
4.In a large bowl, using a handheld mixer, beat together the cream cheese and peanut butter until smooth. Beat in the remaining ¾ cup of the erythritol, eggs, and vanilla.
5.Spoon the batter into the springform pan and smooth out the top.
6.Place a wire rack in the slow cooker and place the springform pan on the wire rack.
7.Cover and cook on low for 5 to 6 hours, or until the cheesecake doesn't jiggle when shaken.
8.Cool completely before removing from pan.
9.Chill the cheesecake completely before serving.

Apple Tapioca

Prep time: 15 to 20 minutes | Cook time: 3 to 4 hour | Serves 8 to 10

8 to 10 tart apples
½ cup sugar
4 tablespoons minute tapioca
4 tablespoons red cinnamon candy
½ cup water
Whipped topping, optional

1. Pare and core the apples. Cut into eighths lengthwise and place in the slow cooker.
2. Mix the sugar, tapioca, candy, and water in a bowl. Pour over the apples.
3. Cook on high for 3 to 4 hours.
4. Serve hot or cold. Top with whipped cream.

Cherry Molton Cake

Prep time: 15 minutes | Cook time: 5 hours | Serves 2

1 cup all-purpose flour
½ cup brown sugar
½ cup granulated sugar
¼ cup cocoa powder
1½ teaspoons baking powder
Pinch salt
½ cup chocolate milk
2 tablespoons melted butter
1 teaspoon vanilla
½ cup cherry preserves
3 tablespoons honey
1 cup boiling water
Nonstick cooking spray

1. Spray the slow cooker with the nonstick cooking spray.
2. In the slow cooker, combine the flour, brown sugar, granulated sugar, cocoa powder, baking powder, and salt.
3. Whisk in the chocolate milk, butter, and vanilla.
4. Drop the cherry preserves by small spoonfuls over the batter.
5. Drizzle with the honey and pour the boiling water over them. Do not stir.
6. Cover and cook on low for 5 hours, or until the cake looks done (toothpick tests will not work since there is a layer of sauce on the bottom).
7. Scoop out of the slow cooker to serve.

Easy Apple and Walnut Pie

Prep time: 5 minutes | Cook time: 2 to 3 hours | Serves 10 to 12

1 (21-ounce / 595-g) can cherry or apple pie filling
1 package yellow cake mix (regular size)
½ cup butter, melted
⅓ cup chopped walnuts, optional

1. Place the pie filling in the slow cooker. Combine the cake mix and butter (mixture will be crumbly) in a small bowl, then sprinkle over filling. Sprinkle with walnuts, if desired.
2. Cover and cook on low for 2 to 3 hours. Serve in bowls.

Raspberry and Lime Custard Cake

Prep time: 15 minutes | Cook time: 3 hours | Serves 8

1 teaspoon coconut oil
6 eggs, whites and yolks separated
2 cups heavy (whipping) cream
¾ cup granulated erythritol
½ cup coconut flour
¼ teaspoon salt
Juice and zest of 2 limes
½ cup raspberries

1. Lightly grease a springform pan with the coconut oil.
2. In a large bowl, using a hand mixer, beat the egg whites until stiff peaks form, about 5 minutes.
3. In a large bowl, whisk together the yolks, heavy cream, erythritol, coconut flour, salt, and lime juice and zest.
4. Fold the egg whites into the mixture.
5. Transfer the batter to the springform pan and sprinkle the raspberries over.
6. Place a wire rack in the slow cooker and place the springform pan on the wire rack.
7. Cover and cook on low for 3 hours, or until a toothpick inserted in the center comes out clean.
8. Remove the cover and allow the cake to cool to room temperature.
9. Place the springform pan in the refrigerator for at least 2 hours until the cake is firm.
10. Carefully remove the sides of the springform pan. Slice and serve.

Apple Crumble

Prep time: 10 minutes | Cook time: 5 to 6 hours | Serves 4 to 5

4 to 5 cooking apples, peeled and sliced
⅔ cup packed brown sugar
½ cup flour
½ cup quick-cooking dry oats
½ teaspoon cinnamon
¼-½ teaspoon nutmeg
⅓ cup butter, softened
2 tablespoons peanut butter

1. Place the apple slices in the slow cooker.
2. Combine the brown sugar, flour, oats, cinnamon, and nutmeg in a large bowl.
3. Cut in the butter and peanut butter. Sprinkle the mixture over the apples.
4. Cover and cook on low for 5 to 6 hours.
5. Serve warm or cold.

Simple Pound Cake

Prep time: 10 minutes | Cook time: 5 to 6 hours | Serves 8

1 tablespoon coconut oil
2 cups almond flour
1 cup granulated erythritol
½ teaspoon cream of tartar
Pinch salt
1 cup butter, melted
5 eggs
2 teaspoons pure vanilla extract

1. Lightly grease a loaf pan with the coconut oil.
2. In a large bowl, stir together the almond flour, erythritol, cream of tartar, and salt, until well mixed.
3. In a small bowl, whisk together the butter, eggs, and vanilla.
4. Add the wet ingredients to the dry ingredients and stir to combine.
5. Transfer the batter to the loaf pan.
6. Place the loaf pan in the slow cooker.
7. Cover and cook until a toothpick inserted in the center comes out clean, about 5 to 6 hours on low.
8. Serve warm.

Hearty Seven Layer Bars

Prep time: 5 to 10 minutes | Cook time: 2 to 3 hours | Serves 6 to 8

¼ cup butter, melted
½ cup graham cracker crumbs
½ cup chocolate chips
½ cup butterscotch chips
½ cup flaked coconut
½ cup chopped nuts
½ cup sweetened condensed milk

1. Layer all the ingredients in a cake pan that fits in the slow cooker. Do not stir.
2. Cover and bake on high for 2 to 3 hours, or until firm. Remove pan and uncover. Let stand 5 minutes.
3. Unmold carefully on plate and cool before serving.

Gingerbread

Prep time: 10 minutes | Cook time: 3 hours | Serves 8

1 tablespoon coconut oil
2 cups almond flour
¾ cup granulated erythritol
2 tablespoons coconut flour
2 tablespoons ground ginger
2 teaspoons baking powder
2 teaspoons ground cinnamon
½ teaspoon ground nutmeg
¼ teaspoon ground cloves
Pinch salt
¾ cup heavy (whipping) cream
½ cup butter, melted
4 eggs
1 teaspoon pure vanilla extract

1. Lightly grease the slow cooker with coconut oil.
2. In a large bowl, stir together the almond flour, erythritol, coconut flour, ginger, baking powder, cinnamon, nutmeg, cloves, and salt.
3. In a medium bowl, whisk together the heavy cream, butter, eggs, and vanilla.
4. Add the wet ingredients to the dry ingredients and stir to combine.
5. Spoon the batter into the slow cooker.
6. Cover and cook on low for 3 hours, or until a toothpick inserted in the center comes out clean.
7. Serve warm.

Mixed Fruit Curry

Prep time: 10 minutes | Cook time: 8 to 10 hours | Serves 8 to 10

1 can pears, undrained
1 can apricots, undrained
1 can peaches, undrained
1 can black cherries, undrained
1 large can pineapple chunks, undrained
½ cup brown sugar
1 teaspoon curry powder
3 to 4 tablespoons quick-cooking tapioca

1.Combine the fruit in a large bowl. Toss to mix well. Let stand for at least 2 hours, or up to 8 hours, to allow flavors to blend. Drain. Place in the slow cooker.
2.Add the remaining ingredients. Mix well.
3.Cover. Cook on low for 8 to 10 hours.
4.Serve warm.

Gold Almond Cake

Prep time: 15 minutes | Cook time: 3 hours | Serves 8

½ cup coconut oil, divided
1½ cups almond flour
½ cup coconut flour
½ cup granulated erythritol
2 teaspoons baking powder
3 eggs
½ cup coconut milk
2 teaspoons pure vanilla extract
½ teaspoon almond extract

1.Line the slow cooker with aluminum foil and grease the aluminum foil with 1 tablespoon of the coconut oil.
2.In a medium bowl, mix the almond flour, coconut flour, erythritol, and baking powder.
3.In a large bowl, whisk together the remaining coconut oil, eggs, coconut milk, vanilla, and almond extract.
4.Add the dry ingredients to the wet ingredients and stir until well blended.
5.Transfer the batter to the slow cooker and use a spatula to even the top.
6.Cover and cook on low for 3 hours, or until a toothpick inserted in the center comes out clean.
7.Remove the cake from the slow cooker and cool completely before serving.

Rhubarb and Strawberry Compote

Prep time: 10 minutes | Cook time: 1 to 2 hours | Serves 6

1 pound (454 g) rhubarb, peeled and sliced 1 inch thick
¼ cup honey
2 tablespoons water
1 teaspoon vanilla extract
Pinch salt
4 cups strawberries, hulled and quartered
1 tablespoon unsalted butter
2 pints vanilla ice cream or frozen yogurt

1.Combine the rhubarb, honey, water, vanilla, and salt in the slow cooker.
2.Cover and cook until the rhubarb is softened and sauce is thickened, 1 to 2 hours on high.
3.Stir strawberries and butter into the compote and let sit until heated through, about 5 minutes.
4.Portion the ice cream into individual bowls and spoon the compote over. Serve.

Pot De Crème

Prep time: 10 minutes | Cook time: 3 hours | Serves 6

6 egg yolks
2 cups heavy (whipping) cream
⅓ cup cocoa powder
1 tablespoon pure vanilla extract
½ teaspoon liquid stevia

1.In a medium bowl, whisk together the yolks, heavy cream, cocoa powder, vanilla, and stevia.
2.Pour the mixture into a baking dish and place the dish in the slow cooker.
3.Pour in enough water to reach halfway up the sides of the baking dish.
4.Cover and cook on low for 3 hours.
5.Remove the baking dish from the slow cooker and cool to room temperature on a wire rack.
6.Chill the dessert completely in the refrigerator. Serve chilled.

Crispy Pineapple and Mango

Prep time: 5 minutes | Cook time: 2½ hours | Serves 6

4 tablespoons unsalted butter, cut into tiny pieces, plus more for greasing the slow cooker
3 cups diced pineapple, drained if canned
2 cups diced mango
½ cup packed brown sugar
¼ cup orange or pineapple juice
2 tablespoons dark rum
¼ cup chopped candied ginger (optional)
2½ cups granola

1.Generously grease the slow cooker with butter.
2.In the slow cooker, combine all the ingredients except the granola and remaining 4 tablespoons of butter.
3.Scatter the butter pieces on top of the fruit and sprinkle the granola on top of the butter.
4.Cook on low for 5 hours or on high for 2½ hours, until the fruit is tender.
5.Serve hot.

Super Lemony Rice Pudding

Prep time: 10 minutes | Cook time: 6 hours | Serves 2

1 cup long-grain white rice
⅔ cup granulated sugar
4 cups milk
1 cup water
⅓ cup freshly squeezed lemon juice
2 teaspoons lemon zest
Pinch salt
4 tablespoons butter, melted
Nonstick cooking spray

1.Spray the slow cooker with the nonstick cooking spray.
2.In the slow cooker, combine all the ingredients and stir.
3.Cover and cook on low for 6 hours, or until the rice is very tender and the mixture has thickened, and serve.

Pumpkin and Mixed Berry Compote

Prep time: 10 minutes | Cook time: 3 to 4 hours | Serves 10

1 tablespoon coconut oil
2 cups diced pumpkin
1 cup cranberries
1 cup blueberries
½ cup granulated erythritol
Juice and zest of 1 orange
½ cup coconut milk
1 teaspoon ground cinnamon
½ teaspoon ground allspice
¼ teaspoon ground nutmeg
1 cup whipped cream

1.Lightly grease the slow cooker with the coconut oil.
2.Place the pumpkin, cranberries, blueberries, erythritol, orange juice and zest, coconut milk, cinnamon, allspice, and nutmeg in the slow cooker.
3.Cover and cook on low for 3 to 4 hours.
4.Let the compote cool for 1 hour and serve warm with a generous scoop of whipped cream.

Pecan-Crusted Blueberry Crisp

Prep time: 10 minutes | Cook time: 3 to 4 hours | Serves 8

5 tablespoons coconut oil, melted, divided
4 cups blueberries
¾ cup plus 2 tablespoons granulated erythritol
1 cup ground pecans
1 teaspoon baking soda
½ teaspoon ground cinnamon
2 tablespoons coconut milk
1 egg

1.Lightly grease the slow cooker with 1 tablespoon of the coconut oil.
2.Add the blueberries and 2 tablespoons of erythritol to the slow cooker.
3.In a large bowl, stir together the remaining ¾ cup of the erythritol, ground pecans, baking soda, and cinnamon until well mixed.
4.Add the coconut milk, egg, and remaining coconut oil, and stir until coarse crumbs form.
5.Top the contents in the slow cooker with the pecan mixture.
6.Cover and cook on low for 3 to 4 hours.
7.Serve warm.

Creamy Pumpkin Pie Custard

Prep time: 15 minutes | Cook time: 7 hours | Serves 2

1½ cups light cream
1 (15-ounce / 425-g) can solid-pack pumpkin
½ cup brown sugar
¼ cup granulated sugar
2 eggs, beaten
3 tablespoons melted butter
2 teaspoons vanilla
⅓ cup all-purpose flour
½ teaspoon baking powder
1 teaspoon ground cinnamon
¼ teaspoon ground nutmeg
¼ teaspoon ground allspice
3 large sugar cookies
Whipped cream, for garnish
Nonstick cooking spray

1. Spritz the slow cooker with the nonstick cooking spray.
2. In a large bowl, gradually add the light cream to the pumpkin, beating with a hand mixer.
3. Beat in the brown sugar, granulated sugar, eggs, butter, and vanilla.
4. Add the flour, baking powder, cinnamon, nutmeg, and allspice.
5. Pour the mixture into the slow cooker. Cover and cook on low for 7 hours, or until the mixture is set.
6. Crumble the sugar cookies on top of each serving and serve with whipped cream.

Chocolate Brownie Cake

Prep time: 10 minutes | Cook time: 3 hours | Serves 12

½ cup plus 1 tablespoon unsalted butter, melted, divided
1½ cups almond flour
¾ cup cocoa powder
¾ cup granulated erythritol
1 teaspoon baking powder
¼ teaspoon fine salt
1 cup heavy (whipping) cream
3 eggs, beaten
2 teaspoons pure vanilla extract
1 cup whipped cream

1. Generously grease the slow cooker with 1 tablespoon of the melted butter.
2. In a large bowl, stir together the almond flour, cocoa powder, erythritol, baking powder, and salt.
3. In a medium bowl, whisk together the remaining ½ cup of the melted butter, heavy cream, eggs, and vanilla until well blended.
4. Whisk the wet ingredients into the dry ingredients and spoon the batter into the slow cooker.
5. Cover and cook on low for 3 hours, then let the cake sit for 1 hour.
6. Serve warm with the whipped cream.

Chapter 11 Side Dishes

Herbed Mashed Potatoes

Prep time: 15 minutes | Cook time: 2 to 3 hours | Serves 10

4 pounds (1.8 kg) Yukon Gold potatoes (about 12 medium), peeled and cubed
1 (8-ounce / 227-g) package cream cheese, softened and cubed
1 cup sour cream
½ cup butter, cubed
⅓ cup heavy whipping cream
3 tablespoons minced chives
3 garlic cloves, minced
1 tablespoon minced fresh parsley
1 teaspoon minced fresh thyme
½ teaspoon salt
¼ teaspoon pepper

1.Place the potatoes in a Dutch oven and cover with water. Bring to a boil. Reduce heat. Cover and cook for 10 to 15 minutes or until tender. Drain. Mash the potatoes with the cream cheese, sour cream, butter and cream. Stir in the remaining ingredients.
2.Transfer to a greased slow cooker. Cover and cook on low for 2 to 3 hours or until heated through.
3.Serve warm.

Braised Beans and Bacon

Prep time: 15 minutes | Cook time: 6 to 8 hours | Serves 12

1 (1-pound / 454-g) package sliced bacon, chopped
1 cup chopped onion
2 (15-ounce / 425-g) cans pork and beans, undrained
1 (16-ounce / 454-g) can kidney beans, rinsed and drained
1 (16-ounce / 454-g) can butter beans, rinsed and drained
1 (15¼-ounce / 432-g) can lima beans, rinsed and drained
1 (15-ounce / 425-g) can black beans, rinsed and drained
1 cup packed brown sugar
½ cup cider vinegar
1 tablespoon molasses
2 teaspoons garlic powder
½ teaspoon ground mustard

1.In a large skillet, cook the bacon and onion over medium heat for 4 minutes, until the bacon is crisp. Remove to paper towels to drain.
2.In a slow cooker, combine the remaining ingredients. Stir in the bacon mixture. Cover and cook on low for 6 to 8 hours or until heated through.
3.Serve hot.

Creamy Potato Mash

Prep time: 15 minutes | Cook time: 3 to 3 ½ hours | Serves 10

3 pounds (1.4 kg) potatoes (about 9 medium), peeled and cubed
1 (8-ounce / 227-g) package cream cheese, softened
1 cup sour cream
½ cup butter, cubed
¼ cup 2% milk
1½ cups shredded Cheddar cheese
1½ cups shredded Pepper Jack cheese
½ pound (227 g) bacon strips, cooked and crumbled
4 green onions, chopped
½ teaspoon onion powder
½ teaspoon garlic powder

1.Place the potatoes in a Dutch oven and cover with water. Bring to a boil. Reduce heat. Cover and cook for 10 to 15 minutes or until tender. Drain. Mash the potatoes with the cream cheese, sour cream, butter and milk. Stir in the cheeses, bacon, onions and seasonings. Transfer to a large bowl. Cover and refrigerate overnight.
2.Transfer to a greased slow cooker. Cover and cook on low for 3 to 3 ½ hours.
3.Serve hot.

Hash Brown Potatoes in Cream

Prep time: 5 minutes | Cook time: 3½ to 4 hours | Serves 12 to14

1 (32-ounce / 907-g) package frozen cubed hash brown potatoes, thawed
1 (10¾-ounce / 305-g) can condensed cream of potato soup, undiluted
2 cups shredded Colby-Monterey Jack cheese
1 cup sour cream
¼ teaspoon pepper
⅛ teaspoon salt
1 (8-ounce / 227-g) carton spreadable chive and onion cream cheese

1.Place the potatoes in a lightly greased slow cooker. In a large bowl, combine the soup, cheese, sour cream, pepper and salt. Pour over the potatoes and mix well.
2.Cover and cook on low for 3 ½ to 4 hours or until potatoes are tender. Stir in the cream cheese.

Potato and Black Bean Gratin

Prep time: 15 minutes | Cook time: 8 to 10 hours | Serves 6

2 (15-ounce / 425-g) cans black beans, rinsed and drained
1 (10¾-ounce / 305-g) can condensed cream of mushroom soup, undiluted
1 medium sweet red pepper, chopped
1 cup frozen peas, thawed
1 cup chopped sweet onion
1 celery rib, thinly sliced
2 garlic cloves, minced
1 teaspoon dried thyme
¼ teaspoon coarsely ground pepper
1½ pounds (680 g) medium red potatoes, cut into ¼-inch slices
1 teaspoon salt
1 cup shredded Cheddar cheese

1.In a large bowl, combine the beans, soup, red pepper, peas, onion, celery, garlic, thyme and pepper. Spoon half of the mixture into a greased slow cooker. Layer with half of the potatoes, salt and cheese. Repeat layers. Cover and cook on low for 8 to 10 hours or until potatoes are tender.
2.Serve hot.

Spicy BBQ Beans and Corn

Prep time: 10 minutes | Cook time: 5 to 6 hours | Serves 12

1 (16-ounce / 454-g) can kidney beans, rinsed and drained
1 (15¼-ounce / 432-g) can whole kernel corn, drained
1 (15-ounce / 425-g) can garbanzo beans or chickpeas, rinsed and drained
1 (15-ounce / 425-g) can black beans, rinsed and drained
1 (15-ounce / 425-g) can chili with beans
1 cup barbecue sauce
1 cup salsa
⅓ cup packed brown sugar
¼ teaspoon hot pepper sauce
Chopped green onions (optional)

1.In a slow cooker, combine the first nine ingredients. Cover and cook on low for 5 to 6 hours.
2.Serve topped with the green onions, if desired.

Water Chestnut and Green Bean Casserole

Prep time: 10 minutes | Cook time: 5½ to 6½ hours | Serves 10

2 (16-ounce / 454-g) packages frozen cut green beans, thawed
2 (10¾-ounce / 305-g) cans condensed cream of mushroom soup, undiluted
1 (8-ounce / 227-g) can sliced water chestnuts, drained
1 cup 2% milk
6 bacon strips, cooked and crumbled
1 teaspoon pepper
⅛ teaspoon paprika
4 ounces (113 g) process cheese (Velveeta), cubed
1 (2.8-ounce / 79-g) can French-fried onions

1.In a slow cooker, combine the green beans, cream of mushroom soup, water chestnuts, milk, bacon, pepper and paprika. Cover and cook on low for 5 to 6 hours or until the beans are tender.
2.Stir in the cheese. Cover and cook for 30 minutes or until the cheese is melted. Sprinkle with the French-fried onions. Serve warm.

Tangy Banana-Raisin Applesauce

Prep time: 10 minutes | Cook time: 3 to 4 hours | Makes 5½ cups

8 medium apples, peeled and cubed
1 medium ripe banana, thinly sliced
1 cup raisins
¾ cup orange juice
½ cup packed brown sugar
¼ cup honey
¼ cup butter, melted
2 teaspoons pumpkin pie spice
1 small lemon
1 envelope instant apples and cinnamon oatmeal
½ cup boiling water
Cooking spray

1.Place the apples, banana and raisins in a slow cooker coated with cooking spray. In a small bowl, combine the orange juice, brown sugar, honey, butter and pie spice. Pour over apple mixture.
2.Cut ends off lemon. Cut into six wedges and remove the seeds. Transfer to the slow cooker. Cover and cook on high for 3 to 4 hours or until apples are soft.
3.Discard the lemon. Mash the apple mixture. In a small bowl, combine the oatmeal and water. Let stand for 1 minute. Stir into the applesauce. Serve.

Creamy Cheddar Spiral Pasta

Prep time: 5 minutes | Cook time: 2½ hours | Serves 15

2 cups half-and-half cream
1 (10¾-ounce / 305-g) can condensed Cheddar cheese soup, undiluted
½ cup butter, melted
4 cups shredded Cheddar cheese
1 (16-ounce / 454-g) package spiral pasta, cooked and drained

1.In a slow cooker, combine the cream, soup and butter until smooth. Stir in the cheese and pasta. Cover and cook on low for 2½ hours or until cheese is melted.
2.Serve hot.

Sweet Green Beans with Bacon

Prep time: 10 minutes | Cook time: 4½ hours | Serves 12

1 (14-ounce / 397-g) package thick-sliced bacon strips, chopped
1 large red onion, chopped
2 (16-ounce / 454-g) packages frozen cut green beans, thawed
1 (28-ounce / 794-g) can petite diced tomatoes, undrained
¼ cup packed brown sugar
1 tablespoon seasoned pepper
½ teaspoon seasoned salt
1 (16-ounce / 454-g) can red beans, rinsed and drained

1.In a large skillet, cook the bacon over medium heat for 3 minutes, until partially cooked but not crisp, stirring occasionally. Remove with a slotted spoon and drain on paper towels. Discard the drippings, reserving 2 tablespoons. Add the onion to the drippings. Cook and stir over medium-high heat for 4 minutes, or until tender.
2.In a slow cooker, combine the green beans, tomatoes, brown sugar, pepper, salt, bacon and onion. Cook, covered, on low for 4 hours. Stir in the red beans. Cook for 30 minutes longer or until heated through.
3.Serve warm.

Hash Brown Potato Casserole

Prep time: 5 minutes | Cook time: 3¼ to 4½ hours | Serves 8

1 (32-ounce / 907-g) package frozen cubed hash brown potatoes, thawed
1 (10¾-ounce / 305-g) can condensed cream of celery soup, undiluted
1 (10¾-ounce / 305-g) can condensed nacho cheese soup, undiluted
1 large onion, finely chopped
⅓ cup butter, melted
1 cup reduced-fat sour cream

1.In a greased slow cooker, combine the first five ingredients. Cover and cook on low for 3 to 4 hours or until potatoes are tender.
2.Stir in the sour cream. Cover and cook for 15 to 30 minutes longer or until heated through. Serve warm.

Hearty Braised Vegetables

Prep time: 10 minutes | Cook time: 7 to 8 hours | Serves 8

4 celery ribs, cut into 1-inch pieces
4 small carrots, cut into 1-inch pieces
2 medium tomatoes, cut into chunks
2 medium onions, thinly sliced
2 cups cut fresh green beans (1-inch pieces)
1 medium green pepper, cut into 1-inch pieces
¼ cup butter, melted
3 tablespoons quick-cooking tapioca
1 tablespoon sugar
2 teaspoons salt (optional)
⅛ teaspoon pepper

1. Place the vegetables in a slow cooker. In a small bowl, combine the butter, tapioca, sugar, salt (if desired) and pepper. Pour over the vegetables and stir well.
2. Cover and cook on low for 7 to 8 hours or until the vegetables are tender. Serve with a slotted spoon.

Mac 'n' Cheese in Slow Cooker

Prep time: 10 minutes | Cook time: 2 to 3 hours | Serves 9

2 cups uncooked elbow macaroni
1 (12-ounce / 340-g) can reduced-fat evaporated milk
1½ cups fat-free milk
⅓ cup egg substitute
1 tablespoon butter, melted
8 ounces (227 g) reduced-fat process cheese (Velveeta), cubed
2 cups shredded sharp Cheddar cheese, divided
Cooking spray

1. Cook the macaroni in a large pot of boiling water for 8 minutes. Drain and rinse in cold water.
2. In a large bowl, combine the evaporated milk, milk, egg substitute and butter. Stir in the process cheese, 1½ cups of the sharp Cheddar cheese and macaroni.
3. Transfer to a slow cooker coated with cooking spray. Cover and cook on low for 2 to 3 hours or until center is set, stirring once. Sprinkle with the remaining sharp Cheddar cheese.
4. Serve warm.

Buttery Maple Butternut Squash

Prep time: 10 minutes | Cook time: 5½ to 6½ hours | Serves 9

1 medium butternut squash (about 4 pounds / 1.8 kg), peeled, deseeded and cut into 2-inch cubes
4 garlic cloves, minced
1 teaspoon salt
½ teaspoon pepper
½ cup butter, melted
½ cup maple syrup
½ cup heavy whipping cream
¼ cup sliced almonds
¼ cup shredded Parmesan cheese

1. Place the butternut squash in a slow cooker. Sprinkle with the garlic, salt and pepper. Add the butter and maple syrup and stir to coat. Cover and cook on low for 5 to 6 hours or until the squash is tender.
2. Stir in the heavy whipping cream. Cover and cook for 30 minutes longer or until heated through. Sprinkle with the almonds and cheese.
3. Serve warm.

Cheddar Ham and Potatoes

Prep time: 10 minutes | Cook time: 8 to 10 hours | Serves 16

1 (10¾-ounce / 305-g) can condensed Cheddar cheese soup, undiluted
1 (10¾-ounce / 305-g) can condensed cream of mushroom soup, undiluted
1 cup 2% milk
10 medium potatoes, peeled and thinly sliced
3 cups cubed fully cooked ham
2 medium onions, chopped
1 teaspoon paprika
1 teaspoon pepper

1. In a small bowl, combine the soups and milk.
2. In a greased slow cooker, layer half of the potatoes, ham, onions and soup mixture. Repeat layers. Sprinkle with the paprika and pepper.
3. Cover and cook on low for 8 to 10 hours or until potatoes are tender.
4. Serve hot.

Butternut Apples with Currants

Prep time: minutes | Cook time: 4 hours | Serves 10

1 (3-pound / 1.4-kg) butternut squash, peeled, deseeded, and cubed
4 cooking apples, peeled, cored, and chopped
¾ cup dried currants
½ sweet yellow onion, sliced thin
1 tablespoon ground cinnamon
1½ teaspoons ground nutmeg

1. Combine the squash, apples, currants, and onion in a slow cooker. Sprinkle with the cinnamon and nutmeg.
2. Cover and cook on high for 4 hours, or until the squash is tender and cooked through. Stir occasionally while cooking.
3. Serve hot.

Slow Cooked Tzimmes

Prep time: 20 minutes | Cook time: 5 to 6 hours | Serves 12

½ medium butternut squash, peeled and cubed
2 medium sweet potatoes, peeled and cubed
6 medium carrots, sliced
2 medium tart apples, peeled and sliced
1 cup chopped sweet onion
1 cup chopped dried apricots
1 cup golden raisins
½ cup orange juice
¼ cup honey
2 tablespoons finely chopped crystallized ginger
3 teaspoons ground cinnamon
3 teaspoons pumpkin pie spice
2 teaspoons grated orange peel
1 teaspoon salt
Vanilla yogurt (optional)

1. Place the first seven ingredients in a slow cooker. Combine the orange juice, honey, crystallized ginger, cinnamon, pumpkin pie spice, orange peel and salt in a bowl. Pour over the top and mix well.
2. Cover and cook on low for 5 to 6 hours or until the vegetables are tender. Serve with the vanilla yogurt, if desired.

Ranch Red Potatoes

Prep time: 5 minutes | Cook time: 8 hours | Serves 4 to 6

2 pounds (907 g) small red potatoes, quartered
1 (8-ounce / 227-g) package cream cheese, softened
1 (10¾-ounce / 305-g) can condensed cream of potato soup, undiluted
1 envelope ranch salad dressing mix

1. Place the red potatoes in a slow cooker.
2. In a small bowl, beat the cream cheese, soup and ranch salad dressing mix until blended. Stir into the potatoes. Cover and cook on low for 8 hours or until potatoes are tender.
3. Serve warm.

Cheesy Veggie-Stuffed Peppers

Prep time: 10 minutes | Cook time: 8¼ hours | Serves 6

2 (14½-ounce / 411-g) cans diced tomatoes, undrained
1 (16-ounce / 454-g) can kidney beans, rinsed and drained
1½ cups cooked rice
2 cups shredded Cheddar cheese, divided
1 (10-ounce / 284-g) package frozen corn, thawed
¼ cup chopped onion
1 teaspoon Worcestershire sauce
¾ teaspoon chili powder
½ teaspoon pepper
¼ teaspoon salt
6 medium green peppers

1. In a large bowl, combine the tomatoes, beans, rice, 1½ cups of the cheese, corn, onion, Worcestershire sauce, chili powder, pepper and salt.
2. Remove and discard the tops and seeds of the green peppers. Fill each pepper with about 1 cup of the vegetable mixture. Place in a slow cooker. Cover and cook on low for 8 hours.
3. Sprinkle with the remaining ½ cups of the cheese. Cover and cook for 15 minutes longer or until the peppers are tender and the cheese is melted.
4. Serve hot.

Cheesy Corn

Prep time: 5 minutes | Cook time: 4 hours | Serves 8

2 (16-ounce / 454-g) packages frozen corn, thawed
1 (8-ounce / 227-g) package cream cheese, cubed
⅓ cup butter, cubed
½ teaspoon garlic powder
½ teaspoon salt
¼ teaspoon pepper

1.In a slow cooker, combine all the ingredients. Cover and cook on low for 4 hours or until heated through and the cheese is melted.
2.Stir well before serving.

Balsamic Glazed Brussels Sprouts

Prep time: 10 minutes | Cook time: 2⅓ to 3⅓ hours | Serves 4 to 6

2 pounds (907 g) Brussels sprouts, trimmed and halved
2 cups vegetable stock
1 teaspoon sea salt, divided
Black pepper, to taste
2 tablespoons extra-virgin olive oil
¼ cup toasted pine nuts
¼ cup grated Parmesan cheese
Balsamic Glaze:
1 cup balsamic vinegar
¼ cup honey

1.Mix the balsamic vinegar and honey in a small saucepan over medium-high heat. Stir constantly until the sugar has dissolved. Bring to a boil, reduce the heat to low, and simmer until the glaze is reduced by half, for about 20 minutes. The glaze is finished when it will coat the back of a spoon. Set aside.
2.Combine the Brussels sprouts, stock, and ½ teaspoon salt in a slow cooker. Cover and cook on high for 2 to 3 hours, or until the Brussels sprouts are tender.
3.Drain the Brussels sprouts and transfer to a serving dish. Season with the remaining salt and pepper. Drizzle with 2 tablespoons or more of the balsamic glaze and the olive oil, then sprinkle with the pine nuts and Parmesan. Serve hot.

Garlicky Red Potatoes with Rosemary

Prep time: 5 minutes | Cook time: 5 to 6 hours | Serves 4 to 6

2 pounds (907 g) small red potatoes, unpeeled
2 tablespoons extra-virgin olive oil, divided
3 garlic cloves, minced
Salt and pepper, to taste
1 teaspoon minced fresh rosemary

1.Combine the potatoes, 1 tablespoon of the oil, garlic, ½ teaspoon salt, and ¼ teaspoon pepper in a slow cooker. Cover and cook until potatoes are tender, for 5 to 6 hours on low or 3 to 4 hours on high.
2.Stir in the rosemary and remaining 1 tablespoon of the oil. Season with salt and pepper. Serve.

Garlicky Braised Kale with Chorizo

Prep time: 10 minutes | Cook time: 7 to 8 hours | Serves 4 to 6

8 ounces (227 g) Spanish-style chorizo sausage, halved lengthwise and sliced ½ inch thick
2 garlic cloves, minced
1 tablespoon extra-virgin olive oil
1½ cups chicken broth
Salt and pepper, to taste
2 pounds (907 g) kale, stemmed and cut into 1-inch pieces
Vegetable oil spray

1.Lightly coat the insert of a slow cooker with vegetable oil spray. Microwave the chorizo, garlic, and oil in a bowl, stirring occasionally, until fragrant, for about 1 minute. Transfer to the prepared slow cooker. Stir in the broth and ¼ teaspoon salt.
2.Microwave half of the kale in a covered bowl until slightly wilted, for about 5 minutes. Transfer to the slow cooker. Stir in the remaining kale, cover, and cook until kale is tender, for 7 to 8 hours on low for or 4 to 5 hours on high. Season with salt and pepper. Serve.

Sweet Potato Casserole

Prep time: 10 minutes | Cook time: 5 to 7 hours | Serves 6

2¼ pounds (1 kg) sweet potatoes, peeled and cubed
¾ teaspoon salt
⅛ teaspoon pepper
1 cup peach pie filling
2 tablespoons butter, melted
¼ teaspoon ground cinnamon
½ cup granola without raisins (optional)
Cooking spray

1. Place the sweet potatoes in a slow cooker coated with cooking spray. Toss with salt and pepper. Top with the pie filling and drizzle with the butter. Sprinkle with the cinnamon.
2. Cover and cook on low for 5 to 7 hours or until potatoes are tender. Sprinkle with the granola, if desired. Serve.

Braised Leeks in Cream

Prep time: 10 minutes | Cook time: 3 to 4 hours | Serves 4 to 6

3 pounds (1.4 kg) leeks, white and light green parts only, halved lengthwise, sliced thin, and washed and dried thoroughly
1 tablespoon vegetable oil
2 garlic cloves, minced
2 teaspoons minced fresh thyme or ½ teaspoon dried
Salt and pepper, to taste
1 cup heavy cream
½ cup dry white wine
¼ cup grated Pecorino Romano cheese

1. Microwave the leeks, oil, garlic, thyme, 1 teaspoon salt, and ¼ teaspoon pepper in a bowl, stirring occasionally, until leeks are softened, for 8 to 10 minutes. Transfer to a slow cooker. Stir in the cream and wine, cover, and cook until leeks are tender but not mushy, for 3 to 4 hours on low or 2 to 3 hours on high.
2. Stir the Pecorino into the leek mixture and season with salt and pepper. Let sit for 5 minutes until slightly thickened. Serve.

Lemony Brussels Sprouts with Bacon

Prep time: 10 minutes | Cook time: 2 to 3 hours | Serves 4 to 6

2 pounds (907 g) Brussels sprouts, trimmed and halved through root end
2 cups chicken broth
Salt and pepper, to taste
4 slices bacon, chopped
2 tablespoons unsalted butter, melted
2 teaspoons grated lemon zest plus 1 tablespoon juice
1 teaspoon minced fresh thyme

1. Combine the Brussels sprouts, broth, and ½ teaspoon salt in a slow cooker. Cover and cook until Brussels sprouts are tender, for 2 to 3 hours on high.
2. Line the plate with a double layer of coffee filters. Spread the bacon in an even layer on filters and microwave until crisp, for about 5 minutes.
3. Drain the Brussels sprouts and return to the slow cooker. Stir in the melted butter, lemon zest and juice, and thyme. Season with salt and pepper. Sprinkle with the bacon and serve.

Buttery Spaghetti Squash

Prep time: 5 minutes | Cook time: 6 hours | Serves 8

1 small spaghetti squash, washed
½ cup chicken stock
¼ cup butter
Salt, to taste
Freshly ground black pepper, to taste

1. Place the squash and chicken stock in the insert of a slow cooker. The squash should not touch the sides of the insert.
2. Cook on low for 6 hours.
3. Let the squash cool for 10 minutes and cut in half.
4. Scrape out the squash strands into a bowl with a fork. When finished, add the butter and toss to combine.
5. Season with salt and pepper and serve.

Root Veggies with Thyme

Prep time: 20 minutes | Cook time: 6 to 8 hours | Serves 8

6 carrots, cut into 1-inch chunks
2 yellow onions, each cut into 8 wedges
2 sweet potatoes, peeled and cut into chunks
6 Yukon Gold potatoes, cut into chunks
8 whole garlic cloves, peeled
4 parsnips, peeled and cut into chunks
3 tablespoons olive oil
1 teaspoon dried thyme leaves
½ teaspoon salt
⅛ teaspoon freshly ground black pepper

1.In a slow cooker, mix all the ingredients. Cover and cook on low for 6 to 8 hours, or until the vegetables are tender.
2.Serve warm.

Green Bean and Mushroom Casserole

Prep time: 10 minutes | Cook time: 6 hours | Serves 6

¼ cup butter, divided
½ sweet onion, chopped
1 cup sliced button mushrooms
1 teaspoon minced garlic
2 pounds (907 g) green beans, cut into 2-inch pieces
1 cup vegetable broth
8 ounces (227 g) cream cheese
¼ cup grated Parmesan cheese

1.Lightly grease the insert of the slow cooker with 1 tablespoon of the butter.
2.In a large skillet over medium-high heat, melt the remaining butter. Add the onion, mushrooms, and garlic and sauté until the vegetables are softened, for about 5 minutes.
3.Stir the green beans into the skillet and transfer the mixture to the insert.
4.In a small bowl, whisk the broth and cream cheese together until smooth.
5.Add the cheese mixture to the vegetables and stir. Top the combined mixture with the Parmesan.
6.Cover and cook on low for 6 hours.
7.Serve warm.

Braised Spinach with Cheese

Prep time: 10 minutes | Cook time: 5 to 6 hours | Serves 6 to 8

2 (10-ounce / 284-g) packages frozen chopped spinach, thawed and well drained
2 cups 4% cottage cheese
1½ cups cubed process cheese (Velveeta)
3 eggs, lightly beaten
¼ cup butter, cubed
¼ cup all-purpose flour
1 teaspoon salt

1.In a large bowl, combine all the ingredients. Pour into a greased slow cooker.
2.Cover and cook on high for 1 hour. Reduce heat to low and cook for 4 to 5 hours longer or until a knife inserted near the center comes out clean.
3.Serve warm.

Cauliflower-Bacon Casserole with Pecans

Prep time: 15 minutes | Cook time: 6 hours | Serves 6

1 tablespoon extra-virgin olive oil
2 pounds (907 g) cauliflower florets
10 bacon slices, cooked and chopped
1 cup chopped pecans
4 garlic cloves, sliced
½ teaspoon salt
½ teaspoon freshly ground black pepper
2 tablespoons freshly squeezed lemon juice
4 hard-boiled eggs, shredded, for garnish
1 scallion, white and green parts, chopped, for garnish

1.Lightly grease the insert of a slow cooker with the olive oil.
2.In a medium bowl, toss together the cauliflower, bacon, pecans, garlic, salt, and pepper.
3.Transfer the mixture to the insert and drizzle the lemon juice over the top.
4.Cover and cook on low for 6 hours.
5.Garnish with the hard-boiled eggs and scallion and serve.

Mozzarella Spaghetti Squash

Prep time: 5 minutes | Cook time: 6¼ to 8¼ hours | Serves 4

1 medium spaghetti squash
1 cup sliced fresh mushrooms
1 (14½-ounce / 411-g) can diced tomatoes, undrained
1 teaspoon dried oregano
1 teaspoon salt
¼ teaspoon pepper
¾ cup shredded part-skim Mozzarella cheese

1.Cut the squash in half lengthwise and discard the seeds. Place the squash, cut side up, in a slow cooker. Layer with the mushrooms, tomatoes, oregano, salt and pepper. Cover and cook on low for 6 to 8 hours or until the squash is tender.
2.Sprinkle with the cheese. Cover and cook for 15 minutes or until cheese is melted.
3.When squash is cool enough to handle, use a fork to separate spaghetti squash strands.
4.Serve warm.

Lemony Leafy Greens with Onions

Prep time: 20 minutes | Cook time: 3 to 4 hours | Serves 8

2 bunches Swiss chard, washed and cut into large pieces
2 bunches collard greens, washed and cut into large pieces
2 bunches kale, washed and cut into large pieces
3 onions, chopped
1½ cups vegetable broth
¼ cup honey
2 tablespoons lemon juice
1 teaspoon dried marjoram
1 teaspoon dried basil
¼ teaspoon salt

1.In a slow cooker, mix the Swiss chard, collard greens, kale, and onions.
2.In a medium bowl, mix the vegetable broth, honey, lemon juice, marjoram, basil, and salt. Pour into the slow cooker.
3.Cover and cook on low for 3 to 4 hours, or until the greens are very tender.
4.Serve warm.

Root Veggie Gratin with Barley

Prep time: 10 minutes | Cook time: 7 to 9 hours | Serves 8

2 cups hulled barley
2 onions, chopped
5 garlic cloves, minced
3 large carrots, peeled and sliced
2 sweet potatoes, peeled and cubed
4 Yukon Gold potatoes, cubed
7 cups vegetable broth
1 teaspoon dried tarragon leaves
½ cup grated Parmesan cheese

1.In a slow cooker, mix the barley, onions, garlic, carrots, sweet potatoes, and Yukon Gold potatoes. Add the vegetable broth and tarragon leaves.
2.Cover and cook on low for 7 to 9 hours, or until the barley and vegetables are tender.
3.Stir in the cheese and serve.

Spicy Corn-Ham Pudding

Prep time: 10 minutes | Cook time: 2 hours | Serves 6 to 8

4 cups fresh corn kernels, divided
1 teaspoon coarse salt
3 scallions, white and pale green parts only, thinly sliced, plus more for serving
1 (4-ounce / 113-g) can diced green chiles
¾ cup diced Black Forest ham
3 tablespoons all-purpose flour
2 cups grated manchego cheese or extra-sharp white Cheddar
5 large eggs, at room temperature
⅔ cup heavy cream

1.Butter the insert of a slow cooker.
2.Purée 3 cups of the corn in a blender or food processor. Transfer to a large bowl and stir in the remaining 1 cup of the corn, salt, scallions, chiles, ham, flour, and 1 cup of the cheese.
3.In another bowl, whisk together the eggs and cream just until combined. Stir into the corn mixture. Pour the batter into the slow cooker and top with the remaining 1 cup of the cheese. Cover and cook on low for until pudding is set, for 2 hours, uncovering for last 15 minutes.
4.Let cool for 30 minutes before serving, topped with the sliced scallions.

BBQ Collard Greens with Tofu

Prep time: 10 minutes | Cook time: 4 hours | Serves 6 to 8

¼ cup canola or safflower oil, divided
¾ cup finely chopped sweet onion
4 ounces (113 g) smoked or regular firm tofu, cut into 1-inch pieces
2 bunches collard greens (about 1 pound / 454 g each), tough stems and ribs removed, leaves cut into ½-inch ribbons
¾ cup barbecue sauce
¼ cup apple cider vinegar
Coarse salt and freshly ground pepper, to taste
3 cups boiling water

1.Heat 2 tablespoons of the oil in a large skillet over high heat. Add the onion and tofu, and cook until lightly browned, for about 8 minutes. Transfer to a slow cooker.
2.In the same skillet, heat 1 tablespoon of the oil over high heat. In two batches, cook the collards for about 4 minutes, or until wilted, adding the remaining 1 tablespoon of the oil between batches.
3.Transfer the collards to the slow cooker. Stir in the barbecue sauce and vinegar, and season with salt and pepper. Add the boiling water, cover, and cook on high for 4 hours or on low for 8 hours, or until very tender. Season with salt and pepper, and serve.

Garlicky Balsamic Glazed Onions

Prep time: 20 minutes | Cook time: 8 to 10 hours | Serves 12

10 large yellow onions, peeled and sliced
20 garlic cloves, peeled
¼ cup olive oil
¼ teaspoon salt
2 tablespoons balsamic vinegar
1 teaspoon dried thyme leaves

1.In a slow cooker, mix all the ingredients. Cover and cook on low for 8 to 10 hours, stirring once or twice.
2.serve warm.

Medjool Acorn Squash with Shallots

Prep time: 15 minutes | Cook time: 3 hours | Serves 4 to 6

2 small acorn squash (about 2 pounds / 907 g), halved, deseeded, and cut into wedges
6 shallots, quartered
10 dates, pitted and thinly sliced
6 thyme sprigs
¼ cup plus 2 tablespoons extra-virgin olive oil
¼ cup pure maple syrup
1 teaspoon coarse salt
⅛ teaspoon freshly ground black pepper
⅛ teaspoon red pepper flakes

1.Combine the squash, shallots, dates, and thyme in a large bowl. Drizzle with the oil and maple syrup, and sprinkle with salt, black pepper, and red pepper flakes. Toss well with and transfer to the slow cooker.
2.Cover and cook on high for about 3 hours or on low for 6 hours, turning the squash once or twice during cooking, until squash is tender. Transfer to a large bowl and serve.

Mashed Squash with Garlic

Prep time: 20 minutes | Cook time: 6 to 7 hours | Serves 8

1 (3-pound / 1.4-kg) butternut squash, peeled, deseeded, and cut into 1-inch pieces
3 (1-pound / 454-g) acorn squash, peeled, deseeded, and cut into 1-inch pieces
2 onions, chopped
3 garlic cloves, minced
2 tablespoons olive oil
1 teaspoon dried marjoram leaves
½ teaspoon salt
⅛ teaspoon freshly ground black pepper

1.In a slow cooker, mix all the ingredients. Cover and cook on low for 6 to 7 hours, or until the squash is tender when pierced with a fork.
2.Use a potato masher to mash the squash right in the slow cooker. Serve.

Lemony Beets with Rosemary

Prep time: 10 minutes | Cook time: 8 hours | Serves 7

2 pounds (907 g) beets, peeled and cut into wedges
2 tablespoons fresh lemon juice
2 tablespoons extra-virgin olive oil
2 tablespoons honey
1 tablespoon apple cider vinegar
¾ teaspoon sea salt
½ teaspoon black pepper
2 sprigs fresh rosemary
½ teaspoon lemon zest

1. Place the beets in the slow cooker.
2. Whisk the lemon juice, extra-virgin olive oil, honey, apple cider vinegar, salt, and pepper together in a small bowl. Pour over the beets.
3. Add the sprigs of rosemary to the slow cooker.
4. Cover and cook on low for 8 hours, or until the beets are tender.
5. Remove and discard the rosemary sprigs. Stir in the lemon zest. Serve hot.

Citrus Carrots with Leek

Prep time: 15 minutes | Cook time: 7 to 8 hours | Serves 9

1½ pounds (680 g) whole small carrots
1 leek, white part only, sliced
3 garlic cloves, minced
¼ cup vegetable broth
2 tablespoons freshly squeezed lemon juice
2 tablespoons orange juice
2 tablespoons honey
½ teaspoon lemon zest
½ teaspoon orange zest
½ teaspoon salt
⅛ teaspoon freshly ground black pepper

1. Peel the carrots and cut off the roots. Trim off the tops, if the carrots have them. Put the carrots in the slow cooker.
2. Add the leek and garlic, and stir. Then add all the remaining ingredients and stir.
3. Cover and cook on low for 7 to 8 hours, or until the carrots are tender.

Pecan-Stuffed Acorn Squash

Prep time: 5 minutes | Cook time: 5 to 6 hours | Serves 4

1 acorn squash
1 tablespoon honey
1 tablespoon olive oil
¼ cup chopped pecans or walnuts
¼ cup chopped dried cranberries
Sea salt, to taste

1. Cut the squash in half. Remove the seeds and pulp from the middle. Cut the halves in half again so you have quarters.
2. Place the squash quarters, cut-side up, in the slow cooker.
3. Combine the honey, olive oil, pecans, and cranberries in a small bowl.
4. Spoon the pecan mixture into the center of each squash quarter. Season the squash with salt. Cook on low for 5 to 6 hours, or until the squash is tender.
5. Serve hot.

Sweet Pumpkin-Carrot Pudding

Prep time: 15 minutes | Cook time: 6 hours | Serves 6

1 tablespoon extra-virgin olive oil
2 cups finely shredded carrots
2 cups puréed pumpkin
½ sweet onion, finely chopped
1 cup heavy cream
½ cup cream cheese, softened
2 eggs
1 tablespoon granulated erythritol
1 teaspoon ground nutmeg
½ teaspoon salt
¼ cup pumpkin seeds, for garnish

1. Lightly grease the insert of the slow cooker with the olive oil.
2. In a large bowl, whisk together the carrots, pumpkin, onion, heavy cream, cream cheese, eggs, erythritol, nutmeg, and salt.
3. Cover and cook on low for 6 hours.
4. Serve warm, topped with the pumpkin seeds.

Mexican Corn with Pimentos

Prep time: 10 minutes | Cook time: 2¾ to 4¾ hours | Serves 8 to 10

2 (10-ounce / 284-g) packages frozen corn, partially thawed
1 (4-ounce / 113-g) jar chopped pimentos
⅓ cup chopped green peppers
⅓ cup water
1 teaspoon salt
¼ teaspoon pepper
½ teaspoon paprika
½ teaspoon chili powder

1. Combine all the ingredients in a slow cooker.
2. Cover. Cook on high for 45 minutes, then on low for 2 to 4 hours. Stir occasionally.
3. Serve warm.

Honey Parsnips and Carrots

Prep time: 15 minutes | Cook time: 5 to 7 hours | Serves 8

6 large carrots, peeled and cut into 2-inch pieces
5 large parsnips, peeled and cut into 2-inch pieces
2 red onions, chopped
4 garlic cloves, minced
2 tablespoons olive oil
1 tablespoon honey
½ teaspoon salt

1. In a slow cooker, mix all the ingredients and stir gently. Cover and cook on low for 5 to 7 hours, or until the vegetables are tender.
2. Serve warm.

Cheesy Carrot Casserole

Prep time: 5 minutes | Cook time: 4 to 5 hours | Serves 4 to 5

4 cups sliced carrots
1 medium onion, chopped
1 (10¾-ounce / 305-g) can cream of celery soup
½ cup Velveeta cheese, cubed
¼ to ½ teaspoon salt

1. Mix all the ingredients in a slow cooker.
2. Cover and cook on low for 4 to 5 hours, or until carrots are tender but not mushy.
3. Serve hot.

Orange Cauliflower with Herbs

Prep time: 10 minutes | Cook time: 4 hours | Serves 8

2 heads cauliflower, rinsed and cut into florets
2 onions, chopped
½ cup orange juice
1 teaspoon grated orange zest
1 teaspoon dried thyme leaves
½ teaspoon dried basil leaves
½ teaspoon salt

1. In a slow cooker, mix the cauliflower and onions. Top with the orange juice and orange zest, and sprinkle with the thyme, basil, and salt.
2. Cover and cook on low for 4 hours, or until the cauliflower is tender when pierced with a fork.
3. Serve warm.

Garlicky Squash Curry

Prep time: 15 minutes | Cook time: 6 to 7 hours | Serves 8

1 large butternut squash, peeled, deseeded, and cut into 1-inch pieces
3 acorn squash, peeled, deseeded, and cut into 1-inch pieces
2 onions, finely chopped
5 garlic cloves, minced
1 tablespoon curry powder
⅓ cup freshly squeezed orange juice
½ teaspoon salt

1. In a slow cooker, mix all the ingredients. Cover and cook on low for 6 to 7 hours, or until the squash is tender when pierced with a fork.
2. Serve warm.

Slow Cooker Button Mushrooms

Prep time: 10 minutes | Cook time: 6 hours | Serves 8

3 tablespoons extra-virgin olive oil
1 pound (454 g) button mushrooms, wiped clean and halved
2 teaspoons minced garlic
¼ teaspoon salt
⅛ teaspoon freshly ground black pepper
2 tablespoons chopped fresh parsley

1. Place the olive oil, mushrooms, garlic, salt, and pepper in the insert of the slow cooker and toss to coat.
2. Cover and cook on low for 6 hours.
3. Serve topped with the parsley.

Creamy Mashed Pumpkin

Prep time: 10 minutes | Cook time: 7 to 8 hours | Serves 6

3 tablespoons extra-virgin olive oil, divided
1 pound (454 g) pumpkin, cut into 1-inch chunks
½ cup coconut milk
1 tablespoon apple cider vinegar
½ teaspoon chopped thyme
1 teaspoon chopped oregano
¼ teaspoon salt
1 cup Greek yogurt

1. Lightly grease the insert of the slow cooker with 1 tablespoon of the olive oil.
2. Add the remaining 2 tablespoons of the olive oil with the pumpkin, coconut milk, apple cider vinegar, thyme, oregano, and salt to the insert.
3. Cover and cook on low for 7 to 8 hours.
4. Mash the pumpkin with the yogurt using a potato masher until smooth.
5. Serve warm.

Peppery Broccoli with Sesame Seeds

Prep time: 15 minutes | Cook time: 6 hours | Serves 8

2 pounds (907 g) fresh broccoli, trimmed and chopped into bite-size pieces
1 clove garlic, minced
1 green or red bell pepper, cut into thin slices
1 onion, cut into slices
4 tablespoons light soy sauce
½ teaspoon salt
Dash of black pepper
1 tablespoon sesame seeds, for garnish (optional)

1. Combine all the ingredients, except for the sesame seeds, in a slow cooker.
2. Cover and cook on low for 6 hours. Top with the sesame seeds.
3. Serve warm.

Thai-Flavored Green Vegetables

Prep time: 10 minutes | Cook time: 3 to 3½ hours | Serves 10

1½ pounds (680 g) green beans
3 cups fresh soybeans
3 bulbs fennel, cored and chopped
1 jalapeño pepper, minced
1 lemongrass stalk
½ cup canned coconut milk
2 tablespoons lime juice
½ teaspoon salt
⅓ cup chopped fresh cilantro

1. In a slow cooker, mix the green beans, soybeans, fennel, jalapeño pepper, lemongrass, coconut milk, lime juice, and salt. Cover and cook on low for 3 to 3½ hours, or until the vegetables are tender.
2. Remove and discard the lemongrass. Sprinkle the vegetables with the cilantro and serve.

Spiced Potato and Corn

Prep time: 15 minutes | Cook time: 5 to 6 hours | Serves 8

4 cups potatoes, diced and peeled
1½ cups frozen whole-kernel corn, thawed
4 medium tomatoes, deseeded and diced
1 cup sliced carrots
½ cup chopped onions
¾ teaspoon salt
½ teaspoon sugar
¾ teaspoon dill weed
¼ teaspoon black pepper
½ teaspoon dried basil
¼ teaspoon dried rosemary

1. Combine all the ingredients in a slow cooker.
2. Cover. Cook on low for 5 to 6 hours, or until vegetables are tender.
3. Serve warm.

Chapter 12 Stocks, Broths, and Sauces

Beef Bone Broth

Prep time: 15 minutes | Cook time: 8½ to 10½ hours | Makes 16 cups

4 pounds (1.8 kg) beef bones
4 carrots, chopped
3 celery stalks, chopped
2 onions, chopped
6 garlic cloves, smashed
1 teaspoon black peppercorns
1 bay leaf
2 tablespoons freshly squeezed lemon juice
1 teaspoon salt
14 cups water

1. In a large roasting pan, roast the bones at 400°F (205°C) for about 20 to 25 minutes, or until browned.
2. In the slow cooker, add the bones and the remaining ingredients.
3. Cover and cook on low for 8 to 10 hours, or until the broth is a deep brown.
4. Remove the solids using tongs and discard. Strain the broth through cheesecloth into a very large bowl.
5. Refrigerate the broth overnight. Remove the fat that rises to the surface and discard.
6. Divide the broth into 1-cup portions and freeze up to 3 months.

Herbed Chicken Stock

Prep time: 10 minutes | Cook time: 8 hours | Makes 12 cups

4 pounds (1.8 kg) mixed chicken bones
2 large onions
3 celery stalks, cut into large chunks
8 garlic cloves, unpeeled
2 bay leaves
½ bunch parsley, stems and leaves
1 teaspoon dried thyme
2 tablespoons peppercorns
1 teaspoon kosher salt, plus more for seasoning
12 cups or more cold water, enough to submerge meat and vegetables

1. Bring a large stockpot filled with water to a boil over high heat. Add the chicken bones and boil for 10 minutes. Drain the bones into a colander and rinse thoroughly with cold water.
2. Put the chicken bones into the slow cooker along with the onions, celery, garlic, bay leaves, parsley, thyme, peppercorns, salt, and water. Cover and cook on low for 8 hours.
3. Using a fine-mesh sieve or cheesecloth-lined colander, strain the broth and discard the solids. Season with additional salt, if needed. If using the stock right away, use a ladle or large spoon to skim and discard the fat that rises to the top. Otherwise, cover and store the stock in the refrigerator for up to 3 days and skim the solidified fat before using.

Fish Fennel Stock

Prep time: 10 minutes | Cook time: 6 hours | Makes about 1 quart

2 pounds (907 g) fish scraps (bones, fish heads, seafood shells)
1 teaspoon kosher salt, plus more for seasoning
1 medium onion, chopped
1 large fennel bulb, trimmed and diced
1 celery stalk, chopped
2 garlic cloves, minced
4½ cups water
½ cup dry white wine
5 fresh parsley sprigs
2 bay leaves
½ teaspoon peppercorns

1. Put the fish scraps into the slow cooker along with the salt, onion, fennel, celery, garlic, water, wine, parsley, bay leaves, and peppercorns. Stir to combine. Cover and cook on low for 6 hours.
2. Using a fine-mesh sieve or cheesecloth-lined colander, strain the stock and discard the solids. Season with additional salt, if needed, before using.

Tomato and Mushroom Soup

Prep time: 10 minutes | Cook time: 6 hours | Makes 8 cups

1 onion, chopped
2 celery stalks, chopped
¼ cup chopped celery leaves
1 garlic clove, sliced
1 large tomato, chopped
1 cup chopped cremini mushrooms
1 bay leaf
1 teaspoon dried thyme leaves
¼ teaspoon salt
4 peppercorns
6 cups cool water

1.In the slow cooker, combine the onion, celery stalks, celery leaves, garlic, tomato, mushrooms, bay leaf, thyme, salt, and peppercorns; then add the water.
2.Cover and cook on low for 6 hours.
3.Strain into a large bowl, pressing on the ingredients to get all the liquid.
4.Serve immediately, or cover and refrigerate for up to 4 days.

Scotch Lamb Broth

Prep time: 10 minutes | Cook time: 8 hours | Serves 4 cups

2 tablespoons olive oil
1½ pounds (680 g) lamb shanks (about 2 medium shanks)
3 bay leaves
3 medium garlic cloves
1 cup finely chopped onion
2 medium carrots, finely chopped
1 medium parsnip, finely chopped
2 celery stalks, finely chopped
1 medium russet potato, finely diced
8 cups chicken stock or low-sodium if store-bought
1 teaspoon kosher salt, plus more for seasoning
⅓ cup pearl barley
2 tablespoons finely chopped fresh parsley leaves
Freshly ground black pepper,to taste

1.In a skillet over medium-high heat, heat the oil until shimmering. Season the lamb shanks with salt and pepper, and brown, about 5 minutes per side.
2.Put the shanks in the slow cooker along with the bay leaves, garlic, onion, carrots, parsnip, celery, potato, stock, and salt. Cover and cook on low for 8 hours, until tender.
3.Using a ladle or large spoon, skim the fat during the final 45 minutes of cooking, and discard. At this point, transfer the shanks to a cutting board. When they are cool enough to handle, but still warm, tear the meat from the bones and discard the bones. Return the meat to the slow cooker and add the barley. The barley should be tender when done.
4.Season with additional salt and pepper, as needed. Stir in the parsley and serve.

Mole Sauce

Prep time: 15 minutes | Cook time: 6 hours | Makes 8 cups

4 dried ancho chiles, stemmed
4 dried chipotle chiles, stemmed
3 corn tortillas, thinly sliced
3 cups chicken stock divided
2 tomatoes, chopped
1 onion, chopped
⅓ cup peanut butter
5 garlic cloves, minced
2 jalapeño peppers, minced
1 tablespoon chili powder
½ teaspoon ground cumin
2 tablespoons cocoa powder
1 teaspoon dried oregano leaves
1 teaspoon salt
⅛ teaspoon freshly ground black pepper

1.In a blender or food processor, process the ancho chiles, chipotle chiles, tortillas, and 1 cup of stock until smooth.
2.Put the mixture in the slow cooker. Add the remaining 2 cups of stock and the remaining ingredients and stir to combine.
3.Cover and cook on low for 6 hours, or until the sauce has blended. At this point you can purée the sauce by using an immersion blender or leave it as is.
4.Cool for 30 minutes, and then serve, cover and refrigerate for up to 4 days, or freeze in ½-cup portions for up to 3 months.

BBQ Sauce

Prep time: 20 minutes | Cook time: 6 to 7 hours | Makes 7 cups

3 cups ketchup
1 (8-ounce / 227-g) can tomato sauce
½ cup Dijon mustard
3 tablespoons coarse ground mustard
1 onion, chopped
3 garlic cloves, minced
2 jalapeño peppers, minced
½ cup brown sugar
¼ cup honey
2 celery stalks, finely chopped
3 tablespoons chopped celery leaves
3 tablespoons freshly squeezed lemon juice
2 teaspoons chili powder
1 teaspoon ground smoked paprika
1 teaspoon salt
⅛ teaspoon freshly ground pepper

1.In the slow cooker, combine all the ingredients. Stir to mix well.
2.Cover and cook on low for 6 to 7 hours.
3.Cool and serve, or cover and refrigerate for up to 4 days.

Lush Fruit Sauce

Prep time: 20 minutes | Cook time: 8 hours | Makes 7 cups

2 (12-ounce / 340-g) packages fresh cranberries
2 Granny Smith apples, peeled and chopped
2 pears, peeled and chopped
1 cup brown sugar
⅓ cup orange juice
2 tablespoons freshly squeezed lemon juice
2 teaspoons orange zest
2 teaspoons ground cinnamon
½ teaspoon salt

1.In the slow cooker, combine all the ingredients and stir.
2.Cover and cook on low for 8 hours, or until the cranberries have popped and the sauce is slightly thickened.
3.Cool and serve, cover and refrigerate for up to 4 days, or freeze in ½-cup portions for up to 4 months.

Roasted Roma Tomato Sauce

Prep time: 20 minutes | Cook time: 9 to 11 hours | Makes 13 cups

4 pounds(1.8 kg) Roma tomatoes, seeded and chopped
2 onions, chopped
5 garlic cloves, minced
3 tablespoons extra-virgin olive oil
2 cups bottled tomato juice
3 tablespoons tomato paste
2 teaspoons dried basil leaves
½ teaspoon salt
⅛ teaspoon white pepper

1.In a slow cooker, place all the tomatoes. Partially cover the slow cooker and cook the tomatoes on high for 3 hours, stirring the tomatoes twice during cooking time.
2.Add the remaining ingredients. Cover and cook on low for 6 to 8 hours longer, until the sauce is bubbling and the consistency you want.
3.Divide the sauce into 2-cup portions and freeze up to 3 months.

Salsa Verde

Prep time: 15 minutes | Cook time: 4 hours | Makes 7 cups

2½ pounds (1.1 kg) tomatillos, husks removed, rinsed, and chopped
1 green bell pepper, chopped
2 onions, chopped
3 garlic cloves, minced
2 jalapeño peppers, minced
½ cup chopped fresh cilantro leaves
1 teaspoon salt
⅛ teaspoon freshly ground black pepper
1 cup Vegetable Broth or water

1.In the slow cooker, combine all the ingredients and stir.
2.Cover and cook on low for 4 hours.
3.Cool and serve, refrigerate for up to 4 days, or freeze in ½-cup portions for up to 3 months.
Appendix 1: Measurement Conversion Chart
Appendix 2: Recipes Index

Nacho Cheese Sauce

Prep time: 10 minutes | Cook time: 3 hours | Serves 10

1 (2-pound / 907-g) box original Velveeta cheese, cut into chunks
8 ounces (227 g) sharp Cheddar cheese, shredded
1 pound (454 g) hot breakfast sausage, browned
1 (4-ounce / 113-g) can chopped green or red chiles
1 teaspoon kosher salt
1 teaspoon freshly ground black pepper
1 tablespoon chili powder
1½ teaspoons ground cumin
½ teaspoon onion powder
¼ teaspoon garlic powder
¼ teaspoon dried oregano
¼ teaspoon red pepper flakes

1.To the slow cooker, add the Velveeta and Cheddar, browned sausage, chiles, salt, pepper, chili powder, cumin, onion powder, garlic powder, oregano, and red pepper flakes. Cover and cook on low for 3 hours.
2.Season with additional salt and pepper as needed before serving.

Pepper Steak Sauce

Prep time: 10 minutes | Cook time: 6 hours | Makes 2 cups

3 large red peppers, seeded and roughly chopped
2 garlic cloves, smashed
¼ cup ketchup
¼ cup orange juice
2 tablespoons tomato paste
2 tablespoons Dijon mustard
2 tablespoons balsamic vinegar
2 tablespoons Worcestershire sauce
1 tablespoon brown sugar
1 tablespoon raisins
½ teaspoon celery seed
½ teaspoon kosher salt, plus more for seasoning
¼ teaspoon freshly ground black pepper, plus more for seasoning

3 tablespoons all-purpose flour

1.To the slow cooker, add the peppers, garlic, ketchup, orange juice, tomato paste, mustard, vinegar, Worcestershire sauce, brown sugar, raisins, celery seed, salt, and pepper. Cover and cook on low for 6 hours.
2.About 1 hour before serving, transfer ¼ cup of sauce to a small bowl. Whisk in the flour until no lumps remain. Pour the mixture into the slow cooker, cover, and continue cooking until the sauce begins to thicken.
3.Season with additional salt and pepper, if needed. Use an immersion blender or transfer to a blender to purée the sauce. Use the sauce immediately, or cover and store in the refrigerator for up to 1 week.

Alfredo Sauce

Prep time: 10 minutes | Cook time: 4 to 6 hours | Serves 4

½ quart heavy (whipping) cream
¼ cup chicken stock
¼ cup butter, melted
2 garlic cloves, minced
1 cup finely shredded Parmesan cheese, plus more for garnish
2 tablespoons dry sherry
¾ teaspoon kosher salt, plus more for seasoning
½ teaspoon freshly ground black pepper, plus more for seasoning
3 tablespoons all-purpose flour
Cooking spray or 1 tablespoon extra-virgin olive oil

1.Use the cooking spray or olive oil to coat the inside (bottom and sides) of the slow cooker. Add the cream, chicken stock, butter, garlic, Parmesan, sherry, salt, and pepper and whisk to combine. Cover and cook on low for 4 to 6 hours.
2.About 30 minutes before serving, whisk in the flour. Leave the lid ajar and continue cooking until the sauce begins to thicken. Season with additional salt and pepper if needed before serving.

Italian Meat Gravy

Prep time: 15 minutes | Cook time: 8 to 10 hours | Serves 6

2 tablespoons extra-virgin olive oil
4 boneless beef short ribs
1¼ teaspoons kosher salt, plus more for seasoning
1½ pounds (680 g) hot Italian sausage
1 large onion, finely chopped
1 celery stalk, finely chopped
1 large carrot, peeled and finely chopped
3 garlic cloves, minced
2 (28-ounce / 794-g) cans crushed tomatoes
2 tablespoons tomato paste
2 teaspoons Italian seasoning
2 bay leaves
Freshly ground black pepper, to taste
Pasta (any kind), for serving
½ cup grated Parmesan cheese, for garnish

1.In a skillet over medium-high heat, heat the oil until shimmering. Season the short ribs with salt and pepper, and brown, along with the Italian sausage, about 3 minutes per side.
2.Put the ribs and sausage in the slow cooker, along with the onion, celery, carrot, garlic, canned tomatoes, tomato paste, Italian seasoning, bay leaves, and salt. Stir to combine. Cover and cook on low for 8 to 10 hours.
3.Remove the lid and discard the bay leaves. Season with additional salt and pepper, if needed. Pour the sauce on pasta, toss, and serve immediately, passing the Parmesan at the table as a garnish.

Buffalo Wing Sauce

Prep time: 5 minutes | Cook time: 6 hours | Makes enough for 3 pounds of wings

1 (12-ounce / 340-g) bottle hot sauce
½ cup (1 stick) unsalted butter
2 tablespoons Worcestershire sauce
2 teaspoons garlic powder
2 teaspoons onion powder
¼ teaspoon cayenne pepper
¼ teaspoon kosher salt, plus more for seasoning
Freshly ground black pepper, to taste

1.To the slow cooker, add the hot sauce, butter, Worcestershire sauce, garlic powder, onion powder, cayenne, and salt. Stir to combine. Cover and cook on low for 6 hours.
2.Season with additional salt and pepper as needed before serving.

Appendix 1: Measurement Conversion Chart

VOLUME EQUIVALENTS(DRY)

US STANDARD	METRIC (APPROXIMATE)
1/8 teaspoon	0.5 mL
1/4 teaspoon	1 mL
1/2 teaspoon	2 mL
3/4 teaspoon	4 mL
1 teaspoon	5 mL
1 tablespoon	15 mL
1/4 cup	59 mL
1/2 cup	118 mL
3/4 cup	177 mL
1 cup	235 mL
2 cups	475 mL
3 cups	700 mL
4 cups	1 L

VOLUME EQUIVALENTS(LIQUID)

US STANDARD	US STANDARD (OUNCES)	METRIC (APPROXIMATE)
2 tablespoons	1 fl.oz.	30 mL
1/4 cup	2 fl.oz.	60 mL
1/2 cup	4 fl.oz.	120 mL
1 cup	8 fl.oz.	240 mL
1 1/2 cup	12 fl.oz.	355 mL
2 cups or 1 pint	16 fl.oz.	475 mL
4 cups or 1 quart	32 fl.oz.	1 L
1 gallon	128 fl.oz.	4 L

TEMPERATURES EQUIVALENTS

FAHRENHEIT(F)	CELSIUS(C) (APPROXIMATE)
225 °F	107 °C
250 °F	120 °C
275 °F	135 °C
300 °F	150 °C
325 °F	160 °C
350 °F	180 °C
375 °F	190 °C
400 °F	205 °C
425 °F	220 °C
450 °F	235 °C
475 °F	245 °C
500 °F	260 °C

WEIGHT EQUIVALENTS

US STANDARD	METRIC (APPROXIMATE)
1 ounce	28 g
2 ounces	57 g
5 ounces	142 g
10 ounces	284 g
15 ounces	425 g
16 ounces (1 pound)	455 g
1.5 pounds	680 g
2 pounds	907 g

Printed in Great Britain
by Amazon